Charles Mackay

**Forty Years' Recollections of Life**

Literature, and Public Affairs, from 1830 to 1870: Vol. I.

Charles Mackay

**Forty Years' Recollections of Life**
*Literature, and Public Affairs, from 1830 to 1870: Vol. I.*

ISBN/EAN: 9783337056339

Printed in Europe, USA, Canada, Australia, Japan

Cover: Foto ©ninafisch / pixelio.de

More available books at **www.hansebooks.com**

# FORTY YEARS' RECOLLECTIONS

OF

## Life, Literature, and Public Affairs.

FROM

## 1830 TO 1870.

BY

## CHARLES MACKAY, LL.D.

AUTHOR OF "EGERIA," "A MAN'S HEART," "STUDIES FROM THE ANTIQUE," &c., &c.

IN TWO VOLUMES.

VOL. I.

LONDON:

CHAPMAN & HALL, 193, PICCADILLY.

1877.

# CONTENTS.

# FORTY YEARS' RECOLLECTIONS.

## INTRODUCTORY.

In the early summer of the year 1832 a young man who had just completed his eighteenth year arrived in London, from Brussels, where he had passed the previous four years in study. He had high hopes, great ambition, vigorous health, and immense inexperience. He had, moreover, a few—a very few—pounds in his pocket, and a small—a very small—credit at an army agency in Westminster, which last was a fund which was only to be available upon occasion of the utmost urgency. This youth had come to London to make, or endeavour to make, his way in literature and journalism. He had once thought of studying law, but had abandoned the idea. He had no taste for theology and divinity and did not think that he was fitted for the pulpit. He had speculated on the possibility of becoming a physician, but did not think on cool reflection that that was his true vocation; and he had an unwise objection to trade. His ancestors, as far back as he could trace them, had all been soldiers, but he lacked interest to obtain a commission, or having had interest it had slipped from his grasp, though he would not have objected to a military career. His education had been of the most miscellaneous kind—picked up by himself, rather than prescribed or enforced upon him by extraneous power or wisdom. He knew little Latin or Greek, though he had painfully studied both, but to make amends for this deficiency, he spoke and wrote French with the fluency of a native ; could converse in German, and enjoy a German book without the aid of a dictionary ; and had taught himself to read and understand Italian and Spanish. He was acquainted with all the best poetry in the English, French, and German languages, and had read whole libraries of romance. He had a brave heart, though he did not know it at the time, and a self reliance, which might either have been called sublime or ridiculous by any wiser person who had studied his character.

This young man, so rash, so hopeful, so slightly indebted to fortune for any aids to climb up the slippery heights of ambition, is the writer of the following pages. The Recollections, which he brings before the public, both as warning and incentive to others who unwisely depend upon the rewards of literature for their daily bread—as he unluckily has done—are not those of disastrous chances, moving accidents, or hair-breadth escapes, like those which so charmed the tender Desdemona, but those of a student of men and books; of one who, though sometimes loving solitude, was never a recluse, and who realised to some extent the dream of his youthful ambition by playing a part in the politics and literature of his time.

In speaking of myself, it is not my intention to assume the place of the hero of my story, but to appear in it merely as the string on which I can collect and exhibit such beads of memory and experience as may illustrate the dangers as well as the successes of a literary career, reflect the spirit and manners of the age in which my lot was cast, and make better known to such readers as may choose to be companions of my way, the great, the good, and the brilliant men and women with whom my avocations brought me into the contact, either of business, of friendship, or of social intercourse.

I was born in the city of Perth, in the year 1814, but in my early manhood I was so ambitious of the tardy maturity that seemed to my impatient eagerness to be much too long in coming, that I endeavoured to persuade myself and others that I was at least three years older. My father was an officer in the Royal Artillery, the second son of Captain Hugh Mackay, of the Royal Marines, a member of the great Clan of Mackay, that at one time occupied nearly the whole county of Sutherland. He and his ancestors came from that part of the district called the "Reay Forest," and "the Mackay country." A few words about this gentleman and my father may not be out of place, as an introduction to the history of a life cast in a mould and amid scenes very different from theirs.

My grandfather, when a stripling, served in the army of the Duke of Cumberland, "the Butcher Cumberland" of Jacobite story and song. In this respect he was true to the training and traditions of his ancestors, for the Mackays were one of the very few Highland clans who sided with the Hanoverian dynasty and faithfully adhered to the principles of the Revolution of 1688. My grandfather, when in his teens, held the rank of ensign, and was present at the battle of Drummossie Muir, better known as Culloden, in 1745, which finally shattered the fortunes of the Stuarts, and left the House of Hanover in unmolested possession of the throne. At a later period he exchanged the military for the semi-naval service of the Crown, and attained the rank of Captain of Marines. He commanded a company of that force on board the "Royal George," under Admiral Kempenfeldt. Though accustomed to the sword, he was not unaccustomed to the pen, had decided literary tastes and acquirements, which he exhibited by writing an epic poem—which never saw the light—and whole volumes of songs and sonnets to Miss Jeanie or Jane Rose, of Kilravock, near Inverness. Although my grandfather's effusions never blossomed into print, they served the, to him, important purpose of gaining the heart and hand of an accomplished and beautiful woman. The Roses of Kilravock, though an untitled family, holding no higher rank than that of country gentlemen, have since the thirteenth century been known to their neighbourhood as "the Barons of Kilravock." They never assumed the title, though they might possibly, if so disposed, have obtained it for the asking. By this lady he had a family of six children. Captain Mackay had influential connections and fair prospects of advancement when an accident occurred which blighted a happy life, and put a sudden end to his professional career, and all his worldly chances of success. In consequence of some trivial dispute at the mess table, leading to the interchange of angry words, he was challenged by Colonel Campbell, his superior officer, to fight a duel. In those days it was impossible even for a private gentleman to refuse a challenge without incurring the social disgrace of being what is called "sent to

Coventry," and though a private gentleman might possibly choose to incur this risk, rather than the greater risk of committing a murder, no officer in the King's service could refuse a challenge without drawing upon his devoted head an amount of obloquy and disgrace that every officer and gentleman considered to be worse than death. The duel was fought, in spite of the efforts of the seconds to prevent it, and the unfortunate Colonel Campbell received a mortal wound, of which he died shortly afterwards. The result was that my grandfather, who would have been ruined if he had *not* fought, was ruined because he *did* fight. Thus one gallant gentleman lost his life, and another gallant gentleman lost his position and his peace of mind, all for a hasty word, which, had it not been for unreasoning pride, might have been forgotten, or apologised for, as soon as it was spoken. A military investigation was held, the upshot of which was that the challenged officer was recommended to retire from the service on half-pay. In his disgust at what he called the unmerited punishment visited upon him, for what he considered more of a misfortune than a crime, and partly perhaps from motives of economy, he resolved to leave England and all his old associations, and chose for his future residence the cheap little town of Venlo, in Holland, where his poor half-pay could go further than it would at home. He was attracted to Venlo by previous knowledge, and by his acquaintance with the Dutch Mackays, with whom he claimed kindred. These were the descendants of the famous General Hugh Mackay, of Scowry, the model hero and great favourite of King William III., the same who fought the memorable

battle of Killicrankie, against the gallant Dundee—the
"bonnie Dundee" of Scott's dashing lyric. General
Mackay lost the battle, and Dundee lost his life, as all
readers of English history are aware. General Mackay
was afterwards killed at the battle of Steenkirk. My
grandfather had not been settled for many months in his
Dutch home, in close intimacy and friendship with his
Dutch relations, when news reached him (1782) that his
old ship, the "Royal George," had gone down suddenly
in harbour, with eight hundred—some accounts said a
thousand—souls, including the gallant Admiral Kempenfeldt, and a great number of women and children, who
had been permitted to come on board to visit the sailors.
The admiral was writing in his cabin at the time, unsus-
picious of danger. As Cowper sang at the time,—

> "His sword was in its sheath,
> His fingers held the pen,
> When Kempenfeldt went down
> With twice four hundred men."

It was the common belief of the day, and is so recorded in Cowper's ballad, that the timbers of the unfortunate vessel were quite sound, and that she might at a
future time be raised to float again, and sound the martial
thunder-peals of England over the oceans of two hemis-
pheres. Investigation, however, brought out the disgraceful fact that the wood-work was utterly rotten, and that
the weight of her guns, when they were all injudiciously
moved to one side, turned her over completely, and actually tore the side out of her worm-eaten hull. Admiral
Milbank declared at the Court of Inquiry that he had
seen the "Royal George" in dock at Plymouth, and that

her timbers were so rotten that the officers of the dock-
yard informed him they could scarcely find fastening for
the repairs which she had to undergo, a statement which
was confirmed by Admiral Jervis. This, too, was
Captain Mackay's recollection of his old ship, and my
father heard him more than once declare, quoting Shakspeare, that there was " a soul of goodness in things evil,"
and that his lamentable duel, whatever ill consequences
it might have drawn upon his devoted head, had at least
been the means of saving his life, as, but for his dispute
with Colonel Campbell, he would in all probability have
been on board with his company, and gone to the grave
with Kempenfeldt.

In 1793, when he had attained the age of fourteen, my
father, who spoke Dutch, French, and English with equal
fluency, and had moreover picked up a little Spanish,
was told that the time had come when he must leave the
paternal roof and make choice of a profession. Great
Britain was at war with the French Republic, and needed
the aid of all her gallant youth to maintain her position
in the fore-front of the European powers, and as my
father was of a martial family and race, his only difficulty
was to decide whether his future life should be passed in
the army or the navy. No idea of any other profession ever
entered his mind. It turned out afterwards that he had
to devote the best years of his youth to the navy, and the
best years of his manhood to the army. This, however,
he did not know. His first choice was the navy, and on
the evacuation of Toulon by the British and their allies
in 1793, he served as a midshipman on board His
Majesty's sloop, the " Scout," one of the fleet under the

command of Vice-Admiral Hood. The "Scout" cruised about in the Mediterranean, employed for many months in various duties, chiefly off the coast of Corsica, and was present, with the remainder of the fleet, to assist General Paoli in his attempt to throw off the yoke of the French revolutionary government. The towns of St. Fiorenzo and Bastia surrendered in succession to the combined attacks of the British army and fleet, aided by a body of Corsican volunteers under Paoli. In consequence of these successes, the whole island, with the exception of the citadel of Calvi, submitted to the British arms. The citadel made an obstinate resistance for several weeks, but finally capitulated, the garrison being allowed to march out with the honours of war. The little middy of fourteen and a half greatly enjoyed this kind of life, and took a keen interest in all the events of the war.

In July of the same year, the "Scout" was appointed to protect a certain number of boats destined for the coral fishery. (These and the following facts are gleaned from a "Narrative," written by my father, "of an Escape from French Captivity in 1798, by a British Officer," privately printed at Brussels in 1826.) "Having received on board a four months' supply of provisions, we weighed anchor with our convoy, which consisted of about forty latine sailed boats, each manned with four Corsican fishermen, and provided with a species of dredge, for the purpose of disengaging the coral from the rocks. Our outset was very agreeable, a vast concourse of people being assembled on the beach to witness our departure, invoking all the saints in the calendar to grant us a prosperous voyage.

"On the 14th of July we came to an anchor with our convoy off the city of Cagliari—the capital of the island of Sardinia, where we received a deputation from the principal inhabitants, inviting us ashore. We were welcomed on our landing by the civil and military authorities, all zealous in their protestations of respect for the British flag—and all equally ardent in their expressions of hatred towards the French Republic. * * * After a few days' jollity on shore, we set sail towards Bona in Africa; and thence to Tripoli, intending to make that place the rendezvous of our coral fishers in case of separation. When about three leagues from Bona, the man at the masthead descried two strange vessels to leeward, which shortly afterwards were ascertained to be frigates. These vessels hoisted Spanish colours as they bore down upon us. Our captain knowing I could speak a little Spanish, placed the speaking trumpet in my hands, that I might answer such questions as the 'Spaniards' might put. When nearly within pistol-shot, we were asked from whence we came, and whether we had any news of the fleet under Lord Hood? To which I replied—in very indifferent—but still very intelligible Spanish, eked out with French—that his lordship had sailed with the squadron to Elba, and that we had left Corsica with our convoy, after witnessing the surrender of the fortress of Calvi. No sooner had I communicated this unwelcome intelligence, than down came the Spanish colours with a bang, and up went the French tricolor like a flash of lightning, and we received a whole volley of musketry from the enemy's marines. The vessels proved to be two French frigates, the 'Alceste' and the

'Vestale,' by the crews of which we were speedily
boarded. Overpowed by vastly superior numbers, we
were forced to surrender, and were all taken prisoners.
We were scurvily treated on board—at least I was. The
captain of the 'Alceste,' to whose clutches I was unfortunately consigned, on the way to the French prison at
Toulon, treated me worse than a dog, and took an especial
objection to me because I was fond of reading. Seeing
me with a book in my hand, he snatched it from me with
an oath, and threw it into the sea, exclaiming to his lieutenant, 'Ces b—— gres d'Anglais sont tous des philo-
sophes.' Young as I was, I accepted the unintentional
compliment as more than an equivalent for the loss of
my book."

The capture of the "Scout" was an unfortunate incident
in my father's career; and were I telling his story rather
than my own, I might, from his little printed volume—
which is now extremely scarce—extract many stirring
particulars of his life during four years as a prisoner of
war in the interior of France, and of his many unsuccessful attempts to escape to England by way of Switzerland
and Germany. In these attempts—continually frustrated
by the ubiquitous French gendarmerie—he traversed
France on foot, from north to south, and from east to
west, living, as he trudged wearily along the road, threadbare and desolate, upon the kindness of the peasantry, to
whom he never hesitated to disclose his nationality, his
story, and his desire to return home, and from whom he
invariably received the most generous aid and sympathy.
He sometimes varied his adventures, as Oliver Goldsmith
had done before him, by striking up on a pocket flageolet,

which he played very well, some of the tender melodies of his native Scotland, for such fee and reward as his performances might bring from the simple and kind-hearted people. He forded rivers, let himself down from dungeon walls by ropes of bedding, and ran innumerable dangers for the sake of liberty, and the yearning, uncontrollable desire of revisiting home. After many adventures, both painful and ludicrous, he succeeded at last in reaching Stuttgart, where the British ambassador, Sir J. Stuart, introduced him to the notice of his Serene Highness the Grand Duke of Wirtemberg, the husband of the Princess Matilda of Great Britain. The duke received him very kindly, and listened with the greatest interest to the story of his adventures in France, and was particularly amused at a document given to him by the famous General Kellerman. The general, intending to give my father a free pass, asked him, somewhat suddenly, what was the English for monsieur? My father answered " sir," and received a permit, commanding the authorities, civil and military, to allow "Sir George Mackay" to pass without let or hindrance. " His highness," says my father in his Narrative, " was seized with such an immoderate fit of laughter at my being knighted in this absurd manner as to make me apprehensive lest he might experience the fate of the fat licentiate while listening to the comic adventures of Gil Blas. On my part, I could not repress a smile when I contrasted my almost fleshless frame with the huge mass of mortality before me. Certainly I thought if a superabundance of fat upon his bones entitled a man to the appellation of great, his Serene Highness was unquestionably the greatest prince in Christendom. He was, however, exceedingly kind;

and after conversing with me for nearly an hour, rang the
bell for refreshments. The gorgeous domestic placed so
large a quantity of eatables and drinkables before me, that
I thought he must have imagined I had an appetite as
greedy as his master's. Though I would have preferred
to take my repast elsewhere than under his highness's
eyes, I made the best of circumstances, and possibly
satisfied the duke that he had really fed a very hungry
man, and that the very hungry man had really enjoyed
the feast. As I was leaving his presence he slipped a
folded paper into my hand, which I judged by its weight
to contain gold; then shook hands with me and said,
' When you arrive in England tell your countrymen that
the Grand Duke of Wirtemberg made you a present of
all the money he had in his pocket.' "

From Wirtemberg the wanderer made his way on foot
to Heidelberg, Darmstadt, Frankfort, Cassel, Göttingen,
Einbeck, Hanover, Bremen, and Cuxhaven, receiving aid
at all, or most of these places, from the British Consular
or Vice-Consular authorities to help him homewards;
and finally took a passage from the last-mentioned port,
on board of a packet bound for Great Yarmouth, where
he arrived towards the end of the year 1798. His
object in coming to England instead of going to Venlo
was to report himself to the Admiralty, and learn whether
he was still to be considered in the naval service of his
Majesty, and had any chance of an appointment to another
ship. His maternal uncle, the Rev. Mr. Rose, was rector
of the parish of St. James's, Piccadilly, but on calling at
that gentleman's house in Clarges-street to ascertain news
of his father, he learned that Mr. Rose had died some
months previously, and that *one* friend on whom he had

relied for advice and support was removed from his path
for ever. On calling at the office of his father's agent he
learned that Captain Mackay had removed from Venlo,
had lost his wife, had married again, and gone to reside
at Düsseldorf. The loss of his mother—his first great
grief, and the fact of his father's second marriage—coupled
with that of his own penniless condition, decided him not
to go to Düsseldorf, but to make every effort to procure
a ship, and get to sea as soon as possible. Men in those
days were urgently needed, both for the army and navy;
and my father, after a short struggle, and the use of all
the influence he could command, found himself once more
in the naval service of his sovereign. His ship was the
"Hydra," commanded by Captain, afterwards Admiral Sir
Francis Laforey. My father discovered, however, after
his four years' vagrancy on land, that his heart was not
in the sea-service, and he gradually grew more and more
discontented with it, and the prospects which it offered.
In after life he described the "Hydra" as a "hell upon
the waters," and the brutal flogging of the sailors for the
most trivial offences as something too horrible for contemplation. "Often," he used to say, "have I wondered
that men, who were treated as if they had neither hearts
nor souls, should yet in the hour of danger and of duty,
forget their wrongs and indignities, act like true heroes,
and pour out their heart's blood with sublime unselfish-
ness for a country that treated them so detestably." It
was not, however, until he had had six years' experience
of a sea life that he finally abandoned it; and, in a fit
of desperation, without home or friends, enlisted in the
army. The superiority of his attainments soon made him
known to the officers of his regiment, who, having learned

his family history and connections, exercised such influence
on his behalf that he was presented by H.R.H. the Duke
of York, at that time Commander-in-Chief, with an
ensign's commission. He served in the ill-judged and
unfortunate expedition to Walcheren, where, with many
hundreds of others, he was invalided with fever and
ague, caught amid the malaria of the marshes, and had
to return to England. Years after his restoration to
health he was on military duty in Perth, where he made
the acquaintance of, and married my mother, a lineal
descendant, as I have heard, of that famous Donald
Cargill, who ranks both as saint and hero in the spiritual
army of the Covenanters, and in that city I was born. I
unfortunately lost my mother in childhood, and had
what is, even under favourable circumstances, the dis-
advantage of being consigned to the care of strangers.
Yet I was not unfortunate; for of her who acted the
part of mother to me in my tender years, I have
every reason to speak with respect and affection. She
was a Perth woman, whose maiden name was Grace
Stuart, and was married to sergeant Thomas Threlkeld,
of my father's regiment, a sturdy and stalwart Cumbrian,
who on leaving the army after the peace of Waterloo, had
settled in Woolwich, to pursue his original avocation of
a tailor. While my father was still knocking about the
world, without a home to which he could bring his child,
good Mrs. Threlkeld took me to her home and heart, and
treated me with as true and as great a love and care as if
I had been her own. Thus, like Béranger, the great
lyrist of the French people, I passed my earlier years in
the house of a tailor. The French poet has told the
world in one of his songs that a fairy, born of his own

imagination, visited him in the tailor's shop, and predicted his future career. My fairy of the tailor's shop
was a sonsie, buxom, comely Scottish woman, who spoke
the broad Doric of the Lowlands in all its purity, and
had a heart as true and tender as ever beat in a human
bosom. Years afterwards ere I had reached my teens,
she often expressed the notion that I too, like Robert
Burns, whom she was fond of quoting, "was a waly boy,"
predicting, as she crooned the song, in a low sweet voice:

> "Thou'lt hae misfortunes great and sma',
> But still a heart aboon them a';—
> Thou'lt be a credit to us a'
> We'll a' be proud o' Charlie;"

or, as she pronounced it, *Chairlie*. Often in after years
has the kind woman's song re-echoed in my mind, when
encouragement, come whence it might, was a ray of sunshine on a dark place, and when even the remembered
echo of an old song was an aid to a tottering step, and to
a young heart that needed sympathy.

Grace Threlkeld, or, as her husband always called her,
"Girzie," taught me the alphabet, together with the tunes
of many scores, I might say hundreds, of Scotch songs,
which she was fond of singing. Among the rest was the
old Jacobite song of "Charlie is my darling, the young
chevalier." I imagined at the time that this was a song
about myself, and that I was the veritable young Chevalier.
I well remember my astonishment when I was about
six years old, at hearing a blackbird, whose cage hung
from a window in Powis Street, Woolwich, pipe this tune
very correctly as I passed along with a playmate. I
looked at the bird with infantine bewilderment, thinking

that the creature was, as the Scotch say, "no cannie," and that the foul fiend himself had taken up his abode in its tiny throat. The good "Girzie" laughed at my terror, but it was many weeks before I was quite reconciled to the possession of musical abilities by so small a creature, or quite satisfied that it had not formed a deliberate purpose by whistling that particular song, to turn me into ridicule.

Having mastered the alphabet, I was consigned, for more advanced instruction, to the care of one Mrs. Baxter, the widow of a corporal in the Royal Artillery, who kept a "dame school." Here I learned to read, and was instructed in the first mysteries of strokes, pot-hooks, and round o's, those rungs on the ladder of penmanship which we must all climb in our young days, if we would possess the first tools of knowledge. I had great aptitude for learning, and very speedily became dux of the dame school. But on becoming dux, I became dissatisfied, and thought the time had arrived when the schoolmistress should hand me over to a schoolmaster. Possibly this desire arose in me, quite as much from pride, as from the thirst of knowledge, for I well remember offering to fight a boy about my own age, who went to what he called an "academy" for boys, for jeering me on the supposed degradation which I suffered in attending a dame school.

I was, if I remember rightly, about eight years old, when, with several other urchins, I ventured into an empty sugar barrel that stood opposite a grocer's door in the High Street, to scrape off the small remnants of sugar that clung to the seams and sides. We had been thus engaged for several minutes when the indignant grocer came out with a cane, and put an end to the glorious feast. Running as rapidly as I could to avoid the uplifted instrument of correction, I stumbled and fell, and received the fag end of a castigation, as the grocer passed me in pursuit of a bigger boy. But I fell in luck's way, for as I sprawled on the ground, my eye caught a glimpse of something bright in the dirt, which turned out to be half-a-crown. I speedily clutched at it, no other boy being near to cry "halves." Unseen by any one, I deposited it in my pocket, alongside of a top and a few marbles. What was to be done with it? The question was difficult to answer. Should I report my "find" to Mrs. Threlkeld? That was not to be thought of, as the good woman would in all probability confiscate my half-crown to her own uses. Should I go to the pastry-cook's, and take what boys call a "tuck-out" of jams and tarts and other sweets? That was a bright idea, and a sore temptation, but I manfully resisted it. After much cogitation, being somewhat precocious, and I suppose even then of a literary turn, I resolved to go to the theatre, or, as I then called it, the "play." And that I might not be so selfish as to take my enjoyment alone, I resolved to ask my favourite playmate—he was but a year older than myself—to accompany me. He, on his part, was nothing loth—though he put in a word for the pastry-cook's, if it were only to the extent of sixpence! This was agreed upon on my part, and as the price of admission was but a shilling each, the precious half-crown was sufficient for all the purposes to which we had resolved to devote it. We went to the pastry-cook's, had three penny buns each, and were at the door of the theatre half-an-hour before the house opened. We were the first to enter, and though I was afraid the money-taker might object to admit us on account of our infant years, he made no demur, and we both passed in, with joy not unmingled with dread. The theatre was cold, dark, and empty; the lights were low, and threw but a faint illumination on the dreary and, as it appeared to me, vast arena. There was no one in the orchestra, or in all the house that we could see except our small and daring selves. Gradually five or six people dropped in to the pit; gradually three or four into the boxes; gradually about a dozen noisy boys into the galleries, who began to kick and shout and whistle, impatient for the performance to begin. To me it seemed many long hours since I had taken my place in the sombre building, and a draught at my back made me shiver with cold. My courage quickly oozed out of me. My companion was in the same sad plight; and after whispering together for a minute, and taking counsel of each other, we resolved to decamp. Like Wordsworth in the land of the Tweed and Yarrow, "we had a vision of our own," but unlike Wordsworth, we made up our minds to "undo it," and leave tragedy, comedy, and farce, "unseen and unknown." The door-keeper offered us each a return ticket as we passed out, but I threw mine away, and slunk home in the dark evening, afraid of my truancy, and the punishment that might follow it. Conscience had made a coward of me, and finding the door ajar in its usual fashion, I crept in softly like a guilty thing, and hid myself under the great bed in a room that opened from the sergeant's sitting-room and workshop. Here I heard my absence discussed by the married couple, and great alarm expressed by tender-hearted Mrs. Threlkeld, lest I should have been kidnapped or run over. At last, the sergeant determined to go in search of me, and to give the alarm at the watch-house (there was no police force in those days), and to send round the bellman if the watch thought advisable. Mrs. Threlkeld was loud in my praise. I was the " bonniest boy," the " best boy," the " dearest bairn " that ever was seen, &c. On hearing these praises—and a whole torrent of them, uttered hysterically—I coughed under the bed to attract attention. I was speedily discovered, dragged ignominiously out, and having showered upon me preliminary kisses without number, and hugged me to her honest heart, she administered with right good will and *more Scotticè* a castigation that could break no bones, and which I bore stoically until after I was put to bed, when my outraged pride found vent in tears, which nobody saw. Such was the first imping of my wings in the wide air of independent action, and such its results—the loss of my two shillings, the loss of the amusement I anticipated, and a well deserved " skelping."

When I was ten years of age my father came from Brussels where he was then resident, economising on his half-pay, to remove me from the care of Mrs. Threlkeld and her husband, and place me at school in London. The worthy tailor felt unaffected sorrow at my departure, and the tailor's wife shed genuine tears, which she only dried on the solemn promise of my father that I should always spend my holidays at Woolwich—the time being too short to permit of a visit to Brussels, and the journey thither and back being much

too costly for the slenderly furnished pocket of my father.
I felt on my part that a new world was opening before me
which I longed, yet was afraid to enter, and sobbed
grievously when the hour came that I was to leave those
who for the best years of my childhood had been more
than friends and protectors, and whose care and affection
no money could have purchased. I made rapid progress
at school, and before I was thirteen my master predicted
that I should infallibly become a great mathematician.
Arithmetic was to me no trouble but a positive delight:
the extraction of the square and the cube roots, which
was a sore vexation of spirit to my school-mates, was as
easy to me as the multiplication-table; and I soared into
geometry, trigonometry, and algebra, as a bird soars into
the air, and positively revelled in them. But, notwithstanding the auguries of my master, all my love for the
mathematics, high and low, came to nothing; and though
I had begun to love the exact sciences, poetry and romance
stepped in the way, and throwing their glamour over me,
took my heart completely. I was at this time an
omnivorous reader. The poetical extracts in Ewing's
Elocutionist—I think that was the name of the school-
book to which I owed my first introduction to the
beauties of English literature—so took my imagination
that I read and re-read them till they were all as familiar
to me as my name. The quarrel of Brutus and Cassius,
Hamlet's famous soliloquy "To be or not to be,"
Othello's account of his courtship, and other specimens
of the wild and wondrous, but clear and sagacious
Shakspeare; the warlike odes of Thomas Campbell, then
in the full flush of his fame; Pope's "Dying Christian to

his Soul," portions of his "Essay on Man;" copious extracts from "Paradise Lost," episodes from Scott's "Marmion" and the "Lady of the Lake," Goldsmith's "Deserted Village," and a beautiful description of a shipwreck by Professor Wilson, all took my fancy. Some of the juvenile pieces of Kirke White also came home to my heart. Kirke White's poems, from the accident that I had been presented by my father with a complete copy of the works of that author, exercised a peculiar fascination over me, which was weakened but never wholly dispelled, as I gradually made the acquaintance of the most celebrated English poets of the past and of the actual generation. I scarcely remember when I began to write verses myself, and to take more pleasure in the art of composition than in other study, or even in the attractions of the play-ground, but I think I was between thirteen and fourteen when I began to think, like Petrarch, and to say [though not in Italian] "io anche son poeta," and to long for some patient, sympathetic, and appreciative reader or listener, who would encourage me in my favourite pursuits by the expression of his approbation. And such listener I found in the person of a man very eminent in his day, Mr. Andrew Robertson, a fashionable portrait-painter and Royal Academician, renowned for his miniatures on ivory. This gentleman, a friend of my father, encouraged me to call upon him at his studio in Gerrard Street, Soho, and knowing the weakness of school-boys for pocket-money, often gladdened my heart with what is now the fashion of boys to call a "tip," which sometimes disappeared in cakes, apples, and other dainties, and sometimes at old book-stalls in the purchase of poems, fairy tales, bygone

romances (all new to me), and now and then of more solid
and useful works.   Among the treasures that I picked up
in this manner was a copy of Johnson's "Lives of the
Poets," in two small pocket volumes, the perusal of which
formed an era in my young life, and which sent me on
my half-holidays—when being a favourite with the master,
I received permission to go out alone—to Westminster
Abbey and St. Paul's, to muse in Poets' Corner, or to
admire the stalwart form of Samuel Johnson, standing
upon his pedestal in the Cathedral.   But Poets' Corner
was my favourite haunt, where, in the contemplation of
the tombs, busts or statues of the poets, great and small,
but all of them great to me at that time, I fed the fires of
my youthful ambition, and formed the resolve that I too
should be known hereafter as one of the company of
the poets.   I was, I dare say, a precocious little fool;
but as I did not know it, both my folly and my precocity
administered to my pleasure, and possibly kept thoughts
out of my head that might not have been so innocent as
the desire to be enrolled among the illustrious men who
had glorified the English language.   Mr. Robertson's
occasional coins, pleasant as they were, did not yield me
half the gratification that I experienced when, on his
invitation, I read to him my latest productions.   He was
a kind but an impartial critic, and as freely pointed out
their faults as he generously praised what he considered
their merits.   Happily these juvenile efforts have all
perished—consigned by my own hands to ignominious
destruction at a later period of my mind's growth; but I
remember, generally, that they were all on very ambitious
subjects.   One in particular, on which I greatly prided

myself, was entitled "Hamlet amid the Ruins of Palmyra."
I think I was induced to attempt this odd subject by the
perusal of Volney's "Ruins of Empires," which I had
picked up for a few pence at a book-stall, and which Mr.
Robertson took especial pains to inform me was a very
improper book, and one that I ought to commit forthwith
to the flames if I valued my immortal soul. Mr. Robertson
was a strict Presbyterian, and I think, one of the elders of
the Scottish Church, of which the celebrated Edward
Irving was the minister. He was very anxious that my
course of reading should not stray into what he called
"latitudinarian paths." He held all French writers in ab-
horrence, and looked upon Volney, Voltaire, and Rousseau
as the incarnation of all that was detestable in politics,
blasphemous in religion, and abominable in morals. He
was pleased to find that there was no "Volneyism" in
my poem: but urged me, as it sprang from so polluted a
source, to destroy it, adding, as an inducement for me to
do so, that he had mentioned my "poetical gifts" to his
friend Mr. Irving, and would introduce me to that
gentleman in a few days, if I would bring some pieces
which I had previously read to him. Mr. Irving was, he
said, an excellent judge of poetry, a beautiful elocutionist,
and, above all, an intimate friend of the great poet
Coleridge. On the prospect not only of seeing Mr. Irving,
but possibly Mr. Coleridge, I gave my "Hamlet in
Palmyra" to Mr. Robertson to do as he liked with it;
and he forthwith put it in the fire, remarking, "You can do
ten times better than that." I felt that I could, and was
quite consoled for the sacrifice I had made, which was
not after all so great as it might have appeared to Mr.

Robertson if he had known all, inasmuch as I remembered
the whole of it, and could have written it out afresh with
very little trouble.   Of this, however, I said nothing.

It was with a beating heart, on the following Wednesday afternoon—the usual half-holiday—that, instead of
going to Poets' Corner, I knocked at Mr. Robertson's
door in Gerrard Street, with a selection of my verses in
my pocket for the great preacher's perusal.   I so dreaded
the interview, that it was a great relief to learn that Mr.
Irving had not yet arrived—and yet I so longed to see
him that it was a satisfaction to hear that he was every
moment expected.   Mr. Robertson took possession of my
manuscripts, and consigned me to the drawing-room, to
amuse myself as best I might with the books on the
table, while he awaited Mr. Irving's arrival in the studio.
But I was far too anxious to read.   Every carriage, of
which I heard the rumbling of the wheels in the street,
seemed as if it bore the distinguished preacher, and when
it passed and the rumbling was lost in the distance, I
rejoiced that it had gone on its way without stopping at
Mr. Robertson's door.   At last there came a rattling,
prolonged, sharp double knock—or series of knocks that
seemed to my anxious mind to shake the whole house.
I heard a foot upon the stair, and knew that the critical
moment was fast approaching, when I should stand face
to face with one of the most eminent men of the day—
not the least portion of whose glory and eminence, in my
youthful imagination, was the fact that he was the friend
of him who had written " Christabel " and the " Ancient
Mariner."   After an interval of five or six minutes, which
seemed to me to be as many hours, and during which I

had twice or thrice meditated an ignominious flight from the premises, Mr. Irving and Mr. Robertson walked into the drawing-room. Mr. Irving held out his hand, and shook mine kindly—I, on my part, receiving the friendly pressure with fear and trembling, not unmixed with pride and admiration. But he soon placed me at my ease. His fine, tall, handsome figure, his dignified and beautiful face, to which a slight obliquity of vision lent a weird-like expression of power and genius, without the least suggestion of unsymmetry, and the manner, unusual with men at least in that day, of parting his luxuriant black hair down the middle, after the fashion of women, suggested to my youthful mind, fresh from the study of the most poetical passages in the Bible—that here before me stood an Isaiah or an Ezekiel, a Hosea or a Habakkuk. Indeed, for many years afterwards, I thought that if I were a great painter, and had to paint a picture of the inspired prophet Isaiah, I should take Edward Irving for my model. There was something so tender and paternal in the tones of his voice, as he patted me softly on the head, that all my awe of him as a superior being disappeared, and I thought I loved him with all my heart, as he said, still holding my hand in his—" I am pleased to see that you are a reader of your Bible. Among all your compositions, which are full of future promise, and as creditable to your heart, my dear young friend, as they are to your head—that in which you have attempted to dramatize the story of David playing the harp before Saul, to soothe his broken spirit in a paroxysm of madness—appears to me the best." My face glowed, my hand trembled, and my heart beat so loudly with joy, to be thus spoken to by such a man, that after the lapse of many years I can truly say that never again did I experience so much real happiness as I did at that moment. Mr. Irving produced the manuscript, and began to read my verses with so clear and musical a voice—so perfect an emphasis—and with such a variety of modulation as suited the changing spirit of the poem, as to impress me vividly that I had never heard reading before—and was never likely to hear it again unless from the same lips. He brought out beauties in my poor composition that I had never myself suspected, and put meanings into my words which were doubtless latent in them, but which had not been apparent to my own mind, until he had enkindled them. All this exalted me in my own opinion; and I now say it with something like regret, moulded my future career, and made me a man of letters. Mr. Irving invited me to call upon him on my half-holidays, at his house in Claremont Terrace, Pentonville, and if he were not at home, to walk into his library, and amuse myself among his books, promising me that if opportunity served he would introduce me to Mr. Coleridge, warning me, however, that Mr. Coleridge was somewhat of an invalid, and seldom went out. "Your Wednesday half-holidays will suit me best," he added, kindly, "for on Saturdays I am always busy with my sermon."

I profited much by Mr. Irving's kindness, and remember how often he impressed upon my mind the fact, which I have never forgotten to lay to heart, and act upon, that "verse" and "poetry" are words that are not synonymous—that good verse may not be poetry at all ; that good prose consisted of the right words in the right places, and not too many of them; that good verse also consisted of the right words in the right places, with the addition of the music of rhythm ; and that poetry, as distinguished from mere verse, had to conform to all the rules of verse, but to add soul, vigour, origina- lity, animating fire, enthusiasm, concentration. "Verse," he said, "may be a quiet fire in the grate ; but poetry is the lightning flash, and must have thunder along with it."

I had turned fourteen years of age, and was at "home" for the Midsummer holidays at Woolwich, at Mrs. Threl- keld's, when the worthy tailor and his wife were surprised by a violent rat-tat at the door of their humble little house in Thomas Street—a rat-tat such as is only practised by fashionable footmen. Mrs. Threlkeld her- self answered the summons, and saw a handsome carriage and pair of grey horses drawn up before the door. Her first idea was that it was a new customer—and likely, from all appearance, to be a good one—when the footman who had given so loud a knock, enquired for *me*. I was not within at the time, but Mrs. Threlkeld said she knew where I was, and would send for me. A venerable gentle- man, with snow-white hair, got out of the carriage, and said that with her permission he would wait indoors until my return. He announced himself as Major-General Robert Mackay, of the East India Company's service, and uncle of my father. Mr. Threlkeld, who, having been a sergeant, knew full well the awful rank of a major- general, jumped from his shop-board, not to keep so great a man too long in waiting, and hurried off to find

me, engaged in a game of cricket in the open space of
ground behind the Sappers' barracks.  I had often heard
of, but had never seen the General, and was no stranger
to his beneficent character, or to the interest which he
had promised to take in my future welfare.  He received
me with paternal kindness, made many enquiries as to
my tastes and the progress of my education ; and when
I divulged, by hazard rather than by design, that I had
read a great deal of poetry, and enjoyed it, he stopped
me, looked grave, and said, " A very good sign, my child,
but do not get too fond of it.  The love of poetry is a good
thing.  Have you ever attempted to write poetry yourself ? "
I owned that I had.  " Continue to read poetry," he
added, " but don't write it, or you will never make a good
soldier.  I suppose your father has told you that I intend
to procure you a cadetship in the Company's service ? "  I
replied that I had heard of it, but that I was unaware of
the time when I should be eligible.  He enlightened my
ignorance then and there, told me that if I would prepare
myself by study, he would, when I was sixteen years of
age, exercise all his influence to procure me a cadetship.
The kind old gentleman—the most placid, benignant-
looking man I ever saw—(his portrait, life-size, by Sir
William Beechey, is in my possession as I write, and I look
at it to refresh my youthful recollections) after slipping
a sovereign into my hand, informed me that I was to
leave London forthwith, and that arrangements had been
made, partly, if not wholly, at his cost, as I thought at
the time, and as I afterwards knew, that I should be
removed to a superior school at Brussels, under my
father's eye, and be fitted, more or less, for the military

profession. This seemed to be, and ought to have been, a turning point in my career. But it was not so. It was predicted that I should be a mathematician, and I might have been, but I never became one. It was agreed and arranged that I should become a soldier, and go to India. But I never became a soldier, and never went to India, but stuck fast, irrevocably, in literature, till it became the occupation of my life thenceforth and for ever.

All arrangements having been completed—greatly to my satisfaction, for I longed to see the world, even if it were so small a portion of it as was then called Les Pays Bas (the name has since died out, and been replaced by Holland and Belgium)—I took sad farewell of Mr. and Mrs. Threlkeld, and a blithesome farewell of my schoolmaster and schoolmates, and proceeded all alone, as if I were a man—at the mere thought of which I was greatly delighted—from St. Catherine's Wharf to Ostend. It was the first time within my recollection that I had beheld the sea; and though my pleasure in looking upon it was not marred by the penalty so often exacted from those who have weak stomachs, by the demon of the deep, my joy upon the sea, great as it was, was not to be compared to the rapture with which, the morning after my arrival, I wandered upon the beach at Ostend, and heard the sublime roar of the waves as they thundered upon the shingle, and read from a pocket copy of the "Beauties of Byron," which I carried about with me, the magnificent lines, "Roll on, thou deep and dark blue ocean," &c. It had been arranged that my father should meet me at Ostend, but I arrived several hours before him, and employed the interval in solitary happiness, gathering shells and sea-weed, and dreaming day dreams, which I afterwards strove, with doubtless but ill success, to preserve in poetry, or, at all events, in verse. When my father arrived at the pre-appointed hostelry, he informed me that he had made arrangements that he and I should walk to Brussels through the ancient cities of Bruges, Ghent, Antwerp, Malines, and Vilvorde, and that he would despatch my portmanteau—a very lightly furnished one it was, though provided with a second-hand " Shakespeare," a well-thumbed copy of the " Arabian Nights," and three or four other volumes—by the diligence to Brussels. The country, as everybody knows, is not beautiful, but flat and uninteresting, with long straight roads, and a superabundance of windmills. The novelty, however, made it beautiful to me. But possibly it was the old historic towns, with their quaint architecture, that were the attraction and enjoyment, both to my father and myself, though I believe that the mere tramp was a source of pleasure to him. He had acquired the habit of walking during his youthful wanderings in France, and nothing gave him greater satisfaction than a walk of twenty or thirty miles. We took a day to Bruges, though but twelve miles distant, another to Ghent, another to Antwerp, and another to Malines and Brussels. Every day brought me a new joy at the sight of the quaint and picturesque street architecture of these brave old towns, their splendid Hotels de Ville and cathedrals, and at the recital by my father of their early history, of their struggles for liberty, and of the legends of old romance associated with them.

I found my father comfortably situated in Brussels :

was introduced, for the first time, to a mother-in-law, a very notable woman, and first-rate manager, who knew how to make a small income produce more comforts than some people can extract from a large one, and who, having no children of her own, did not look upon me as an unwelcome intruder at her family circle. My father having no settled income beyond his scanty half-pay, having all his time on his hands, and possessing much energy and ability besides, turned his knowledge of languages to account, by teaching Englishmen the French language, and Frenchmen and Belgians the English. He had a considerable number of pupils, among others the two young sons of his Royal Highness the Prince of Orange. The Prince was heir apparent to the throne of the Netherlands, and universally beloved by the people of Brussels, and as popular among the Belgians, generally, as the king was the reverse. He knew my father to be a connection of the Dutch Mackays, and took pleasure in conversing with him in English, which he spoke very well, and in learning from him the opinions and feeling of the Belgian public on the unhappy differences which had arisen between his father and the Belgian people— differences which afterwards culminated in such intense discontent, that a revolution and the separation of Belgium and Holland were the consequences.

Soon after my arrival in Brussels I began the practice, which soon hardened itself into a habit, of walking round the pleasant little park that fills up the space between the Rue Royale and the Rue Ducale on the parallel sides, and between the king's palace and the Houses of the Legislature on the other parallels, five or six times every morning before breakfast. On these occasions I frequently met the Prince, engaged in a similar " constitutional," and though I never had the honour of an introduction to him—my father, I suppose, judging me to be too young [in which judgment I did not agree], I always took off my hat to him as I passed—a courtesy which he invariably returned. I had met the Prince in this manner many scores of times, and performed the same ceremony with the same results each day, when it suddenly flashed across my mind that it must be a bore to his Royal Highness to be continually saluted by the same school-boy, and that I must either forego my walks—walk in the same direction as the Prince, or ' cut him.' I chose the latter alternative, and when I next passed his Royal Highness, pretended not to see him. The Prince looked at me, and went his way as I did mine. On the next day I pretended, or was about to pretend the same absence of mind, when the Prince looking fixedly at me, lifted his hat. Of course I lifted mine; but as I really thought it was a bore to him to be confronted continually by one boy, I lay in wait *perdu*, as it were, and concealed behind a tree, until he had passed the spot, and then came forth, following him at a considerable distance, so that unless he suddenly turned round and came full upon me from the opposite direction, there was no chance of an interchange of salutation.

There are three stages through which all must pass who learn, or wish to learn, a language—first, the knowledge of the names of things, actions, and qualities; second, the power of connecting words into sentences on one's own tongue; and last, the immediate comprehension of these words and sentences when uttered by another. Children of tender years seem to pass through all these stages very rapidly, and learn to speak and understand at one and the same time without any painful effort of the mind. But after the age of childhood the acquisition of a language becomes more difficult, and each of these stages must be laboriously passed before the next stage becomes possible. It took me about three months after my arrival in Brussels to read and understand French. In six months I was able to speak and write it without understanding very clearly what was said to me in return, in consequence of what I erroneously supposed to be the undue rapidity with which the French and Belgians rattled out their words. The mind understood, but the ear required longer time to become familiarized with the sounds. But all at once, and as if by lightning flashes of comprehension, and in much less than a twelvemonth after first commencing the study, I found myself a master of the language to read, to write, to speak, and to hear. I had some thoughts of learning Dutch and Flemish, as I had found French so easy, but bethinking myself that these were but offshoots of the great Teutonic or German, I resolved to apply myself to the latter tongue; and did so. But German, though at first glance easy enough to an Englishman, is not easy after the first entry into the vestibule of the language, and a large temple has to be traversed, in which the student gets no assistance by the way from the corresponding words of his own speech as he does in French. Nevertheless I found German a delightful study, and soon began to revel in Goethe, Schiller, Körner, Uhland; and, more than all, in a German author with a French name, La Motte Fouqué, the author of the fanciful little romance of Undine. I next betook myself to Italian, which, after French, I found comparatively easy. I next tried Spanish, that I might read Don Quixote in the original, though I must own that I found less pleasure in reading Gil Blas in the original than in making the acquaintance of the prose and poetical works of Victor Hugo, who was then budding and blossoming out into his first fame in "Les Orientales," "Le Dernier Jour d'un Condamné," and "Notre Dame de Paris." All this time my devotion to poetry, both in the reading and what I thought the writing of it, suffered no cessation or diminution; and I had planned an epic poem, two or three tragedies, and several tales, after the manner of Byron, all of which projects happily came to nothing. As for studies for the military profession they were never so much as mentioned to me, nor did it appear necessary that I should devote myself to anything of the kind until I got my cadetship. But my cadetship never came. My sixteenth year arrived, but with it no news of my approaching initiation into military life. How it came about I never knew, though I sometimes enquired; but only learned in the vaguest and most unsatisfactory manner that the kind-hearted General and my kind-hearted but somewhat irascible and impetuous father had quarrelled about something or other. My father, though sorry for the quarrel, would not admit that he was in the wrong: he was a poor man, and his pride was certainly equal if not superior to his poverty. So these two walked for the future in separate paths, and my military prospects ended in nothing.

I was not disappointed. On the contrary, I was rather glad; for my heart had long been finally set on the literary career. I had read much of its glories, but had heard little of its perils and pitfalls; or hearing, had taught myself to despise them.

About this time, the General's remittances having, as I supposed, ceased, or been rejected on a point of temper, I was removed from my school, and informed that the time had arrived when I must, if possible, do something for myself. It was towards the close of the year 1829, or the commencement of the year 1830, when I thus, very greatly to my satisfaction, found that I was considered to be a man, and fit to fight my own battle. But it was not much of a battle that I had to fight after all; and I slid very easily into the harness of work and business, finding myself, through my father's influence, installed as secretary to an old English gentleman, who wanted a young man to keep his accounts, answer his letters, read the French and Belgian newspapers to him in English, and accompany him in his drives. I was delighted, as the pay was liberal, the labour light, and the hours of attendance not burdensome.

This gentleman was a remarkable person in his way, and one who has left his name in Belgium as one of the worthies and benefactors of the country: no other than the William Cockerill who was among the first of English working mechanics to carry the nascent machine manufacture of England to the continent of Europe. He was a man of strong natural powers of mind, but of very imperfect education, and a sturdy specimen of what

is now the fashion to call the "self-made man." He
was at this time about seventy-four years of age, and had
three sons—one, John Cockerill, the proprietor of the
famous iron foundry and machine works of Seraing, near
Liege—an establishment in which it was reported the
King of the Netherlands was a partner;—the other,
James Cockerill, a wealthy proprietor of mines and
colleries, who resided at Aix-la-Chapelle, and was the
grandee of the place, famous for his hospitality, his
taste, and his love of horses and horse-racing;—and the
third and eldest, William Cockerill, who resided at
Berlin, and was largely engaged in the manufacture of
iron goods. The old gentleman, who had constructed
several engineering works in St. Petersburg and other
parts of Russia, besides establishing the iron-works at
Seraing, and some important woollen cloth manufactories
at Verviers, had long previously retired from business;
and lived alone with his niece in a large house at the
corner of the Boulevard de Louvain. His accounts were
simple and easily kept, and his correspondence was not
very extensive. He cared nothing for literature, but
took a keen interest in Continental politics; so that I
had but little to do except to read the French newspapers
to him. He cared little about English politics, but
thought that a great deal too much fuss was made about
Daniel O'Connell, Catholic Emancipation, and the
Reform Bill. The old gentleman was fond of a mild
joke; revelled in the oldest of Joe Millerisms, however
often it might be repeated; and invariably called an
English newspaper that was then published at Brussels
as a small rival of *Galignani* under the title of *News*

*from Home*, the "*Knaves* from home," which was the pronunciation of the word "news" by the French and Belgians, and which with a chuckle he affirmed to be a true designation of the English colony that had taken up its abode in Brussels. His own French was exceedingly imperfect, so that it became my business to translate the French news and French leading articles to him, which I soon learned to do with as much ease and quickness as if I were reading from an English paper. Like his son at Aix-la-Chapelle, he was very fond of horses, and would always purchase the best pair of greys or bays for his numerous carriages that money could procure. He was too feeble to walk, but every afternoon took a carriage airing on the Boulevards, the *Allée Verte*, or on the road to Waterloo and the Bois de Soignies; sometimes accompanied by me, and sometimes by his niece and housekeeper, who was then about fifty years of age, and expected, as report would have it, to inherit his large property.

I had not been three months with Mr. Cockerill when an adventure occurred. A gentleman who would give no name desired to see him, and after some delay was admitted. I asked him to take a chair, but he replied that in consequence of an infirmity he could not sit down; that he had not sat for years, and that his usual mode of resting was to lean upon a staff, which, with permission, he would do now. He put a few questions to Mr. Cockerill, which were of no particular significance to me, but which appeared to relate to the affairs of a bygone period of his business life. Mr. Cockerill evidently knew him, and as evidently mistrusted or disliked him;

answered some of his questions in a surly tone, and others not at all; and finally broke off the interview by wishing his visitor good morning, and ringing the bell for his niece to take his arm and lead him to his bed-room. I was left alone with "the man who could not sit down," and whose name I did not learn; who speedily took his departure, after a few remarks about the weather, and an expression of sorrow that Mr. Cockerill was so infirm.

I was aroused from bed at my father's house the next morning about five o'clock by Mr. Cockerill's coachman, who came to say that Mr. Cockerill was up at that unusually early hour, and desired to see me immediately on important business. Much wondering, I dressed myself in all haste, and proceeded to the house on the Boulevards, where I found Mr. Cockerill and his niece at the breakfast-table. I was asked to partake, and then told that I must get ready in an hour, or less if I liked, to start for Seraing. I was to take one of his carriages, and travel post all the way. Having gone to Seraing, with a message to Mr. John Cockerill, I was to proceed as quickly as possible to Aix-la-Chapelle, and deliver the same message to Mr. James Cockerill. This done, I was to return in the same manner to Brussels, with the answer that each of them might give me. The message was a verbal one, and was simply a command to his sons, that if any person applied to them for particulars of their business, or made any request to look at their books, he should be peremptorily refused. I could not help asso-ciating this singular message with the visit of "the man who could not sit down." But I said nothing. Miss Yates, his niece, produced two good-sized bags of five-franc pieces in silver. Each bag was ticketed as containing five hundred francs. With this money I was to pay the posting and other expenses of the trip. If the sum were not sufficient to bring me back, when I reached Aix-la-Chapelle Mr. James Cockerill would let me have any additional money I might require. I was delighted with the prospect of the journey. I was to see the world, or a little of it; had what seemed almost fabulous wealth in my possession; and moreover, I was to travel in state, like a *grand seigneur*. I thought to myself that if my successive postilions did not make their whips crack more merrily than usual at "my" entrance to every town through which "I" had to pass, they should not receive the extra *trink-gelt*, which the members of that now defunct fraternity invariably expected in addition to the usual fee per mile; or at least that I would not behave so munificently to them as I might do in other circumstances.

I was ready to depart in less than the hour; had my instructions emphatically repeated; and was whirled out of the Porte de Louvain amid a cracking of the postilion's whip, which was pleasant to hear, and reached Louvain, fifteen miles distant, in about an hour and three-quarters. At the entrance to every village, I had the satisfaction, not only to hear the postilion's whip ringing and cracking lustily in the air, as if he would announce a personage of importance, but to overhear him tell the ostler at the hotel in Louvain, as I alighted to take refreshment, and to change horses and postilion, that I was a "*jeune milord Anglais.*" Of course, I made up my mind that that par-

ticular postilion should be duly rewarded for his description of me, especially if he passed on the secret of my
"lordship" to his successor. The only drawback to my
silly satisfaction was that, in obedience to instructions, I
had to hurry on as fast as relays of horses could carry
me, and that I was not permitted to stay a few hours in
such interesting old cities as Louvain, Tirlemont, St.
Trond, and Liege, and visit the cathedrals and other
public buildings. Shortly after nightfall, I found myself
on the bank of the Meuse, opposite Seraing, and in waiting for the ferry-boat that was to convey me and the
carriage to the other side. I found Mr. John Cockerill
at home, a rare thing for that busy and restless man,
who was always flying to and fro between Liege and
Berlin, and between Berlin, Warsaw, Moscow, and
St. Petersburg. He received me most kindly, but was
very much puzzled at the oddity of his father's message. He would not hear of my proceeding to Aix-la-
Chapelle that night, and arranged that I should leave in
the morning, after looking over the works, if I felt so
disposed. "You will be at Aix," he said, "by three
o'clock in the afternoon, and to-night you can rest yourself, and tell me, if you can, what made my father take
this unaccountable fancy into his head."

I told him of the "man who could not sit down," and
that in my opinion his visit had some connection with
the matter. "I think so too," replied Mr. Cockerill,
"but my father need not have troubled his mind about
him. I know the man of old. He fancies he has a
grievance; but his grievance has long ago been disposed
of, and has nothing to do with me or my brother." What

the grievance was he did not tell me, but I learned long
afterwards that it arose out of a trade dispute of many
years standing, by which the elder Mr. Cockerill had
bound himself not to establish a woollen manufactory in
the town of Verviers, or within twenty miles of it, which
engagement this "man who could not sit down" con-
tended had been broken, in the spirit, if not in the letter,
by the encouragement which Mr. Cockerill had given to
a near relative to do that which he was forbidden to do
himself. Some legal proceedings had been taken, in
which Mr. Cockerill gained the day; but the subject remained a sore one in the mind of the unwelcome visitor
of the day previous.

In the morning, after having gone through the various
branches of this great establishment, at that time the most
celebrated on the Continent, I started for Aix-la-Chapelle,
travelling in the same luxurious fashion as before, and
feeling very much as if I had really been the "*milord
Anglais*" which my first postilion had represented. I
had an opportunity, ere the day was far advanced, of
airing my German in the Prussian town of Aachen, which
the French call Aix, adding La Chapelle, to distinguish
it from two other towns of the same name, Aix-en-Savoie
and Aix-en-Provence.

Mr. James Cockerill was as hospitable as his brother,
and, like him, expressed great surprise at his father's
message. This, however, was not my affair. I had had
a pleasant journey to Aix, and should have an equally
pleasant journey back again to Brussels, if all went well
on the morrow; and in the meantime had leisure to look
about me in Aachen, to taste its disagreeable medicinal

waters that smelt like rotten eggs, to visit its splendid
cathedral, sacred to the memory of Charlemagne, and
also to a piece of the supposed veritable toe-nail of the
Apostle Peter. Next morning I took my departure,
journeying as rapidly as I could, in order that I might
comfort the mind of old Mr. Cockerill with the assurance
that I had faithfully delivered his message to his sons,
and that both of them had promised implicit obedience.
It turned out, however, that there had been no necessity
for any hurry on my part. On the very day after my
departure, Mr. Cockerill, unable to contend any longer
with his alarm and anxiety, had, to " make assurance
doubly sure," started, along with his niece, for Seraing,
travelling post as I had done. How it was that I did
not pass him on the road, I was unable to explain, except
on the supposition that he had rested for the night at
Louvain, Tirlemont, or St. Trond. Greatly I regretted
my enforced haste, and the consequent loss of the opportunity of profiting, however slightly, by my travel. It
was a fortnight before the old gentleman returned home.
On his way back the coachman drove against some accidental obstruction in the road between St. Trond and
Tirlemont, and upset the carriage. Mr. Cockerill and
his niece were thrown violently to the ground. Strange
to say, the elder and weaker person escaped without a
bruise, while the younger and stronger was severely cut
about the head and face, and returned to Brussels a
pitiable spectacle.

This was not the only journey I was destined to take
with this couple. In the autumn of the year 1829 there
resided in Paris a celebrated oculist, who daily advertised

in *Galignani's Messenger*, whose name I cannot recall; and Mr. Cockerill, who was fast losing the sight of one of his eyes, and was afraid of losing the sight of both, suddenly determined to take a journey to Paris to consult him. It was also determined that I should go with him. I was fresh from reading the history of the Great Revolution of 1789, and the " Reign of Terror " that succeeded it, and promised myself great satisfaction from a visit to the beautiful and historical city, where all these mighty events had occurred. We were to travel by slow stages, with Mr. Cockerill's own favourite greys; and, as the horses could not well accomplish more than forty miles a day, if so many, we would have to stop for the night at many celebrated towns and fortified cities. We slept the first night at Mons, the second at Valenciennes, the third at Cambrai, the fourth at St. Quentin, the fifth at Compiègne, the sixth at Senlis, the seventh at Pontoise, and on the eighth arrived at Paris. The old gentleman slept the greater part of the day, rousing himself up now and then, as I told him the names of the places through which we were passing. Though frail, he was always very ready for his dinner when the horses halted to bait and rest at the way-side inns. I was not a connoisseur in cookery in those early days. All was grist that came to my mill, for health and hunger gave zest to the plainest fare that was placed before me. But Mr. Cockerill, as was natural at his age, was vastly more particular. He required succulent and savoury dishes, and invariably enquired, if we stopped at anything like a pretentious hotel or restaurant, whether we could have *Paté de foie gras, Tête de veau à la maître d'hôtel*, or *Oreilles de cochons à la*

*Ste. Menehould.* We were generally successful enough in finding the first dainty, though it was only once, I think at Cambrai, that we were rewarded with the second or the third. To me, a mere boy, to be treated like a full grown man, to have a choice in ordering the dinner and the wine, and to be allowed to drink of the latter *ad libitum* as if I had been fifty instead of sixteen, was an acknowledgment of my manhood that had great charms for my young imagination. The distances, measured by time rather than by miles in those days when railways were the dreams of enthusiasts, so different from our own swifter epoch when we can dart from London to Paris in eleven hours and a half, and send a message to America in a minute, impressed most people with the magnitude of the world, and not, as in our epoch, with its littleness; and, by the time I reached Paris, I was of opinion that I was a considerable traveller. Old and mature as I thought myself, I was by far too young to take notice of the political agitation in Paris at this time, or to hear even the faintest rumblings of the storm that was destined to overturn the throne of Charles X., and to prepare the way for a series of revolutions that are not yet ended, or likely to be ended until the French learn that the first elements of liberty are patience and self-control. But I revelled in the sights of Paris; visited all its historical buildings, my mind full of the incidents which had rendered them famous, and looking at every celebrated spot with a recollection fresh from my reading of the events which had ennobled, or, it might be, had disgraced it.

The great oculist—if great he were—failed to be of service to Mr. Cockerill, and gave him no hope of the preservation of the one affected eye, and little hope of the preservation of the other ; so he resolved to return to Brussels. A few days before our departure, a tall, elderly gentleman sent in his card to our apartments in the Rue St. Anne, on which was inscribed " Lord Blantyre." Mr. Cockerill was indulging in his afternoon *siesta,* and it became my duty to receive the visitor. His lordship explained that he did not know Mr. Cockerill, personally—but had heard that he was the proprietor of a house in the Rue Royale, Brussels, fronting the park, which he very much wanted to hire for a term of years. Knowing all Mr. Cockerill's affairs, and that he never interfered in the letting of his houses, I referred him to the agent at Brussels. Lord Blantyre ultimately took the house, and I only mention this trifling circumstance, to narrate the melancholy fate of this amiable man, which might have been other than it was, had he been disappointed in hiring this particular mansion. In less than a year after this time, during the short, sharp and terrible struggle in the streets of Brussels, that accomplished the Belgian Revolution of 1830, Lord Blantyre went up into an attic of his house to survey the conflict that was raging at his door and in the park opposite, between the Brussels mob and the troops of the King of the Netherlands ; and unfortunately stretched his head out of the window the better to observe what was going on. A shot, that may have been accidental, but that more probably was fired in mere wantonness, went right through his neck, and he fell back in the arms of his wife, immediately behind him, who had vainly endeavoured to dissuade him from exposing himself.

The shot was fatal; and having seen much of him between his first visit to Mr. Cockerill at Paris and his tragical end, I felt his loss with all the keenness of a personal calamity.

I had influence enough with Mr. Cockerill to persuade him to return to Brussels through a different series of towns than that by which we had reached Paris, but only remember, at this distance of time, that Arras, Lisle, and Tournay were three of them, and that we were, as before, eight days on the journey. The change of route made no difference to him or his niece, but it made the difference to me that I saw new places and gratified my love of travel.

About this time the signs of political strife and approaching convulsions in Belgium were manifest. My father—a Tory of the old school, was a keen partisan of the King of the Netherlands in his ill-judged attempts to assimilate Belgium to Holland in everything, even in the language—and spoke so much and so warmly on the subject, that I could not choose but be fully informed of all that was taking place. His early residence in Holland, where his mother was buried, and his connection with the Dutch Mackays, helped to strengthen his Dutch predilections, and he was all for the king, and against the malcontents. But, my sympathies were with the Belgians. The leader of the Belgian or anti-Dutch party was a M. De Potter, aided very materially by a young lawyer and journalist, named Sylvain Van de Weyer, one of the editors of the *Courier Belge*, afterwards and for many years the highly respected Belgian ambassador to the Court of St. James's. Among the most·

eminent and most obnoxious leaders of the Dutch party
in Brussels was one Libri Bagnano, a bookseller and
publisher in the Rue Montague de la Cour, who wielded
the pen of a ready writer, and wrote a long-continued
series of very trenchant, witty, provocative articles and
pamphlets in defence of the policy of the king. This
gentleman had a hunch-back, and was diminutive in
person, for both of which misfortunes or defects he was
mercilessly held up to ridicule by the Belgian separatist
and revolutionary press. In an evil hour for him, it was
discovered, or at all events it was loudly asserted, that
he had in his youth been condemned to the galleys,
or *bagnes;* that his very name *Bagnano,* was given in
commemoration of the fact; and that he was marked on
the back, (burnt in the ordinary manner), with the
letters T. F., signifying *travaux forcés.* This allegation
was treated as a calumny by the friends of M. Bagnano,
and of the king ; but only met with the scornful response
"let him show his back." The war carried on against
Bagnano by the liberal and Catholic press, for the
Roman Catholics were liberal and revolutionary in
Belgium at that day, in so far, as they desired separation
from Protestant Holland; was bitter in the extreme; and
succeeded in making him the most unpopular man in
Brussels. Next to him, a Dutchman named Felix
Van Maanen, who served the high office of Minister of
Justice in the then existing administration, came in for
the greatest share of popular execration. The mal-
content Belgians with the exception of the priestly
party, did not at that time desire, or at all events ask
for the independence of the country. All they wanted

was its legislative separation from Holland. It was generally thought that even this might not be necessary if the obstinate king would abdicate in favour of the Prince of Orange, who was as popular among the Belgians as among the Dutch, and who, it was thought, would act in a conciliatory spirit and redress all the real grievances of which the Belgians complained, one of which was, that no one, however competent in other respects, should be allowed to keep a school unless he was able to teach the Dutch language. In the midst of the Belgian excitement, and when the temper of the people was rapidly becoming more hostile to the king and his advisers, the French Revolution of July, 1830, exploded with sudden violence, and drove Charles X., the stupidest and most obstinate of all the Bourbons, from the throne which he was unworthy to occupy. The French people contemptuously allowed him to leave the country, an exile for the second time, too old and too broken a man to expect that any turn of the great wheel of Destiny would ever restore him to authority or to home. He took refuge in Great Britain, as his brother Louis XVIII. had done forty years previously, and found an asylum in the melancholy Palace of Holyrood, which was placed at his disposal by King William IV., who had not long previously ascended the throne. The news of the French Revolution fell upon the Belgians like a blazing torch into a powder magazine, and created a commotion and perturbation in men's minds that presaged inevitable explosion. Nor did things at this time, Mr. Cockerill thought, look very favourable in England, where the Reform Bill agitation began to assume formidable dimensions. "All the world is going mad," said the old gentleman, in a despondent tone, "and though I am not surprised at anything the French do, for I look upon them as a nation of monkeys, I am surprised that the English will not let well alone. As for that Daniel O'Connell, and Hunt, the blacking-maker, I would hang them both on the same gallows." It was one night in August, not many weeks after the flight of Charles X., that Auber's splendid opera of "La Muette de Portici," better known to the lyric stage of Italy, England and Germany as "Masaniello," was announced at the Théâtre de la Monnaie, then the principal theatre of Brussels; and my father proposed that he and I should witness the performance. As the incidents of the well-known opera show the progress and success of a democratic uprising, and consequent revolution, there was a general impression all over the city that a political demonstration of some kind or other was likely to be made. Quiet and timid people in the cafés and places of public resort were of opinion that no such too suggestive performance should be allowed, and that the manager ought to be called upon, in the interest of the public peace, to substitute "Fra Diavolo," "Der Freischütz," or some other harmless opera, that was void of political allusion. But the hint was not taken. The crowd in the Place de la Monnaie, half an hour before the opening of the doors, was vast and uproarious. It was with the utmost difficulty that my father and I obtained entrance to the pit, where there was only standing room. The frantic excitement that greeted the overture was such as I

should not have believed possible unless I had witnessed
it, and went on increasing as the performance proceeded.
More than once the whole audience started to their feet
as if by one simultaneous impulse, and cheered and
waved their handkerchiefs, and stamped, and roared,
and gesticulated as if they had been a congregation of
madmen and madwomen—the women, perhaps, being the
maddest of all.

At the finale of the opera, and just as the curtain
descended, someone in the boxes—some said it was a lady
and some affirmed it to be a student—suddenly displayed
and waved the French tricolour flag. At this signal,
which was doubtless preconcerted, the audience raised a
shout, which seemed actually to shake the house, as if
with the concussion of a mighty wind, and ere the sound
died away, was succeeded by a chorus of voices singing
the Marseillaise. This, too, was possibly preconcerted.
The effect was grand and terrible, and the crowd, still
singing the splendid revolutionary anthem, made its
way into the open space before the theatre, formed itself
into a wild irregular procession, to which some unknown
person, with a loud voice, gave a direction by shouting
" *Chez Libri Bagnano!* " My father and I were in
the midst of the moving mass, and followed whither
it impelled us. " It will go badly with poor Bagnano,"
said my father, " if they find him at home. I would not
give sixpence for his life's purchase." Arrived opposite
Bagnano's shop in the Rue Montagne de la Cour, the
crowd halted, broke the windows, and attempted to batter
in the door. Bagnano, forewarned by a few minutes,
escaped in his night clothes from a back window by the

aid of the gutter-pipe, and got clear off. Speedily the
crowd burst open the door and swarmed into the house,
in search of the object of their hatred. They ransacked
his secrétaire, tore down all the books from the shelves
in his library and shop, and threw the fragments into the
street, together with the furniture and utensils. There
was a cry to set fire to the building, but in consequence
of danger to the houses on each side, the design was
abandoned, and the mob contented itself with gutting
the house from top to bottom. Another ominous cry
was raised, " *Chez Van Maanen !* " The distance to be
traversed was not great; and again attuning their rough
voices to the Marseillaise, the crowd tramped heavily
along, keeping time to the music, to the house of the
Minister of Justice. Fortunately he was not at home,
or had managed to escape ; no one knew. But the doors
were rapidly forced in, and the mob poured in like a
torrent. The mirrors, ornaments, and pictures were
smashed, broken, and cast from the windows to the
garden, and the torch applied to the furniture and the
bedding. The house stood alone, so that there was little
or no danger of the fire extending. In less than ten
minutes the mansion was in flames, and thick volumes
of smoke poured upwards to the sky, succeeded by a
lurid glare that lit up all Brussels. Those who passed
the scene of devastation in the morning, discovered
amid the still smoking ruins a huge gallows, from which
depended the effigy of the Minister of Justice, with the
inscription above it, in large letters,

FELIX INFELIX !

The King's palace would doubtless have been attacked,

and shared the fate of the hotel of the minister, but pre-
cautions had been taken, and all the military force at
command was drawn up in the open space between
it and the park; and the crowd had at that time
no desire to draw conclusions with the soldiers. The
gunsmiths' shops, however, were less fortunate than the
palace, and were speedily ransacked. The ironmongers'
shops shared the same fate, and people who could not
procure fire-arms contented themselves for the time
being with scythes, or with long poles to which they affixed
knives, and transformed them into rude but formidable
spears. The other damage done during the night was
inconsiderable, but in the upper or new part of the city
scarcely an eye was closed; and dense crowds swarmed
into the streets as spectators of the mischief. The
animus of the people was decidedly anti-monarchical,
and shouts of *Vive la République* resounded on every
side. In the early dawn there were to be seen hundreds
of French tricolour flags, hastily improvised out of sheets
and table-cloths, smeared with red and blue stripes,
dangling from the windows in the Rue Royale and the
mercantile streets, though nothing of the kind was to be
seen in the aristocratic quarter of the Rue Ducale and
the Boulevards. As the morning wore on, the republican
feeling displayed itself unmistakably. Men climbed up
ladders, with paint-pots and brushes, and effaced the word
"roylae" from the corners where the name of the Rue
Royale was exhibited, and then demolished, or pulled
down the royal arms over the doors of the public buildings,
and called upon the tradesmen who announced that they
were bakers, butchers, grocers, fishmongers, or other

purveyors to the King, to score out the obnoxious words
" king and royal." One violent fellow, with more zeal
than knowledge, seeing the inscription Fabrique de
mi*roirs*, mounted a ladder with a paint-pot and effaced
the letters *roirs*, with the notion apparently that the
peccant syllable was somehow or other connected with
royalty. One M. Leroy, a boot and shoemaker, was
waited upon by a crowd of lads armed with spades and
scythes—one of them, the leader of the band, brandishing
a pistol—and commanded to take down the board over his
shop, on which his name was painted Leroy—and M.
Leroy (King) had no choice but to obey, and the young
wags or scamps disappeared, shouting *Vive la République !*

The tumults of this and several succeeding days greatly
alarmed Mr. Cockerill. The King was at the Hague, and
manifested no disposition to submit to the dictation of
the mob, even when he learned that the disaffection was
not local and confined to Brussels, but general, and that
Louvain, Liége, and other cities had pronounced against
his government. A report was industriously circulated
that his Majesty had resolved to send a Dutch army,
commanded by the Prince of Orange, against rebellious
Brussels ; but the friends of the Prince took especial
pains to contradict it, and to make it known that under
no circumstances would that Prince consent to bear arms
against the Belgians. Within a fortnight of the outbreak
and the establishment of a Provisional Government, it
would have been possible, had the King manifested any
disposition to yield, to have calmed the public excitement,
and saved Belgium and Holland, by the appointment

of the Prince of Orange as Viceroy of Belgium, with
full powers to redress the grievances of the Belgians.
But the King was as obstinate as if he had been a Bourbon
or a Stuart, and, as his elder son would not lend himself
to the military coercion of the better half of the kingdom,
appointed his second son, Prince Frederick, to the command of a large force to besiege Brussels.  Mr. Cockerill,
as soon as he became convinced that force was to be
employed, resolved to leave the country.   His first
thought was to take refuge, with his son at Aix-la-Chapelle.   But the mob of Aix-la-Chapelle shared in the
revolutionary fever of the time, broke out into open insur-
rection, and sacked and destroyed Mr. James Cockerill's
house without provocation or pretence, and for no other
reason than that he was the richest man in the town,
or that, as Marshal Blucher might have said, "his
house was a beautiful one to sack."   But the Aix-la-
Chapelle disturbances soon subsided, and the King of
Prussia took effectual measures to prevent their renewal.
Old Mr. Cockerill, reassured on this point, abandoned a
hasty determination to go to London, and finally decided
to make his home, at least for a while, in Aix.   He
asked my father to allow me to accompany him, and he
and I gladly consented.   There was some difficulty in
procuring post-horses, as every available animal had been
put in requisition by the Provisional Government for the
wants of the army of defence, so Mr. Cockerill resolved to
travel by easy stages with his own team.   We were nearly a
week in reaching Aix, and were duly installed in Mr. James
Cockerill's new mansion, one of the finest in the town,
which he had hired after the destruction of the one still

finer in which he had previously resided. It did not appear that any feeling of political hostility existed towards him, or other leading citizens, or the Prussian Government; but that the outbreak was that of the roughs against the gentlemen, and that of the poor against the rich.

Mr. Cockerill had left Brussels none too soon. A division of the Dutch army, under the command of H.R.H. Prince Frederick, bombarded the city a few days after his departure, to the wild indignation of the inhabitants. The proprietor of the Hôtel de Belle Vue, in the corner of the Place Royale, was in the market in the Grande Place, opposite the Hôtel de Ville, when he heard the booming of the guns, and saw a shot strike against one of the houses, and was seized with such terror that he fell to the ground helpless, and never recovered. An English lad, an apprentice to Mr. Legge, the English saddler of the Prince of Orange, was killed at the door of the shop by a chance ball, and several other fatal calamities occurred, the news of which spread rapidly and increased the exasperation of the people. When the bombarding troops attempted to enter the city, they found that a series of formidable barricades had been erected in the Rue Royale, and the streets that commanded the approaches to the palace of the King, the House of Representatives, the Hôtel de Ville, and other buildings of strategic importance, and that each barricade was defended by hundreds of earnest volunteers, thoroughly armed and provided with ammunition. Capable leaders of the people seemed to spring up as if by magic, and just at the moment when they were wanted, and

one, especially a man with a wooden leg, only known
to the people as *jambe du bois*, wrought wonders at the
head of a body of adherents in repelling the troops. The
fury of the fight was in the Rue Royale and the park,
and all the houses in the line were riddled with shot and
bomb-shells, which, long after the struggle had ended,
were taken out of the walls, and again stuck in, after the
damage had been repaired, to show the indignity to which
the city had been exposed by the troops of its own king,
and to keep up the animosity of the citizens against the
Dutch. The Belgian revolution was not a mere insur-
rection, but an almost unanimous national movement,
as the King discovered when it was too late. On the 4th
of October, the King's troops—having evacuated Brussels
and other cities of Belgium, and retired to the citadel of
Antwerp, whither the French Government sent a force to
besiege them—the Provisional Government proclaimed
the independence of Belgium. The efforts of the veteran
general Lafayette in Paris having stemmed the republican torrent that threatened to overwhelm France,
and diverted the raging waters into the channel of a
constitutional monarchy, of which the presiding genius
was to be a "Citizen King," the Belgian moderates
judged it the wisest and safest policy to imitate the
example, and direct all their efforts to the establishment of a monarchy. In the meantime the Chambers
appointed a Provisional President, or viceroy, with
powers as a king, to form a responsible ministry.
The choice fell upon a venerable country gentleman,
whose name few had ever heard of before, a M. Surlet
de Chokier, whose character inspired the respect of

all parties as a man of intelligence who would do his
duty, neither more nor less, and who did not possess
the slightest taint of personal ambition.  On the 26th
of December it was announced to the Congress, then
sitting in Brussels, that the allied powers of Europe
had recognized the independence of Belgium, and its
permanent separation from Holland.  This was the first
blow to the famous treaty of Vienna, solemnly agreed
to by all the great powers after the battle of Waterloo.
Henceforth that much vaunted document became of no
more value than waste paper, and was set at nought by
every power whose interest or inclination it was to
ignore it.

Such news arrived at Aix-la-Chapelle of the damage
done by the Dutch soldiers in the houses of the wealthier
citizens, during their occupation of the town, that I was
despatched to Brussels to report on what had been done to
the house of Mr. Cockerill on the Boulevards, to instal some
responsible person to take care of it, and to bring to Aix
a favourite travelling carriage and pair of horses which
had been left behind.  Report had not greatly exaggerated
the devastation committed by the troops.  A hundred or
more had been installed in Mr. Cockerill's mansion ; had
drunk up or allowed to run to waste all the wines and
spirits in his cellar, amounting to at least a thousand
bottles ; had smashed all the drawing-room mirrors and
chandeliers ; had ripped up all the pictures on the
walls, and in the most outrageous manner defiled the
beds, and even the tables and chairs, refusing, with
disgusting malice, to make use of the conveniences which
every well-constructed house affords.  The Augean

stables could not have smelt worse than that luckless
house, which was but one of hundreds that had en-
dured the same foul indignities from the hands of the
infuriated blackguards who served in the army of the
King. The carriage had been so hacked and cut, and
otherwise vilely treated by the soldiers who had made
their beds in it, as to be not worth the trouble of removal.
I was a fortnight in Brussels before I could get the
house purified, and place a trustworthy English mechanic
and his wife in possession, and was able, at the end of
that time, to make my way back to Aix-la-Chapelle.

Mr. Cockerill bore the recital of the mischief with
much equanimity, consoling himself with the calcula-
tion that the war damage would doubtless have to be
paid for by the King of Holland, when the final settlement was made between the King and his former subjects.
In casting about them for a king, the first choice of the
Belgians fell upon the Duke de Nemours, a younger son
of Louis Philippe, the newly installed King of the French.
But the King refused his consent on behalf of his son,
a minor, and the Belgians had consequently to proceed
to a new election. In order that the Crown should
not seem to go a-begging, the Provisional Government
prudently made sure beforehand that the person to whom
the perilous gift was to be offered would accept it; and
this having been carefully ascertained, the choice of the
Legislature was duly announced to have fallen upon His
Royal Highness Prince Leopold of Saxe-Coburg Gotha,
widower of the lamented Princess Charlotte, daughter of
George IV. The Prince had previously refused the throne
of Greece, but did not feel himself at liberty to refuse that

of Belgium, the acceptance of which would retain him in the vicinity of England, which he loved so well, and in which he for many years had found a home and friends. The Prince of Orange had once been a suitor for the hand of the Princess Charlotte, but had been rejected in favour of Prince Leopold. "Hang the fellow!" said the Prince of Orange, when he heard upon whom the choice of the Belgians had fallen. "He seems fated to stand in my way! Years ago he deprived me of a wife, and now he has deprived me of a kingdom!"

Prince Leopold ascended the throne in July, 1831, under the title of Leopold I., King of the Belgians; and in the November following, Great Britain, France, Austria, and Prussia, which had previously acknowledged the independence of the little kingdom, concluded a treaty with the King, which was signed at London, in which the boundaries of Belgium were defined, and in which the powers severally and collectively guaranteed to the King the peaceful possession of his kingdom.

My father had, as already stated, always sympathized with the Dutch King and his advisers in their endeavours to retain Belgium, which they might easily have done if they had been wise in time. Though he accepted the fact of the revolution as well as he was able, he never thoroughly reconciled himself to the reign of King Leopold. I sent him from Aix-la-Chapelle some verses which I had written in celebration of King Leopold's accession and inauguration, to which he returned the following reply :—

"83, Montagne de la Cour,
"15th September, 1831.

" My dearest Charles,—

"I received your letter containing the stanzas upon the *inoculation* (inauguration) of Leopold. Without flattery, allow me to say that they are much admired even by better judges than myself. A copy of the poem, illuminated and ornamented, is in the hands of a high official, who has promised to place it under the royal eye. You may suppose that with my opinions as regards the revolution I care but little about this; but you, perhaps, may. We are all down in the mouth here, not even excepting the King himself—*et bouder semble être l'ordre du jour.* Alas, the poor *blouse!* The ci-devant civic guard, hitherto the terror of the house of Nassau, are now called by the populace the *garde sauve qui peut,* in allusion to their ignominious retreat from Louvain. You have, no doubt, heard of the haystack of moustachios left by these Trojans in their flight? The Government of King Leopold intends, it is said, to purchase the lot, to stuff mattrasses for the military hospitals! His Majesty goes regularly to Laeken to dine, sup, and, *perhaps,* sleep. He does not appear to enjoy half as good spirits as I do; and I am quite sure I should be very sorry to change places with him. Write soon, and believe me,

" Yours affectionately,
" George Mackay."

The health of Mr. Cockerill began to fail in Aix-la-Chapelle, and with the view of procuring him fresher air, and greater quiet, he was removed to the Château de

Bernsberg, a kind of castle with a feudal tower, about five miles from the city. The Château belonged to Mr. James Cockerill, who had let the farm-house attached to it and the farm to a worthy German, who made very excellent butter and cheese and did a considerable business in the rearing of cattle. But the change did not operate so favourably as was expected on the health of the invalid, and he sank gradually into so comatose a state as to be scarcely sensible of passing events. He took but the slightest interest in himself or any body else, and listened to what was said or read to him without appearing to understand it. During this interval, which lasted until the commencement of the year 1832, having no duties to perform, I bethought myself that I ought not to eat the bread of idleness at another's expense, and meditated a return to Brussels. But I was over-persuaded by Mr. James Cockerill to remain at the Château de Bernsberg, to transact for his father such light business as had to be transacted; for his niece, who was an excellent nurse, was of very humble origin, and had not the education to act as secretary. To overcome my scruples about the bread of idleness, Mr. James Cockerill, who had a large family, that increased by one annually, or biennially proposed that I should give the elder boys and girls, ranging from fifteen downwards, lessons in arithmetic, the rudiments of mathematics, and English composition. I fell in cheerfully with this arrangement, and devoted all the time that was required, two hours daily, to this pleasant duty. My abundant leisure did not hang heavily on my hands. I read a great deal in French and German—for English books were not easily procurable, especially the new ones—and acquired for my years a wide acquaintance with the masterpieces of both languages. My favourite German poet at this time was Theodor Körner, a young soldier, who had aroused the patriotic fervour of the Fatherland by his stirring war songs, and done even more than even Goethe himself to impress the youth of Germany with the idea that it was nobler to be a German than a Bavarian, a Wurtemburger, a Hanoverian, a Prussian, or an Austrian; and produced slowly, and imperceptibly, the wide prevalence of that patriotic spirit and national *élan* which enabled Bismarck and Moltke, in 1870, to overwhelm France and convert the kingdom of Prussia into the empire of Germany. My favourite French poets were Victor Hugo and Auguste Barbier. I am unable to say which I admired the most, and oftenest read, but I think the latter exercised the greatest influence over my mind, by the splendid fulminations and denunciations of his *Iambes*, a series of poems unequalled in the whole range of French literature for manly vigour of thought and style, and in the blazing light of which the more popular effusions of Béranger, Delavigne, De Lamartine, and other contemporary poets, are but pale lamps compared with the effulgence of the sun. I thought then, as I think now, that the description of the first Napoleon riding the war-horse France, in the passage commencing—

> "O Corse ! à cheveux plats, que la France était belle
> Au beau soleil de Messidor !
> C'était une cavale, indomptable et rebelle,
> Sans frein d'acier ni rênes d'or,"

was one of the noblest images to be found either in

ancient or modern poetry, carried out perfectly in all its parts, and to the smallest accessories of the metaphor.

I endeavoured to be pleased with Béranger, but in vain. The lack of dignity, except in five or six of his many hundreds of songs, and his general frivolity and indecency, either rendered me indifferent or offended me. I remember reading for the first time his particularly French and very lascivious song, "La Bacchante," which, it is to be hoped, no Frenchman or Frenchwoman ever sung; and feeling indignant at such a prostitution of talent—I could not call it genius—to so unworthy a subject. I was lying on a sofa, on a very hot day in July, at the Château de Bernsberg, and turned over the leaves to find something better than the drunken Bacchante to reconcile me to the "poet of the French people," when I lighted upon one entitled "Ma Grand'Mère." Here the disreputable old woman is represented as impressing upon her grand-daughters the necessity of making good use of their youth and charms, and as telling them the numbers of her lovers, and the manner in which she had deceived their grandfather. I was no prude, but this was too much for my modesty and sense of decency. The poem, if it may be so called, appeared to me such treason to the majesty of the poet's calling, that I flung the volume through the closed window, breaking the glass with a violent smash, and resolved to read Béranger no more. Mr. Cockerill's niece was walking in the garden below, heard the crash, and saw the volume fall. She picked it up, and came into my room with an angry frown and petulant voice, and asked the reason of my conduct. I told her, offered to pay for the broken glass, and declared I would have smashed the whole window, instead of only one pane, rather than not do what I had done. She was mollified, said she would accept the offered payment, and said, not too angrily, I thought, that I was a foolish boy.

My wrath against Béranger was somewhat appeased by this relief to my feelings. I did not carry out my threat of reading him no more, and speedily learned to admire his satirical and moral pieces, of which the latter were very few; but came to the conclusion, inexperienced as I was, that he was of his age only, and would not retain either a large or very honourable place in the literature of his country.

I not only read but wrote much at this time. I translated Burns' song, " Ye Banks and Braes o' Bonnie Doon," into German; and endeavoured to translate it into French, but broke down hopelessly, not from ignorance of French, for I wrote it as easily and correctly as I did English, but from the poetic incompatibility of the two languages. English and German are both highly poetical languages, and can melt and fuse one into the other in translation; but French is hard, dry, and prosaic. Even our English Bible, so grand, so noble, and so simple, loses its grandeur in French. Shakspeare in French is but dry stubble, without leaves, or sap, or fruit; and Burns in French, translated by Loève Weimars, is ludicrously grotesque. Besides the labours of translation, I indulged in original poetical composition in both of these languages, as well as in English. But to write French verses was to dance in fetters; and I resolved, after having proved the fact to the satisfaction of my own mind, that I could write French poetry if I liked, to devote myself exclusively to English composition. About this time I translated, or rather paraphrased, Béranger's song, " Mon habit "—a little event, which in an unexpected manner became a turning point in my career, and enabled me to stand on the first rung of the steep and perilous ladder of the literary profession.

Old Mr. Cockerill's state of health was not likely to improve. He never stirred out from the Château de Bernsberg, never inquired after his favourite horses, never inquired after anything; scarcely ever spoke ; but lay on his bed, alive, but so slowly dying, that his physician said he might not die for two or three years. I began to chafe at my position, and long for the day when I might go to London, and embark on the great ocean of authorship. The two younger Cockerills were very kind, and had I been disposed to pursue a mercantile life, a place would probably have been found for me at Seraing with a fair chance of advancement. But as the months wore on, this bright prospect, though I did not consider it bright, darkened palpably before my eyes. The revolution in Belgium had acted injuriously upon the business of that great concern. Trade and manufactures of all kinds suffered, and the pessimists and adherents of the House of Orange predicted that still worse times were impending for Belgium. In this uneasy state of public feeling, the magnitude of an enterprise only rendered it the more liable to financial difficulty and possible collapse. All kinds of sinister rumours were afloat, and

I was ultimately led to understand, though not by any one of sufficient authority, that the King of Holland had given notice of his withdrawal from the partnership at Seraing, and had made such a demand for a settlement of accounts, as would severely test the credit of the great house of Cockerill. Though pressed by my father to make the most I could of the Cockerill connection, and enter into the service of the firm at Seraing, and possibly causing him to consider, like the description of the lad in Pope, that I was

> " A youth condemned his father's soul to cross,
> Who penned a stanza when he should engross,"

or keep accounts and write commercial epistles, I steadily made up my mind to be *aut poeta aut nullus !* I had to atone for the pleasant delusion by years of disappointment and suffering; but fortunately for me, as for all other men, I could not read the future ; and was happy in the present time, and saw the world of fame and fortune stretching before me and around me in a vast panorama of glory and beauty.

The life at the Château de Bernsberg had grown almost insufferably tedious ; and though in a certain sense sorry to see the last of poor old Mr. Cockerill, who had always been good and kind to me while his faculties lasted, I was as impatient as a young bird to try my wings, and finally took leave of Aix-la-Chapelle and the Cockerill family. I had money in my pocket, but I preferred to walk the whole distance from Aix-la-Chapelle to Brussels, and pass the night at each of the great towns on the road, sending on my personal effects by the *diligence*.

I met with companions on the way, who, like myself, were tramping it, and bound for Brussels. They were two young Frenchmen of good family, who had been smitten, after the accomplishment of the Revolution of 1830, with a love for the Poles, then struggling against the gigantic power of Russia for the restoration of the independence of Poland; and who, having volunteered in the Polish army, had, after the final collapse of the hopes of Poland, amid the smoke and grape-shot of the Grand Duke Constantine, made the best of their way homewards, very scantily provided with ready money. They were both two or three years older than myself, but we soon fraternised; slept at the same inns, and made the long way seem pleasant. One of these is still alive, and ranks high in the diplomatic service of his country. The other I long ago lost sight of, though from his talents and high family connections, it is possible, and most probable, that he found o made a good position in his after years.

My father, finding it of no use to argue with me, and perhaps being more or less of my opinion, that London might, after all, be the best place for me, gave his consent to my project; and resolved to accompany me. He had friends, kinsmen, and acquaintances in the great city, to whom he wished to introduce me; among others, the late Lord Panmure, the late Earl of Dundonald, then Lord Cochrane; Eric Mackay, the seventh Lord Reay, the head of the clan—very unpopular among his clansmen, for having cut off the entail of his estates and sold the

Mackay country to the Marquis of Stafford, afterwards
Duke of Sutherland ; Mrs. Somerville, the celebrated
astronomer, and wife of Dr. Somerville, the physician ;
Mr. John Crawfurd, the well-known Asiatic traveller ;
and two or three publishers. He told me also that his
feud with General Mackay need not prevent me from
seeking him out, and cultivating his further acquaintance, and if it were possible, his friendship. We arrived
in London in May, 1832 ; and "the world was all before
me."

THIS once-famous and powerful journal was established in 1769 by twenty gentlemen, got together for the purpose by William Woodfall—a reporter and printer. This was nineteen years before the *Times* came into existence ; and the specialty of the new journal was to be the publication of the debates in Parliament. The reporter's gallery was non-existent and undreamed of. Notes were not allowed to be taken in either house, and the publication of the debates was not only nominally but actually a breach of privilege, at which the Commons sometimes shut their eyes, and which at other times they angrily resented. Woodfall, from his retentive memory called Memory Woodfall, was able without taking a single note to report or rather to summarize with accuracy and tolerable fulness a long debate. But though established for reporting the proceedings of Parliament, the *Chronicle* could claim no monopoly in the practice, and speedily had to encounter the competition of rival papers whose reporters did not rely upon memory, but took notes, at first furtively, and afterwards more openly, and who did not depend upon a single reporter, however able and industrious, but on a succession of hands. Among the most noted of these early reporters was James Perry, a native of Aberdeen, who twenty years after the establish-

ment of the *Morning Chronicle* which had not greatly
prospered under Woodfall's management, entered into
partnership with another Scotsman named Gray, and in
conjunction with him purchased the copyright of the
paper for £150, part if not the whole of which was
advanced by Bellamy, the keeper of the refreshment
rooms in the House of Commons. Perry conducted the
paper with great spirit and success; and made it what it
remained for many years, not only the greatest of the
Whig journals then in existence, but the leading journal
of Great Britain. Perry died in 1821, and his family
and representatives not finding in themselves any inclination or perhaps talent for conducting the enterprise as
Perry had conducted it, disposed of the copyright to Mr.
William Clement, proprietor of *Bell's Life in London,*
and the *Observer.* Under the management of this gentleman its decline was steady, and he disposed of the
copyright in 1835 after fourteen years possession, for
more than a hundred times as much as Messrs. Perry
and Gray had given for it.

The publication of a small volume of juvenile poems,
now happily out of print, and a translation, or rather
paraphrase of Béranger's poem, " Mon Habit," procured
me in that year through the intermediation of Mr.
Robert McWilliam, one of the magistrates of Middlesex,
the acquaintance of Mr. John Black, " the Dr. Black "
of Cobbett's Register, who was at that time and for
several years subsequently, the working editor of the
*Chronicle.* Mr. Black spoke kindly of my paraphrase,
inserted it in the *Chronicle,* and gave me an order for
five guineas for it, saying, " That is as much as Milton's

first payment for 'Paradise Lost,' and I dare say more than ever Béranger received for the original. It is given not so much as a payment, but as a retainer." This was the pleasantest money I ever received before or since—pleasant yet to some extent fatal—for it tended to fasten my inexperienced feet in the thorny pathways of literature, and to confirm me in the confidence that the profession of literature was as profitable as it was noble. At that time the *Chronicle*, of which the circulation had sunk so low as 800 copies a day, had just been purchased from Mr. Clement by three gentlemen, who determined if possible to infuse new life into it and restore it to that high place in the political and literary world, which it had occupied in the brilliant days of Mr. Perry, when it was *de jure* by its talent, and *de facto* by its circulation, the leading journal of Great Britain. These gentlemen were Mr. John Easthope, a stockbroker, who had once been member of Parliament for St. Alban's, and again aspired to legislative honours; Mr. Simon MacGillivray, a warm-hearted and impetuous Highlander, who had been a prosperous merchant in Mexico, and a leading spirit in the Canada and the Hudson's Bay Companies; and Mr. James Duncan, a publisher in Paternoster-row, who had become celebrated and wealthy by the publication of the most accurate Hebrew text of the Old Testament. It has been said of many publishers that they never cared to read the books they sold; but it was said with more truth of Mr. Duncan that he was totally unable to read the books by which he made his money. These gentlemen, on entering into partnership, found John Black in possession of the editorial chair of the *Chronicle*, and they resolved, prin-

cipally on the emphatic decision of Mr. MacGillivray, to
whose heart the fact of a man's Scottish birth was a sure
passport, that Mr. Black should continue in it. For
many years Mr. Black had performed single-handed the
whole editorial work of the *Chronicle*, lightened now
and then by the aid of Mr. Albany Fonblanque, of
Mr. Serjeant Spankie, Mr. Frederick Dubois, and
by that of any political or literary volunteer who
might happen to turn up, and whose pen Black was
always glad to welcome to the columns of his beloved
journal, provided the work was up to the standard of his
judgment.  Black was a celebrity in his day, but he had
been overburdened with work, and his style had become
somewhat diffuse and rambling from the nightly necessity
of filling up a certain quantity of space with political
matter—space which he did not always occupy with the
work of the pen, but with the proceeds of the scissors and
the paste-pot, cemented by a running commentary. John
Black was a thorough journalist. His whole soul was in his
business. He was a keen politician, and an acute critic; but
his mind had capacity for other things than politics and
criticism, and ran over the whole gamut of literature and
knowledge.  He spoke with the strong border accent of
his native town of Dunse in Berwickshire, and had a fund
of homely humour, which he expressed in the homeliest
and sometimes the coarsest words.  He was an accomplished linguist, and particularly fond of Greek, and used
to boast that he could read off at sight one of his own
or anybody else's leaders into that language.  He would
occasionally recite Greek passages *ore rotundo*, and affirm
with great glee that the music of the language was so
sonorous and so magnificent as to afford pleasure to the

ear, even of one who could not understand a word of it.
But he was not merely a learned man; he had a heart
overflowing with kindness, and a warm sympathy with all
literary talent. Nothing delighted him more than to
find a young man of genius and good conduct whom he
could help to ascend the steps of the difficult ladder of
worldly fortune. At this period of his life he resided
rent free with Mrs. Black on the upper floors of the
*Morning Chronicle* office, at No. 322, Strand, now the
printing-offices of the *Weekly Times* and the *London
Journal*; and had besides a little cottage at Lewisham
Hill, on the skirts of Blackheath to which he resorted
every Friday night, or rather Saturday at two or three
in the morning, when the material of the Saturday's
paper was in the printer's hands. He used to walk the
distance, whatever might be the season or the weather,
and remain in rural idleness until the Sunday evening,
when he walked up to town to resume his usual round at
the mill-wheel of his business.

I dwell thus particularly upon him, not only because
he was my first literary friend, but because he was the
last of the London editors of the old school, and had
made his way by sheer ability and force of character to
the influential position which he held. He used to tell
that he had walked with a few pence in his pocket all the
way from Berwickshire to London to try his fortune in
the great metropolis, and lived on the way upon the hospitality of farmers and farmer's wives, to whom he had
never hesitated to tell his story, and by whom he had
been generally made welcome to a slice of bread
and a bowl of milk or a night's lodging when he needed

it. Mr. Black's abilities had been discovered early by
Mr. Perry, by whom he was rapidly advanced to posi-
tions of importance on the paper.

Mr. Black, at an early period of our acquaintance, told
me that he would do his utmost to procure me an engagement, and urged upon me the desirability of cultivating
a good prose style to which he said the writing of verse
was an admirable apprenticeship. He had not only the
will, but he knew the way to serve me, and in less than
six months I was made through his instrumentality
assistant sub-editor. I had for my immediate superior
Mr. George Hogarth, the son-in-law of Mr. George
Thomson, widely known as the George Thomson to whom
so many of the letters of Robert Burns were addressed,
and as the editor of the famous Scottish songs, which
had helped to render the name of Burns immortal. Mr.
Hogarth was above all things a musician and a musical
critic, a most excellent, amiable, and accomplished man;
and I worked under him with much pleasure as long as
he remained sub-editor.

The time at which Messrs. Easthope, MacGillivray
and Duncan assumed the management of the *Morning
Chronicle* was an important epoch in English history,
and especially in that of the Whig and Liberal party.
"It was a time" to use the eloquent words of Macaulay
in a speech on the Reform Bill, which had been carried
by a reluctant House of Lords, and consented to most
unwillingly by a still more reluctant king, "when everything abroad and at home foreboded ruin to those who persisted in a hopeless struggle against the spirit of the
age—a time when the crash of the proudest throne of

the continent was still ringing in people's ears ; a time
when the roof of the Palace of Holyrood afforded an
ignominious shelter to the exiled heir of forty kings—
when on every side ancient institutions were subverted
and great societies dissolved, but when the heart of England was still sound," and when king and peers—not a
moment too soon—warned by the fate of Charles X. had
prevented revolution by conceding reform.   As Macaulay
had adjured, the old unreformed Parliament had "taken
counsel, not of prejudice—not of party spirit—not of the
ignominious pride of a fatal consistency, but of history,
of reason, of past ages and the signs of the living time,
and pronounced in a manner worthy of the expectation
with which the great Reform debates had been anticipated."   He had called upon both houses to "renew the
youth of the state, to save property, divided against
itself; to save the multitude, endangered by their own
passions ; to save the aristocracy, endangered by its own
unpopular power; to save the greatest, and fairest, and
most highly civilized community that ever existed, from
calamities which might in a few days have swept away all
the rich heritage of so many ages of wisdom and glory."
The appeal—only one of a hundred others—made by
other statesmen and orators, with equal wisdom though
not perhaps with equal eloquence, had not been made in
vain, and Great Britain had just begun to enter upon a
new and hitherto untried career of popular government.
Though the Reform question had been settled for a time,
other questions almost as vital were looming dark and
large upon the political horizon.   Under the leadership
of Daniel O'Connell, whose unwelcome aid was essential

to the ministerial existence of the Whig and Liberal party, that would gladly have dispensed with it had that been possible, Ireland was almost in a state of rebellion. The labouring classes of England and Scotland, under the pressure of bad trade, low wages, and high prices of bread, were, if not exactly rebellious, very much inclined to become so. Though the Roman Catholic Emancipation Bill had long since happily passed, the Roman Catholics of the South and West of Ireland, not content with political and religious equality with the Protestants of the North, thirsted for domination over them, and with a view of acquiring it clamoured for a repeal of the Union, while the masses of the British public, not satisfied with the Parliamentary Reform from which so much had been predicted, but which had as yet produced no improvement in their social condition, began to demand other and greater changes and to put forward pretensions which seemed, even to persons not easily frightened, to partake of revolution and to foreshadow a time when the three estates of the realm should be reduced to one—and that one, the uneducated and prejudiced multitude. The Corn Law question had become troublesome to the minds of easy-going men, though as yet it had made no great way with the people, who it might be supposed were most interested. Thomas Moore had written not long previously—

> " What, still those two infernal questions,
> That with our meals, our slumber mix !
> That spoil our tempers and digestions,
> Eternal Corn and Catholics !

> " Gods ! were there ever two such bores !
> Nothing else talked of night or morn,
> Nothing *in* doors, or *out* of doors,
> But endless Catholics and Corn ! "

Lord Brougham and his coadjutors in the " Society for the Diffusion of Useful Knowledge " had broken ground on the great question of the Education of the People, but had scarcely done more.  His happy phrase that "the schoolmaster was abroad " was germinating, however, in the public mind, and many earnest spirits were awakening to the perception, that of all the tasks reserved for a near future to accomplish, that of education was the most important.  The philanthropic legislation of later years for the abridgment of the hours of labour and for the protection from undue and exhaustive toil of women and children, had hardly gathered a parliamentary following.  Few railroads had been constructed beyond the little line connecting Manchester and Liverpool, at the opening of which Mr. Huskisson had lost his life.  The old semaphore still corresponded from the top of the Admiralty with the old semaphore at Greenwich, and that with a succession of other old semaphores all the way to Dover ; the postage of a letter to Cornwall was tenpence, and to Edinburgh one and twopence, and to John o' Groat's house half-a-crown, for Mr. Rowland Hill, even if he had imagined or planned the great Reform for which the country was afterwards to bless his name, had not yet brought it before the public.  It was a transition period from the old England to the new ; and when the slow civilization of our grandfathers was giving place to the far more active, prying, aggressive civilization of the present day—the day of steam, electricity, and engineering, and of material rather than of intellectual or moral progress.

The *Chronicle,* as the leading journal of the Whig and

Liberal party, had abundance of work before it under its new proprietary, and set about its task with vigour as well as wisdom, to keep its party well together after its long banishment from power ; and to educe out of the Reform Act the social benefits for the sake of which far-seeing minds had advocated a change which had been so long and obstinately resisted.

When I joined the *Chronicle* there was on its Parliamentary staff a young reporter named Charles Dickens, universally reputed to be the rapidest and most accurate short-hand writer in the Gallery; and who was known to a few, and among others to John Black, as an essayist and humorist of highly original genius. It was proposed in the summer of 1837, to establish an *Evening* as well as a *Morning Chronicle*, and George Hogarth was appointed to the editorship. The proprietors were desirous that the *Evening Chronicle* should not be a mere abridgment and re-issue of the *Morning Chronicle*, but that it should contain, in addition to the news of the afternoon, some original article or articles of a political or literary character, of a nature to attract the public attention. There were five other daily evening papers then in existence, three of them in the Whig and Liberal interest, namely, the *Sun*, the *True Sun*, and the *Globe*, and two in the Tory, namely, the *Courier* and the *Standard*. Bethinking themselves that a fourth Liberal paper ought to justify its existence, or in the literary slang of 1875, its " raison d'être," by some specialty, the proprietors took counsel with John Black on the subject, and on his recommendation entered into negotiations with Mr. Dickens, who was then writing for the *Monthly Magazine*

a series of articles signed " Boz," to contribute under
the same signature to the *Evening Chronicle*.   Mr. Hogarth was charged with the conduct of the negotiation,
and received from Mr. Dickens the following letter :—

"13, FURNIVAL'S INN,
"Tuesday Evening, January 20th.

" MY DEAR SIR,

" As you have begged me to write an original
sketch for the first number of the new evening paper, and
as I trust to your kindness to refer my application to the
proper quarter, should I be unreasonably or improperly
trespassing upon you, I beg to ask whether it is probable that if I commenced a series of articles, written
under some attractive title for the *Evening Chronicle*, its
conductors would think I had any claim to *some* additional remuneration (of course of no great amount) for
doing so ?

" Let me beg of you not to misunderstand my meaning.
Whatever the reply may be, I promised you an article,
and shall supply it with the utmost readiness, and with
an anxious desire to do my best, which I honestly assure
you would be the feeling with which I should always
receive any request coming personally from yourself.   I
merely wish to put it to the proprietors, first, whether a
continuation of light papers in the style of my ' Street
Sketches ' would be considered of use to the new paper ;
and, secondly, if so, whether they do not think it fair and
reasonable that, taking my share of the ordinary reporting business of the *Chronicle* besides, I should receive
something for the papers beyond my ordinary salary as a
reporter.

"Begging you to excuse my troubling you, and taking this opportunity of acknowledging the numerous kindnesses I have already received at your hands since I have had the pleasure of acting under you,

"I am, my dear Sir,

"Very sincerely yours,

"CHARLES DICKENS.

"George Hogarth, Esq."

As I had repeatedly heard Mr. Black predict the future greatness of the writer, I begged the MS. of Mr. Hogarth, after he had answered it, and it has since remained in my possession. The modest request which it preferred was complied with, and in addition to his salary of five guineas per week, as Parliamentary reporter, the embryo novelist, who was destined to achieve the greatest popularity ever enjoyed by any author of modern time, except Sir Walter Scott, received an extra two guineas for his "Sketches." These laid the firm foundations of his future fame. In the preface to "Sketches by Boz—illustrative of every-day life, and every-day people," forming one of the volumes of "The Charles Dickens edition," the author makes no allusion to the *Evening Chronicle*, but merely says, "The whole of these sketches were written and published, one by one, when I was a very young man. They were collected and republished while I was still a very young man, and sent into the world with all their imperfections (a good many) on their heads."

At this time there was no daily paper in the British isles, published out of London : and the London dailies had neither the circulation, the wealth, nor the political

power which they have since acquired. They were bur-
dened with a stamp duty of fourpence per copy, were
sold at sevenpence, and were not half their present size.
The *Times* and *Chronicle*, the two great rivals, were what
is called single papers—of four pages—and only published eight pages at rare intervals on great occasions, or
when there was a pressure of advertisements. In addition to the stamp duty, there was an advertisement
duty of three-and-sixpence for each advertisement, long
or short; and an excise duty of three-halfpence per
pound upon the fabric of the paper. Their circulation
was small, though thought to be large at the time. I
well remember the consternation excited in the office of
the *Morning Chronicle*, of which the daily issue was
about nine thousand, when it was proved on the authority
of the Parliamentary returns, that the circulation of the
*Times* was eleven thousand. This was the first intima-
tion the public received that the *Times* had shot ahead
of the *Chronicle*. But the proprietors of the *Chronicle*,
though alarmed, were not disheartened; and after the
first feeling of disappointment had subsided, set themselves to work to improve their journal in all its departments. Their chief care was to secure the excellence
and extend the fulness of their reports of the proceedings
in Parliament, in which for many years the *Chronicle* was
far superior to its only rival, the *Times*. This was so
well known to all the Parliamentary celebrities, and to
the political public of the day, as to send them to the
*Chronicle* in the first instance to read the reports of all
great debates. The next care of the proprietors was to
secure the services of competent writers for their editorial

articles, and to relieve Mr. Black of three-fourths of his labour, leaving him, however, all the more time for the supervision of his colleagues, and the harmonisation of the labours of different minds into one consistent whole. Among the *Chronicle* writers at, and after this time, who had either obtained, or afterwards achieved, political renown, were Mr. Charles Buller, M.P., who became President of the Poor Law Board; Mr. W. J. Fox, M.P. for Oldham, the Unitarian preacher and lecturer, and one of the most eloquent speakers as well as writers of the day; Mr. Albany Fonblanque, editor of the *Examiner*, who wrote one leader per week for the *Chronicle*, for which, it was reported in the office he received what was considered the enormous fee of fifteen guineas; Mr. Eyre Evans Crowe, author of "A History of France;" Mr. James Wilson, M.P., a Scotsman, from Hawick, who wrote the City or Money Article, and afterwards filled a distinguished position in successive liberal administrations; Mr. Thomas Hodgskin, a well known political economist; and Mr. Thomas Gaspey, a voluminous novelist, and formerly editor of the *Sunday Times*. Among the parliamentary reporters were Mr. Thomas Beard, who always ran in harness with Mr. Dickens whenever there was special or extraordinary work to be done at great public meetings, or other political celebrations in the provinces; Mr. John Payne Collier, the well known antiquary and Shakspearean critic; Mr. William Hazlitt, son of the celebrated essayist and critic, and afterwards and now a Registrar in the Court of Bankruptcy; Mr. W. B. MacCabe, a novelist; and at a later period Mr. Alexander Mackay, author of the "Western

World;" Mr. Angus B. Reach, and Mr. Shirley Brooks. Mr. Thackeray long held a floating connection with the *Morning Chronicle*, but was never on the staff. Among the occasional contributors of poetical *jeux d'esprit* were Thomas Moore and Thomas Campbell.

When the *Chronicle* and the *Times* were running a hard and a close race for the premiership of the press, and when it was difficult to decide which would win, an incident occurred, which, had the *Chronicle* taken advantage of, it might, perhaps, have given it the superiority. The Americans had been making claims to the whole of the great western territories on the Pacific, including what is now called British Columbia, Vancouver's Island, and Oregon, and agitating the question in so bad a spirit as to render the relations between Great Britain and the United States unpleasant, if not threatening. In those days, when the electric telegraph was but a dream of science, the annual Message of the President to Congress was usually expected in London a few days before Christmas. The Oregon difficulty had unsettled public opinion; and the money market was sensitive, lest, unfortunately, the Americans should prove so unreasonable as to render a war inevitable. The President's Message was consequently looked for with more than usual anxiety, and speculation was eager to know whether its tone would be peaceable or hostile. One night, or rather morning, about an hour and a half after midnight, when all the staff of the *Chronicle*, except Mr. Black and myself, had gone home to bed, an unexpected visitor appeared at the office. Mr. Black had been dissatisfied with a leader sent in by one of his colleagues, and finding it impossible to

patch or alter it, he had sat down after midnight to write
a new one, with directions that he should not be disturbed.
It was my business to wait until Mr. Black had given up
his last page of "copy," and then to arrange with the
printer if he had more matter than would fill the paper,
what miscellaneous articles should be either abridged or
omitted. I was asleep on a sofa, when I was suddenly
aroused by the night porter, who announced that a
gentleman, in a great hurry, who had just arrived from
New York, desired to see the editor on urgent business.
The gentleman declared that he had not even a minute to
spare ; and the porter thought, after Mr. Black's strict in-
junctions to be left alone, that it was better to bring him to
me. I directed that he should be shown up to my room,
and invited him to take a chair, and explain his business.
He would not sit down : he had no time ; and proceeded
to say that he had a copy of the *New York Herald* in his
pocket, containing the President's Message. The steamer
from New York by which he was a passenger, had put
into Queenstown to remain for four hours, before proceeding on her voyage. At that moment an ordinary
steam-packet between the two ports was about to start for
Liverpool ; and without hesitation he had transferred his
luggage from the larger to the smaller steamer, carefully
secured the *New York Herald* in his pocket, and sped
on his way. On arriving at Liverpool he had engaged
a special train all to himself, for which he had paid eighty
guineas ; and here he was, with the President's Message,
at the service of the *Morning Chronicle*, for the sum of
500*l*. Fully alive to the importance of the offer, I made
my way to Mr. Black, and told him the news. He became

greatly excited. "I wish Mr. Easthope were here," he
said. "What am I to do? It is a large sum. Ask the
gentleman to wait ten minutes while I think it over." I
returned to the traveller, and told him what Mr. Black
had said. "I can't wait ten minutes," he replied. "If
the *Chronicle* won't do business with me I must do business
somewhere else; but I like the politics of the *Chronicle*
and give it the first offer. But as I am thirsty and weary,
I will go to Short's tavern next door, and wait five minutes
while I have a glass of brandy and water. Not another
minute can I spare." I reported this to Mr. Black, who
was in a state of much perturbation of spirit, and walked
hurriedly up and down the room, speaking by fits and
starts. "I am afraid that I shall be blamed by the
proprietors if I agree to pay so large a sum. And after
all, it would be well worth 500*l.* to have the Message
exclusively! We'll have it! No! I am afraid we
cannot! It would be hard upon me to have my bargain
repudiated! If MacGillivray were sole proprietor I would
not hesitate. What shall I do?" "Risk it," said I.
And while we were talking the news-bearer came back,
was shown into the room, and exhibited the *New York
Herald*, containing ten or twelve long columns of the
important document. At the last moment Mr. Black
reluctantly refused the offer. The stranger folded up his
paper, curtly said "Good night," and vanished. He had
not been gone two minutes when Mr. Black asked me to
run after him and bring him back. I sprang down stairs
as fast as I could, but the stranger had jumped into a
cab, and was rattling away in the direction of Fleet Street.
There was no other cab on the stand, or I would have

followed him; but pursuit on foot was vain, so I returned to Mr. Black and announced the fact. "It is just as well," he said, " and now let me finish my leader."

That morning the President's Message appeared in the *Times*, and procured for that journal an amount of commendation for its spirit and energy, which, at that critical moment was of the utmost value to its character, and which in like degree was damaging to its rival. At the usual four o'clock meeting of the *Chronicle* staff the subject was discussed; and though no blame was cast upon Mr. Black, so much regret was expressed at the victory of the *Times*, that he looked upon the remarks that were made as equivalent to a reproof for his mistake. "I tell you what it is, Mr. Easthope," he said, "if I had been dealing with my own money and not yours I should not have hesitated a moment. Indeed I think I should have paid a thousand pounds rather than have allowed the *Times* to gain an advantage over the *Chronicle*. And it's my opinion that every chief editor of a great London newspaper ought to be a part proprietor, so that he might act without hesitation in an emergency." Here the subject dropped, and was not again revived in the councils of the *Chronicle*.

It is curious and not flattering to the public to reflect, that no newspaper ever yet published in London, or England, or Scotland, or anywhere else within the compass of our isles, has ever been able to pay its way by the profits of its circulation. If for any reason the traders of the country took it into their heads to spend no money upon advertising, there is not an existing paper that would be able to live. It is trade alone that supports political literature, that pays for all the news that arrives from every part of the world, that enables newspapers to keep reporters in the galleries of the Lords and Commons, and in the law courts, and to make known to civilization what is done and said in its centres, whether at home or abroad. Even when the old stamp duties and other taxes on knowledge, or the vehicles of knowledge, were in existence, and when newspapers were small, and conducted with less than half the spirit, and perhaps not a tithe of the expenditure of the present time, the profits on a sevenpenny paper, from which the State took fourpence, were insufficient, without the aid of the advertiser, to keep it in a state of solvency. Forty years ago advertising had not reached the large proportions which it has now assumed; but even at that period, there were some leviathans of trade who considered advertising as one of the fine arts, and who were the real patrons, and sometimes when they dared—the controllers or masters of the newspapers. Among these, George Robins, the famous auctioneer of Covent Garden, stood conspicuous as a person who was not to be offended without danger, and whose countenance was to be courted by every means, as Burns says of money, that were "justified by honour." It was said that his weekly expenditure for advertisements of land, houses, and estates, of which he had the disposal, sometimes amounted to as much as 5000*l*. There are no such advertisements issued in our day as those which were drawn up by George Robins, and which sometimes filled a whole page of the *Chronicle* or *Times*, with flowery, high-flown, and wordily profuse descriptions of the various terrestrial paradises, bowers of bliss, and palatial man-

sions, which were to be knocked down to the highest
bidder at the tap of his potent and busy hammer. Among
other great advertisers of that and the preceding period
were Robert Warren, the blacking-maker, of No. 30,
Strand, the site of whose house and premises is now
occupied by the court yard in front of the Charing Cross
hotel, where stands the beautiful fac-simile of the old cross,
erected by King Edward to the memory of Queen Eleanor.
It was Warren who boasted that he kept a poet to write
his rhymed advertisements, after the fashion of the floriline
advertisements of the present day. Warren expended
many thousands of pounds on making known the merits
of his commodity; and doubtless got them all back
again, with as many thousands more upon their backs in
the shape of profits. He carried on his business for
many years, and paid his poets so well, that, in the zenith
of Lord Byron's fame, in the second half of the first
quarter of the nineteenth century, some malicious wag
spread abroad a report that the author of Childe Harold
himself did not disdain to write advertisements for Warren
at a guinea a line, a report at which, it is said, Lord
Byron was wise enough to laugh. Day and Martin were
also great advertisers of a similar article, as was one Henry
Hunt, a famous radical in the days when radicalism was
more perilous to the radical than to the nation, and who
was afterwards Member of Parliament for Preston. In
our day we may look in vain for the advertisements of the
blacking-makers. The columns of the newspaper, and
even the bill-posters of the street, and the walls of the
railway stations know them no more. Almost, if not the
very last of this race of advertisers are Rowland and Son,

who, forty years ago, rivalled George Robins and the
blacking-makers in his lavish expenditure in making
known to the admiring world the merits of his macassar
oil, his kalydor, and his odonto.   It is not the fashion
for men in our day to anoint their hair with oil or grease.
Possibly the cultivation of the beard is one of the
reasons for the wholesome neglect of this ancient practice.
The fashion is going out even among the ladies, who
have discovered that nothing is better for the hair than
pure cold water.  Macassar, however, is not wholly a
thing of the past, and has left its traces in the word
" anti-macassar," not yet admitted into the dictionaries ;
an article that supplies much elegant work to fingers that
might otherwise be idle, and that preserves from the
desecration of grease the arm-chairs and sofas of our
drawing-rooms.   The advertisers, by profession, no
longer seek to polish our boots, or oil our heads, but
in the persons of the proprietors of Holloway's, Morrison's, and Old Parr's pills attack credulity on even
a weaker side than its head or its heels—the most
imaginative side of humanity—the stomach.

An early incident of my connection with the *Morning
Chronicle* was the sudden and mysterious disappearance
of John Black from his editorial chair ; and the equally
sudden and mysterious disappearance of Mr. Simon
MacGillivray from the daily meetings of the editors and
proprietors.   There were many nods and whispers about
it, and various unsuccessful attempts to curb the curiosity
of those who were not in the secret.  But it soon oozed
out that John Black had gone to fight a duel with Mr.
John Arthur Roebuck, member for Bath ; and that Mr.

MacGillivray was to act as his second.  Mr. Black was
the challenger, and the cause of offence was an attack by
Mr. Roebuck in a series of pamphlets entitled, "Pamphlets for the People," then in course of publication, on
the whole body of editors, contributors, and reporters of
the London press, especially those of the *Morning
Chronicle*.  In this attack he singled out Mr. Black by
name ; and Black's impetuous friend MacGillivray decided
that nothing was left for the honour of London journalism
but that Black should be its champion, and challenge Mr.
Roebuck.  The duel took place on the 10th of November,
1835, near Christchurch, in Hampshire.  Two shots
were exchanged ; neither combatant was injured, honour
was declared to be satisfied, and Black and MacGillivray
returned to London to MacGillivray's rooms in Salisbury
Street, Strand, where they were reported to have celebrated the event in copious libations of mountain dew, of
the merits of which both of them were excellent
judges.

Black had a fine Newfoundland dog, named Cato, a
great favourite, who usually lay at his feet while he
wrote his articles, accompanied him home in the early
grey of the morning, and was always the companion of
his long Saturday and Sunday walks in Kent and Surrey,
when he forgot politics and literature, and every thing
but his keen enjoyment of exercise, fresh air, and rural
scenery.  He was invited on one occasion to stay a week
at Fonthill, the seat of Mr. Morrison, head of the house
of Morrison, Dillon, and Co., of Fore Street, a rich merchant, then in Parliament, and a constant visitor to the
*Morning Chronicle* office.  Black, on accepting the invita-

tion, stipulated that his dog Cato might be allowed to accompany him. His friend Mr. MacGillivray, always ready for a joke, or a tumbler of toddy, prevailed upon Black's *locum tenens* in the editorial chair, to give his *imprimatur* to a paragraph under the head of " Fashionable Intelligence," to the effect that " John Black, Esq., and —— Cato, Esq., had gone on a visit to Mr. Morrison, of Fonthill." The little joke passed unnoticed until the following Saturday, when the *Age* newspaper, very notorious in its day, happily long passed, and edited by Mr. John Molloy Westmacott, appeared with a furious article, denouncing the insult to the aristocracy of England, committed by that vile, radical journal, the *Morning Chronicle.* " Will it be believed," said the indignant editor, " that —— Cato, Esq., is no other than the Editor's big black dog? The intention to insult not only the king, who is the fountain of honour, but the whole aristocracy, is palpable." The logic of this diatribe was not at all palpable; but the attention directed to the paragraph was exceedingly unpleasant to Messrs. Easthope and Duncan, who called the acting editor to account for the joke, and even went so far as to threaten him with dismissal. Under these circumstances Mr. MacGillivray came to the rescue, avowed himself the originator of the jest, and took all the blame upon himself. The case was altered immediately. " That, which in the captain's but a choleric word, is in the soldier rank blasphemy ; " and the other co-partners came at once to the conclusion that no harm had been done after all, and that the editor of the *Age* was a blockhead for trying to make a mountain out of a mole hill.

Black was accustomed to say that every man was the better for the possession of a hobby; and that devotion to it gave a zest to life, which, unlike other condiments, grew in flavour the more earnestly it was indulged. His hobby was the collection of old books, of which he had a vast and heterogeneous store, amounting, it was said, to upwards of 50,000 volumes. In the later years of his connection with the *Morning Chronicle*, when he had apartments at the top of the great house in Salisbury Street, the last on the right-hand side, overlooking the river, now occupied as a private hotel, he had no space to arrange his library, and could not easily find a book when he wanted it. Sitting-rooms, bed-rooms, pantries, closets, staircases, passages, every available inch of space overflowed with books in all languages and on all subjects. In one department of literature his collection was unusually rich—that which second-hand booksellers, with a euphemism, call "Facetiæ"—but which a barrister, prosecuting a delinquent under Lord Campbell's Act, might appropriately describe by a harsher and correcter word. Black had many thousands of such volumes in Italian, as many in French, and a few in English. The latter he did not greatly care about, as he alleged that their grossness was too gross, and was unaccompanied by any degree of wit, or even of humour, to atone for their indelicacy. It was his design to bequeath his whole library to his native town of Dunse, including the facetiæ—a design which he imparted to his particular friend and crony, Mr. John Ramsay MacCulloch, the well-known political economist and voluminous statistical writer—afterwards Comptroller of the Stationery Office.

"Lord save us, man!" said MacCulloch, in broad Scotch
—much broader than Black's own; "if you do, it's to be
hoped the provost and bailies will make a bonfire of your
books, or, at all events station a force of police constables at
the library door to prevent anybody from going in.   Such
a collection is enough to poison the whole Border!"

"No, no!" said Black, "there's not a soul in Dunse,
or within twenty miles of it, that can read either French
or Italian, and the facetiæ will do no harm.   There may
be a minister or two who can read French, and it's a
kind of literature that ministers like."

"Eliminate the facetiæ," replied MacCulloch, "and
when you die they will 'roup' at auction for a good
round sum, and excite a keen competition among the
rich old reprobates of London.   Give the good books
to Dunse if you like, but keep your facetiæ for your
executors!"

Black employed the leisure hours of several years in
making a catalogue of his books, little thinking that
Dunse would never possess any of them, the good, the
bad, or the indifferent; that the auction which his friend
MacCulloch foresaw in the dim distance would become
necessary during his life-time; and that the beloved
volumes which he had taken such pleasure in collecting would have to come to the hammer to provide him
with bread in his old age.   But Black was an easy
philosopher; and if perchance he cared for the
morrow, seldom extended his thoughts so far into
futurity as the day after.   It was fortunate for him that
he did not.

During the first and second periods of the premiership

of Lord Melbourne, it was Black's duty to wait upon his
lordship occasionally in Downing Street, to obtain information, or consult with him upon points of ministerial
policy, to be advocated in the columns of the *Chronicle*.
"Lord Melbourne has a very high opinion of Mr. Black,"
said Mr. Joseph Parkes, who at that time acted as confidential parliamentary agent for the Whig party, "and
wishes 'he would call upon him oftener than he does.
He likes to talk to him, and thinks he possesses a
greater fund of miscellaneous knowledge than any man
he ever met.   And with all his knowledge, said his lordship to me, he is as simple as a child.   Lord Melbourne
frightened him a little the other day, and was quite
amused at his bewilderment.   After a long and pleasant
talk, chiefly ethnological, his lordship said to him somewhat abruptly, 'Mr. Black, I think you forget who I
am!'   'I hope not, my lord!' replied Mr. Black, in a
tone of alarm; 'I trust I have not said or done anything
to show that I am not fully aware of your position, or to
make you think I am wanting in proper respect.'   'Mr.
Black,' said his lordship, solemnly, 'you forget that I
am the Prime Minister, and treat me in a manner that is,
to say the least of it, somewhat uncommon.'   Mr. Black
looked more puzzled than before as his lordship went
on.   'Yes, somewhat uncommon!   Here am I, as I have
said, in the position of Prime Minister, in confidential
intercourse with you, and always glad to see you.   I
have patronage at my disposal, and you never so much as
hint to me that you would like me to give you a place.
And, Mr. Black,' he added, 'there is no man living to
whom I would sooner give a place than yourself.'   'I

thank you, my lord,' said Mr. Black, with the utmost
simplicity and *bonhommie*, 'but I do not want a place.
I am Editor of the *Morning Chronicle*, and like my work
and the influence it gives me, and do not desire to change
places with anybody in the world—not even with your
lordship.' 'Mr. Black,' said Lord Melbourne, shaking
hands with him very heartily, 'I envy you; and you're
the only man I ever did.'"

Mr. Parkes brought this story fresh from Lord Melbourne's lips to the *Chronicle* office, from a dinner table
at which he, Lord Melbourne, and Mr. Simon MacGillivray were guests. At a later period, when it became
necessary that he should leave the *Morning Chronicle*,
Mr. Black's friends applied for the editorship of the
*London Gazette*, as a fitting reward for his long, consistent, and arduous services to the party; but Lord
Melbourne was not then in power, and the application
was unsuccessful.

During the last two years of the reign of William IV.
and the first five years of the reign of Queen Victoria,
Mr. Joseph Parkes was a constant visitor to the editorial
rooms of the *Chronicle*—a privileged interloper, who
brought the latest social news, and sometimes got political news in exchange. Mr. Parkes had been an attorney
in Birmingham, and, like Mr. Black, had the honour of
being abused in "Cobbett's Register," where he was
always designated as "*Pis aller* Parkes." He had played
a prominent part in the Reform Bill agitation in his
native town, where he or his leader, Mr. Attwood, had
proposed that the Birmingham people, to the number of
100,000, should march upon London, and demand the

Reform in Parliament, which the Duke of Wellington's
Government had offensively refused. After the passing
of the Reform Bill, Mr. Parkes settled in London as a
solicitor, and was trusted by the leaders of the Whig and
Reform party as a confidential agent, or what the Americans call "a wire puller," doing the work that had to be
done, and in which the hands of the real doers were not
to be seen. Mr. Parkes, who was a stanch friend and
admirer of Black, and who adhered to him loyally in bad
fortune as well as in good, had, as Black said, the luck to
have a hobby. His hobby was the mystery of the authorship of the "Letters of Junius," about which he was never
weary of talking. Upon the *questio vexata* of the identity
of Junius with Sir Philip Francis, with the Earl of Chat-
ham, with Colonel Barré, and others, he had collected a
considerable library; omitting no book, or pamphlet, or
even newspaper article, that touched upon this, to him,
all-absorbing topic. He was also an industrious retailer
of the jokes and *bon mots* of society, and was always ready
to tell the last new story. At that time, 1837, many
stories were current about the good-natured king, who
had outlived the short and not very vehement popularity
that greeted his accession to the throne. It was the
custom to call him "Silly Billy," and "Poor old Billy
Barlow," and to hold him up generally to a ridicule
which he did not deserve. Two of these stories recur
to my memory, as told by Mr. Parkes.

"Human nature," said he, "is the same in kings as
in other folk, and the king is a very good fellow, though
not the wisest of men. I have just heard a story of him
and his son, which tickled my fancy. One of the Fitz-

clarences was desperately in need of £100, and applied to
his father for a gift or a loan of that sum.   The king
pleaded poverty; but the son's poverty was still greater.
Wearied by his importunity, and in his heart desiring to
assist him, the king opened a secrétaire and took out a
couple of rouleaux of sovereigns neatly done up in paper.
Counting out fifty sovereigns from each, he spread them
upon the table in piles of ten.   He looked upon them
lovingly, as well as sadly, for a little time, and then took
them up quickly and put them back into the secrétaire.
' Dang it !' he said, ' I can't let you have the gold; I
really can't.  I'll give you a cheuqe instead.'   And he
wrote out the cheque accordingly."

The other story concerned a deputation of the baronets
of Nova Scotia, who had waited upon his Majesty by appointment at Windsor Castle, to prefer some grievance
relative to their order, and petition for redress.   When the
baronets arrived, the king was at breakfast alone, reading
the *Morning Chronicle*.   The page in waiting announced
the baronets, who had come by appointment.   The king
looked up from the paper, took a sip of tea, glanced at the
attendant, said nothing, and again began reading.   After
an interval of twenty minutes, that doubtless to the
baronets appeared a very much longer time, the page,
prompted perhaps by the deputation in the ante-room,
ventured once again to remind his Majesty that the
baronets were in attendance.   Again the king looked
up, poured out a cup of tea, and resumed his reading.
Another interval, and more impatience on the part of
the baronets.   Next a third attempt on the part of the
page, goaded to action, it is to be presumed, by the

impatient dignitaries, to gain the king's attention. "The baronets, please your Majesty, have come by appointment." "I wish," said the king quietly, and just lifting his eyes for a moment from the broad sheet, "that you would kick their ***** ;" using a phrase common among the sailors amid whom his Majesty's youthful days had been passed, but which is never heard in polite society.

On the 24th of May, 1836, a band of musicians serenaded her Royal Highness, the Princess Victoria, under her windows in Kensington Palace, where she resided with her mother, the Duchess of Kent. The occasion was that of her nineteenth birthday, and the complimentary verses recited or sung on the occasion spoke of her as the budding rose and expectancy of the fair State. In less than a month afterwards the "budding rose" of the State expanded into the full flower of royalty. William IV., whose malady was reported to be hay fever, expired on the 20th of June, in the seventh year of his reign, and the sixth year of his unpopularity ; and the young Princess ascended the throne amid universal good wishes for her personal happiness and the glory of her reign. The Liberal party were particularly elated ; for the late king had been a very uncertain liberal, and when he adhered to a Liberal measure, he had, like the personification of Fear, in Collins's Ode, only struck the string, "to back recoil, even at the sound himself had made."

# THE ANTI-CORN-LAW AND FREE-TRADE
## PARTY—1838–1844.

———◆———

THE new Sovereign had been trained in a different
school from that in which the last had been nurtured.
Her father, the Duke of Kent, was a Liberal in days
when Liberalism was dangerous; had incurred the displeasure of George III., and had been allowed to pine
and wither in the cold shadow of disfavour. His widow
and daughter had found a friend and mentor in one of
the ablest and most fascinating men of his time, who hid,
under the gay and apparently cynical or careless exterior
of a man of the world, not only the wisdom, but the tact
of far-seeing statesmanship, and as kindly a heart as
ever beat in a human bosom. Under the guidance of
Lord Melbourne, the future Sovereign of Great Britain
had been carefully prepared to fulfil her high functions,
and taught how to reign without attempting to govern,
and to walk without deviation in the path of the Constitution.

The circumstances of the time were not of happy
augury either for the country or its new ruler. There
were difficulties, obvious and palpable to all but the most
careless observers of events, which presaged a stormy
time in the near future. Lord Melbourne was Prime
Minister when William IV. died, and Queen Victoria

retained him in that position, as both duty and inclination bound, leaving it to the new Parliament, summoned
as a matter of course at the commencement of a new
reign, to decide by its votes whether the Minister or his
party possessed its confidence.   The first Parliament of
Victoria had a Liberal majority, but not so large a
majority as the last Parliament of William IV.—a
circumstance which was not encouraging to the Whigs
and Liberals of the day, inasmuch as it proved that they
were losing the popularity acquired by the passing of the
Reform Bill, or that a Conservative reaction had commenced, as reactions always do in Great Britain when any
one party has long been in power.   It is the tendency of
power, under a democratic or popular form of government,
to depopularise itself, as may be seen in the history of
Great Britain, the United States, and all free countries.
The tendency, however, works well for the public interest ; for it gives the " outs " the chance of coming " in,"
and thus keeps them in good humour ; and it impresses
upon the " ins " the certainty that sooner or later they
will be " out," and so teaches moderation in their pride
of place, and effectually imposes a certain amount of fair
play and courtesy in political warfare.

 After the first novelty of the young Queen's accession
had worn off, and parties had marshalled themselves
under new circumstances to strive for the possession of
power, it became evident that politics would not rage
less violently than before, because the Sovereign was of
the gentler sex.   The Reform accomplished in Parliament
was not wide and deep enough to satisfy the extremists,
who began to clamour for the five points of what they

called the "Charter;" and beneficent as the Reform
Act was, it had not yet produced any sensible improvement in the condition of the people. Ireland, under
O'Connell's agitation, was a constant source of dis-
quietude to statesmen of both parties—to Lord Melbourne as to Sir Robert Peel and the Duke of Wellington. The working classes throughout England were
dissatisfied with their condition, and vainly looked to
Parliament for relief from the combined pressure of low
wages and dear bread. The Free Traders had not yet
become a party, but a party was rapidly growing up of
which the first object was the repeal of the Corn Laws—
an object not to the mind either of the Whigs or the
Tories—a middle-class and manufacturers' question,
which did not find particular favour with the working
classes, whom it was so greatly calculated to benefit.
Ebenezer Elliott, the Sheffield poet and blacksmith,
every line of whose poems and songs were like thumps
upon his own anvil, and who poured out the full vials
of his wrath on the aristocracy, whom he called "the
bread-tax eaters," wrote a Coronation Ode for the new
Queen, which, perused by the lights of this generation,
seems harsh and ungrateful. He spoke of her as
"Victoria, cypress-crowned"—as "the Queen of new-
made graves," in allusion to the Canadian rebellion—and,
coming to the condition of the people at home, broke out
lugubriously into

> "Here too, oh Queen, thy woe-worn people feel
>   The load they bear is more than they can bear,
> Beneath it twenty million workers reel,
>   While fifty thousand idlers rob and glare,
> And mock the sufferings which they yet may share.

" The Drama soon will end ; four acts are pass'd,
  The curtain rises o'er embracing foes,
  But each dark smiter hugs his dagger fast,
  While Doom prepares his match and waits the close :—
  Queen of the Earthquake ! wouldst thou win or lose ? "

" The embracing foes " in these lines meant the Whig
and Tory leaders, who agreed in their opposition to
the repeal of the Corn Laws.    The poet's ire was
especially excited by the Marquis of Chandos—afterwards Duke of Buckingham—who had recently said,
with something very like a sneer, that "he expected to
hear no more about the Corn Laws."   But the Queen
was to be no "Queen of the Earthquake ; " but the
Queen of the peaceful solution of a difficulty that to
many earnest and fervid men at that time, to Ebenezer
Elliott among the rest, appeared unsurmountable, except by violence and revolution.    The men of the
present scarcely know how much they are indebted
to the men of the last generation for their skilful
conduct of this great question, and for the patience
and the ability with which they conducted it—through
storm and obstacle—through ill-report and contumely
—through every species of moral, as well as of physical, obstacle — to that triumphant issue the inestimable blessings of which the Empire is enjoying at
this hour.

The agitation for a repeal of the Corn Laws—or, as it
was the fashion in early days to call them "The Bread
Tax"—began long before the establishment or inception of
the Anti-Corn-Law League.    There were warriors before
Agamemnon, and Free Traders before Messrs. Cobden
and Bright.    Not to go so far back as Adam Smith,

there were first and foremost the small minority in the House of Commons in the year 1815, who steadily, but ineffectually, opposed the Corn Act of that year, which endeavoured to perpetuate high prices, and consequent high rents, by the creation of an artificial scarcity, and the prohibition of the import of foreign corn to feed the people, until the price of home-grown corn was eighty shillings the quarter. Any one who desires to read the early history of these selfish and unwise laws will find the facts in "Knight's Political Dictionary," published in 1845, to a time but shortly precedent to their auspicious abolition, and the admission of corn into the British Isles, free of duty, from all parts of the world. Among the pioneers of that great reform, which prevented a revolution that threatened to be sanguinary, were Mr. Huskisson, Mr. Ricardo, General Peyronnet Thomson, who wrote "The Catechism of the Corn Laws ; " Ebenezer Elliott, the sturdy poet of Sheffield ; and the Right Honourable Charles Pelham Villiers—all of whom helped to prepare the way and facilitate the task of Messrs. Cobden and Bright, who, in their turn, prepared the way for Sir Robert Peel, and provided him with the arguments that justified him in deserting his party, for the sake of saving his country. The utmost efforts of such early reformers of the Acts regulating the importation of corn, as Mr. Canning and Mr. Charles Grant, afterwards Lord Glenelg, went no further than the imposition of such a sliding-scale as should keep out foreign corn until the home price threatened a famine. If home-grown wheat were to rise to seventy-three shillings per quarter, foreign wheat might be admitted at a duty of one shilling; but if the home price fell so low as fifty-three shillings, all foreign supplies were to be subjected to a duty of thirty-four shillings according to Mr. Canning's plan, and of thirty-three shillings and eightpence according to Mr. Charles Grant's of 1828. In the year of the Queen's accession, the price of corn had so greatly fluctuated that the sliding-scale of duties underwent no less than thirty variations in eleven months, and in two veeks in November was as low as one shilling, and as nigh as ten shillings and eightpence. The agriculturists continually complained of distress; the working classes of the great towns and cities as continually complained of semi-starvation; the corn trade partook more of the character of betting at a horse-race, or on a game of whist or écarté, than of a legitimate business; and nobody was satisfied with the existing state of things, except the statesmen and members of Parliament who followed the lead of Sir Robert Peel, and possibly some few farmers, who did not particularly like the operation of the Corn Laws, but who would have stood aghast at the suggestion of their total repeal, as something fraught with all the horrors of the first French Revolution.

The question of Corn Law repeal was prominently before the country in the last year of William IV., but gained a new impetus immediately after the accession of Queen Victoria. The Honourable Charles Pelham Villiers, M.P., brother of the Earl of Clarendon—the ablest, almost the sole, champion in the House of Commons, not alone of the repeal of these laws, but of the freedom of trade—had done the cause great service. He was not a trader or a manufacturer, and had no interest in the question beyond that of a citizen, a philosopher, and a statesman. He brought to its consideration not only great talents and power of debate, but the prestige of aristocratic connection; so that when he declaimed on the impolicy and injustice of the Corn Laws, he argued with all the advantages of a perfect disinterestedness, and from a serener sphere, than the merchants and manufacturers, who afterwards, for their own purposes, entered heart and soul into the agitation. But valuable support was approaching for Mr. Villiers and the small band who voted with him in the House of Commons. A public dinner was given in Manchester on the 18th of September, 1838, to Dr. (afterwards Sir John) Bowring, a friend, disciple, and associate of Jeremy Bentham, and editor of the *Westminster Review*. Dr. Bowring, though not in Parliament, aspired to be, and was well known at the time for his enlarged ideas on all subjects of foreign commerce; and had been employed by Earl Grey, and afterwards by Lord Melbourne, as Commercial Commissioner to report on the trade of France, Italy, the Germanic States of the Zollverein, the Levant, and Switzerland, in which capacity he had drawn up several able reports, which had been printed by order of the House of Commons. There were between fifty and sixty gentlemen present at this dinner—all Free Traders by conviction, and opponents of the Corn Laws. Lord Melbourne, in this respect, and perhaps only in this, behind his age, and imbued with all the prejudice of the landowners, had declared that the idea of the repeal of the Corn Laws was "madness." These gentlemen were of opinion, on the contrary, that the repeal of the Corn Laws would be an act of the highest wisdom; and before they separated on that memorable evening, formed themselves into an "Association for promoting the principles of Free Trade." This was the germ of what afterwards became the most powerful political body of its time—the "Anti-Corn-Law League." Six days afterwards, seven of these gentlemen, who had been appointed a Committee to do the preliminary work, met to draw up a code of principles and bye-laws. These being agreed to, and published in the Manchester papers and the *Morning Chronicle,* upwards of a hundred of the leading men of Manchester enrolled their names as members, and subscribed to the funds. On the 25th of October, the first lecture for the enlightenment of public opinion on the question of the injurious operation of the Corn Laws was delivered by Mr. A. W. Paulton, under the auspices and at the expense of the Association. Similar lectures were delivered at Birmingham and other large centres of manufacturing industry; and, in December, the Manchester Chamber of Commerce, after long debates, passed a resolution by a majority of six to one, that in its opinion, "The great and peaceful principle of Free Trade on the broadest scale is the only security for our manufacturing prosperity, and the welfare of every portion of the community." A few days afterwards, the Association, fortified by the resolution of the Chamber of Commerce, issued and circulated an address to the municipalities and people of all the great towns, urging the establishment of auxiliary associations, and the organization into active bodies of all who held views favourable to the repeal of the Corn Laws. The movement did not greatly affect London, then, as now, a difficult place to interest in anything, but spread rapidly elsewhere ; and on the 22nd of January, 1839, a great public dinner was held at Manchester, which was attended by six members of Parliament, and by upwards of eight hundred delegates from various towns and cities throughout the country. Three hundred of these delegates, including those of Manchester, proceeded to London about a week later, to be present at the opening of Parliament ; and on that occasion, for the first time, the Association assumed the name, speedily destined to become historical, of "*The Anti-Corn-Law League.*"

But London held aloof. The newspapers, Tory, Whig, and Radical, gave no encouragement to a movement of which they either disapproved or to which they were indifferent. The Tories were hostile, the Liberals, under Lord Melbourne, followed in the same track. The Whig leaders had not yet sufficiently studied the economic principles which underlie the good government of nations, or having considered them were not yet converted to Free Trade, while the angry Radicals seemed to be of opinion that it was of no use to meddle with such small questions as those of trade, while such great questions as Universal Suffrage, Vote by Ballot, Electoral Districts, Annual Parliaments, the payment of members, and perhaps the abolition of the House of Lords, and the monarchy of which it was the ornament and the buttress, were all before the public, awaiting decision. The *Times* gave no support to the Free Traders; the *Morning Chronicle* gave a little, and a

very little; and the manufacturers of Manchester, with
scarcely a newspaper to support them, had to do a work
which was truly national, and to perform, in their own
interest, a task which ought to have been undertaken by
higher agencies, in the interest of the whole State.   But
the Manchester men were in earnest.   They knew what
they were about, and where to look for the right men to
aid them with money, with intellect, and with labour.
These men appeared in due time, and among them three
stood conspicuously forward,—Mr. George Wilson, Chairman of the League, Mr. Richard Cobden, and Mr. John
Bright, all engaged in manufactures in Manchester, or
near it; all young, or in the prime of life, energetic,
hopeful and eloquent; and all determined to devote their
time, their talent, and their means, to the work which they
had undertaken.   Mr. Villiers still remained the spokesman and leader of the free traders in the House of Commons, while Messrs. Cobden, Bright, and the coadjutors
who rapidly gathered around them, carried on the work
out of doors, by means of public meetings, by the employment of lecturers, by a vigorous propaganda through the
press and the post-office, and by the establishment of the
*Anti-Bread-Tax Circular*, a newspaper wholly devoted to
the cause.   For three years the League pursued its
course, undaunted by opposition, whether it came from
above or from below,—from the landed aristocracy, or
from the Chartists.   The latter were especially troublesome.   Either from ignorance of the importance of the
question; or from the settled obstinacy of theorists,
that whether important or unimportant, right or wrong,
good or bad, Free Trade would have its best, if not its only

chance of consideration, when the five points of the Charter had become the law of the land. Then, and only then, they declared it could be fairly debated, and fairly carried by a legislature competent to understand, and courageous enough to establish it.

At the opening of the Parliamentary Session of 1839, the three hundred delegates of the Anti-Corn-Law League present in London, had taken measures to force discussion in both Houses on the subject they had most at heart. Lord Melbourne, in the debate on the address in answer to the Queen's speech, could not avoid the topic, but being still without a comprehension of its vast importance, and still prejudiced by his early training in a different school, declared that the question was an open one in the Cabinet, in which various members had formed different opinions, and that he wished to avoid any debate upon it. " He would only state, for his own part, that, though he was not prepared to pledge or bind himself to the maintenance of the existing system (the sliding scale) as the best possible, he was not, at the same time, prepared, either as a member of Parliament, or of the government, to pledge himself to any alteration." This was discouraging to the League, as coming from a Liberal Premier. Still more discouraging, perhaps, was a speech in the House of Commons, made by Mr. Wood, Chairman of the Manchester Chamber of Commerce. This gentleman had been selected by the Ministry to second the address, expressly with a view to the conciliation of the discontented manufacturers; but, though he advocated in his speech the repeal of the Corn Laws as a matter alike of good policy and justice, he went out of his way to

demolish one of the great arguments upon which the
League depended; and not only denied that the manufacturing interests were suffering, but asserted, on the
contrary, that they were in a state of progressive prosperity.   Sir Robert Peel, then leader of the Opposition,
and as yet unconverted to Free Trade principles, very
dexterously took advantage of Mr. Wood's unguarded ad-
missions, and complimented him on his knowledge of the
facts, on the extreme clearness with which he stated
them, and on the delivery of " one of the ablest and most
conclusive speeches in favour of the existing system which
he had ever had the good fortune to hear."   The indignation of the League against Mr. Wood was bitter,
and all Manchester shared in the feeling.   He was removed from the chairmanship of the Chamber of Commerce, and the League, goaded by the taunt and the
temporary triumph of Sir Robert Peel, set still more
vigorously to work to extend and intensify the agitation,
not for Corn Law Repeal alone, but for the abolition of all
protection. to native industry, whether displayed in the
pursuits of agriculture or of manufactures.   Mr. Villiers,
in an able speech on the 19th of February, moved that
evidence should be received at the Bar of the House to
prove the injurious effects of the Corn Laws, not alone
on trade and manufactures, but on agriculture itself, and
unrolled and commented upon a voluminous mass of
statistics, to show how mighty were the interests at stake,
and how deeply the moral and physical well-being of the
whole people were involved.   The motion was negatived
by a large majority; but Mr. Villiers, nothing daunted,
and with the great power of the League at his back, gave

notice of a more direct motion on the subject, to the
effect that the House should resolve itself into committee
of the whole, for considering the laws that regulated the
importation of corn. The question came up for discussion
on the 12th of March, and the debates lasted for five
nights. On the fourth night, Sir Robert Peel, who said
all that could be said on the Protectionist side of the
question, admitted that "he considered the statement,
that the condition of the labourer had been rendered worse
by the operation of the Corn Laws a most important one,
and, for his own part, he had no hesitation in confessing that
unless the existence of those laws could be shown to be
consistent, not only with the prosperity of agriculture and
the maintenance of the landlord's interest, but also with
the protection and maintenance of the general interests of
the country, and especially with the improvement of the
condition of the labouring classes, he would look upon
those laws as practically at an end." The motion was
rejected by 342 against 195; but the League accepted
Sir Robert Peel's challenge, and undertook, by means of
renewed meetings, lectures, discussions, letters, pamphlets,
and all the most approved and effective means of political
and literary warfare, to prove what their own injudicious
friend, Mr. Wood, and the Protectionist leader denied,
that the effect of the obnoxious laws was clearly and unmistakably to do everybody harm, and most cruelly to
press upon the working people.

But while the maintenance or abolition of the Corn
Laws might have been the crucial question to decide the
fate of Lord Melbourne's administration, which, on the
admission of its chief, held divided opinions, the danger

came from another quarter. Challenged on their Irish policy, the government obtained a small majority of twenty-two. Challenged again on the measure that in the interest of the emancipated slaves of Jamaica it had introduced, for suspending for five years the constitution of that island, the government obtained a dwindled majority of only five. Lord Melbourne, in the Lords, and Lord John Russell, in the Commons, announced that with such failing support they had found themselves unable to carry on the public business with advantage, and had resigned office. Sir Robert Peel was charged with the duty of forming an administration. But the times were unpropitious for him. If Lord Melbourne had become unpopular,—chiefly because the Queen delighted to honour him, partly because he had been compelled to accept the unwelcome support of Mr. O'Connell and the Irish Roman Catholic party, and partly because he was not able to make up his mind on the paramount question of Free Trade and the feeding of the people,—Sir Robert Peel could scarcely claim to be popular at all. Yet he might perhaps have managed to form a ministry, with a fair chance of stability, had he not wilfully, and indeed ungraciously, run his head against a very hard wall that he might easily have avoided. The Queen first applied for advice to the Duke of Wellington, and, on his recommendation, sent for Sir Robert Peel, to both of whom her Majesty frankly declared that she had parted from her late minister with regret, but that she would loyally give her entire support to a new administration. The list of the names submitted included the Duke of Wellington, Lord Lyndhurst, the Earl of Aberdeen,

Lord Ellenborough, Lord Stanley, Sir James Graham, Sir Henry Hardinge, and Mr. Goulburn. At their very first council, these noblemen and gentlemen, at the instigation, as was believed and alleged, of Sir Robert Peel, adopted a resolution which at once put them in the wrong, as regarded their young sovereign, and rendered it difficult, if not impossible, for her to grant them her cordial confidence. On the following day Sir Robert Peel, in the name of himself and his colleagues, communicated to the Queen their joint opinion, that certain offices in the royal household, held by ladies of the highest rank, appointed by their predecessors, should be vacated, although in some few instances the absence of all political feeling might render a change unnecessary. The two ladies more particularly obnoxious to Sir Robert Peel and his colleagues, as he afterwards stated in Parliament, were the Duchess of Sutherland and the Marchioness of Normanby, the one a sister of Lord Morpeth, Secretary for Ireland, and the other the wife of the Viceroy of Ireland, who were objected to wholly and solely for their relationship to those Whig noblemen. The Queen, then unmarried, and having no friends on whom she could rely for support and advice, except her mother and the very ladies who were complained of, received the notification with surprise and displeasure, and promised to send a written answer. On the following morning, May 10th, 1839, her Majesty wrote to say that, "having considered the proposal made to her to remove the ladies of her bedchamber, she could not consent to adopt a course which she conceived to be contrary to usage, and which was repugnant to her feelings." Sir Robert Peel thereupon relinquished the task of forming an administration, and Lord Melbourne and his colleagues returned to office. These circumstances, partaking as they did of the nature of a scandal, excited much interest in all circles, and the Queen's spirited protest against such unfair dictation, did much to diminish the unpopularity which had gradually been growing around her name, and which was destined, at no distant period, to be splendidly replaced by an amount of favour and respect which no previous sovereign ever enjoyed. It was stated that on the first announcement of the resignation of Lord Melbourne, certain Conservative ladies of high rank, or if not Conservatives themselves, the wives of eminent Conservatives, had spoken of the event as a personal triumph over the Queen, as well as over the Whigs, and that "the majority would now, for the first time, be kept in order." These improper remarks were communicated to the Queen before Sir Robert Peel's official visit, and she naturally felt aggrieved at the idea of subjection to a political party, and to a possible *espionnage* over her private conduct by the ladies who were to be thrust, against her will, into her intimacy.

The Anti-Corn-Law League had some hopes of being able to convince Lord Melbourne; it had no hopes of being able to convince Sir Robert Peel. The return of the former to power was therefore agreeable, though the accession of the latter would have made no difference in their arrangements, unless perhaps it should have spurred them on to redoubled exertion. But the spur was not necessary. The hands of the leaders were upon the plough, and the grip was not to be relaxed until the furrow was drawn straight to its end. But there were yet several years of hard work before the League; for errors, if quick to grow, are difficult to uproot, and the particular error which it was its business to destroy, had twined its roots so deeply into the supposed interests of the most influential and powerful classes in the state, that the task was not so much the eradication of a tree, as of a whole forest.

Viewed in the serener light of the public discussions of the present time, it must be difficult for those whose recollections do not go back to the last generation, to understand the bitterness of party politics in the first years of Queen Victoria. The Tories (for there *were* Tories in those days, who were not, as in ours, merely mild Conservatives) had enjoyed so long a continuance of office under sovereigns who were as Tory as themselves, George III., George IV., and, in a modified degree, William IV., that they did not readily reconcile themselves to a new *régime*, which had received its colour from the Reform Bill. They chafed at the idea of their possible exclusion from office during a whole reign, not remembering that the operation of the Reform Act, giving power more than ever to parliamentary majorities, would, wholly irrespective of the sovereign's private feelings and convictions, give them, if they had the country along with them, as fair a chance as their opponents. They overrated the sovereign's influence, or wrongly judged it by the standard of previous reigns, and, until the auspicious marriage of the Queen, missed no opportunity to throw discredit upon the sovereign. The unfortunate scandal created by the thoughtless, if not cruel conduct of some

of the leaders of the Court, in the case of the hapless and
innocent Lady Flora Hastings, brought out party animosity in a matter which had really no concern with
party, with a virulence that was particularly unfair towards
the young Queen, and impressed all true gentlemen and
good subjects, whatever their politics, with the desirability
of her happy union to a man of her own choice.   One of
the rabid politicians of the ultra Tory party, the member
for the City of Canterbury, went so far as to say that,.
" brought up under the auspices of the citizen King of the
Belgians, who was the serf of France, and guided by his
influence, the Queen thought that if the monarchy lasted
her time, it would be enough.   But he warned her that.
the people of England would never consent that the crown
should be degraded and debased for the inglorious ease
of any created being, nor that the personal wishes and
caprices of the sovereign should direct the conduct of the
executive."   How wrong all this was in point of fact, to
say nothing of its detestable bad taste, subsequent events
made manifest.   Much more trash of the same kind was
spoken.   " I believe, in my conscience," said the irate
member, "that the favourite equerries are younger and
better looking, and better dressed than Sir Robert Peel ;
that Lord Melbourne can tell a tale meet for a lady's
ear, better than the Duke of Wellington, and that neither
Lord Stanley, nor Sir James Graham, can compete with
Lord Normanby in getting up a pageant ; but are these
the qualifications which the people of England prize so
much, as to sacrifice to them their religion, their honour,
and the care of their ancient institutions ? "   This, and
other utterances of the same kind, repeated by members

of his party, gave great annoyance to Sir Robert Peel, who strenuously set himself to work, both publicly and privately, to denounce and discourage such displays of bad taste, bad temper, and disloyalty.

When the announcement of the Queen's approaching marriage to his Royal Highness Prince Albert of Saxe Coburg and Gotha was made in November, 1839, the affair of Lady Flora Hastings, and the persistent attacks made on her Majesty's supposed political and personal predilection for one party in the state, had left unpleasant traces on the public mind. But the marriage was looked upon favourably by all sensible and loyal people, the more so as the high personal character of the bridegroom became better known. It was felt that scandals were not so likely to arise in the Court of a married sovereign as in that of a maiden; that it was not good for the Queen to be alone, and that highly placed as she was, in a sphere where equal friendship with a person of either sex was difficult, if not impossible, the friendship, the love, the support, and the guidance of a good husband, was likely to prove a blessing both to herself and to the state. But bitter party feeling was not all at once to be sweetened. In the debate on the Royal speech at the opening of the session of 1840, the Opposition found fault, that the Royal message did not explicitly state whether Prince Albert was a Protestant. The bill for naturalizing the Prince was objected to, because it was proposed to give him precedence over all Englishmen except the possible heir-apparent of the future; and when it was proposed by Lord Melbourne's ministry to settle upon the Prince an annuity of £50,000,

which was but half the sum settled upon Queen Adelaide,
the widow of William IV., the Opposition, led for the
occasion by Colonel Sibthorp and supported by Sir
Robert Peel and all his party, as well as by a small
section of Liberals led by Mr. Joseph Hume, the Queen's
friend, but also the friend of economy in the national
expenditure, objected to the prodigality of the proposed
annuity. Lord John Russell complained severely of the
tactics of the Opposition, and said, notwithstanding the
expressions of extraordinary loyalty and respect that
came from the other side of the House, he could not
forget that no sovereign of this country had ever been
insulted in such a manner as her present Majesty. Sir
Robert Peel vindicated himself and his party from the
charge of disloyalty and disrespect, and declared for himself that, "not one word, not one breath of disloyalty to
the Crown or any member of the Royal Family, however
adverse their political sentiments to his own, had ever
passed his lips." The Ministry were defeated on this
question, and the Prince's income was fixed at £30,000.
After these small incidents, which seemed to relieve the
minds of the Opposition and cleanse it of the perilous stuff
of disaffection, few or no attacks were made, and few or
no insinuations and innuendoes were indulged in against
the sovereign, and Queen Victoria entered upon a new
and happy path, illuminated by the warm sunshine, first
of popular favour, and afterwards of popular respect, that
deepened, as the years rolled on, into popular affection.

In May, 1841, the Melbourne administration endeavoured to settle the Corn Law question by the abolition
of the sliding scale, and the imposition of a fixed duty

of eight shillings per quarter on the importation of
foreign cereals, whatever the price of the home-grown
commodity might be. Lord John Russell brought forward a motion to that effect on behalf of the Ministry,
though forewarned by the Anti-Corn-Law League that
the compromise would not be satisfactory, and that
nothing less than total abolition would meet the
justice of the case and the growing necessities of the
country. The debate commenced on the 7th of May,
and was continued for eight nights. The Ministry were
defeated by 317 against 281, or by a majority of 36.
Lord Melbourne and his colleagues did not immediately
resign. Lord John Russell gave notice of another
motion on the subject of the Corn Laws for the 4th of
June ensuing, and as it was believed to be the intention
to dissolve Parliament after laying a full exposition of
the new policy before the country, Sir Robert Peel resolved
to frustrate their policy by a direct vote of want of confidence. He brought forward a motion to that effect
on the 27th of May and carried it by 312 votes
against 311, leaving Lord Melbourne in a minority
of one. This sealed the fate of the existing Parliament,
which was forthwith dissolved ; and the struggle between
Free Trade and Protection was transferred from the
House of Commons to the constituencies.

The contest was more than usually bitter. The
Whigs, and that large portion of the Liberals who had
not yet been been converted to the principles of Free
Trade, were disheartened, and, to a certain extent,
politically demoralized by a long lease of power, which
they had not exercised either vigorously or wisely ; while
the Conservatives were exultant and aggressive. They

had found their opportunity, and were resolved to make
the most of it, sparing no exertion in boroughs or counties to secure a majority. Between the two were the
Anti-Corn-Law League—hopeful, defiant, resolved not to
be utterly beaten, and doing its best by all the agencies
in its power, to impress upon Liberals that their best, if
not their only chance of regaining their lost place, was
to adopt cordially and fully the doctrine of commercial
freedom, and to narrow the issue to be decided to the
great and paramount question—of Free Trade or Protection. The one great victory of the League was the
election of its most eminent upholder, the very soul as it
were of the movement, Mr. Cobden, for the borough of
Stockport. Otherwise the Liberals suffered many and
sore reverses. The City of London, which returned four
Liberals to the preceding Parliament, returned two Conservatives and two Liberals, Lord John Russell, the
most eminent man of the party, being at the bottom of
the poll, with a majority of only seven above a third
Conservative candidate. Lord Howick and Lord Morpeth, shining lights of the Liberal party, lost their
seats. Mr. O'Connell, whose dangerous alliance had
worked much mischief to the reputation of the Whigs,
was rejected for Dublin. Out of a hundred and fifty-
nine county members, the Liberals only succeeded in
electing twenty-three; and in the boroughs the Liberal
losses, though not so great, were more than sufficient
to prove that the Conservatives would muster a strong
majority. Lord Melbourne, though fully aware that
his administration could not long survive the meeting
of Parliament (1842), resolved that he would not retire

until compelled to do so by an adverse vote, which he
challenged, it was believed, on the inspiration of Lord
John Russell, by an emphatically Free Trade passage in
the Royal speech. "It has appeared to her Majesty,
after full deliberation," said the Ministry, through the
voice of the sovereign, "that you may at this juncture
properly direct your attention to the revision of the
duties affecting the productions of foreign countries. It
will be for you to consider whether some of those duties
are not so trifling in amount as to be unproductive to
the revenue, while they are vexatious to commerce . . .
Her Majesty is desirous that you should consider the
laws which regulate the trade in corn. It will be for you
to determine whether those laws do not aggravate the
natural fluctuations of supply; whether they do not
embarrass trade, derange the currency, and by their
operation diminish the comfort and increase the priva-
tions of the great body of the community." These
passages were palpably intended to provoke an amendment to the Address, to seal the fate of the Ministry,
and to lance a Parthian arrow to stick in the very ribs or
the heart of the Protectionist party. The proposal of
the amendment was entrusted to Mr. Stuart Wortley, the
successor of Lord Morpeth in the West Riding of Yorkshire. Long and animated debates ensued, which were
rendered memorable by the maiden speech of Mr.
Cobden; a speech that was simple, earnest, impressive,
and convincing, and made manifest to both sides of the
House that a master of debate had come amongst them,
and still further memorable from an admission of Sir
Robert Peel that he would not bind himself to the details

of the existing Corn Law, but reserve to himself the
unfettered discretion of considering and amending that
law. The division on the Address showed 269 votes
in its favour, and 360 in favour of the hostile amendment
of the Conservatives—a majority of 91. The result had
been long anticipated, though not the magnitude of the
majority, and excited neither sensation nor surprise.
Lord Melbourne and his colleagues immediately resigned,
and Sir Robert Peel received Her Majesty's commands
to form an administration. He found no difficulties in
his way; the filling up of the various offices had been
long pre-arranged, and not a hitch occurred in the negotiation. The Duke of Wellington accepted a seat in the
Cabinet, without an office, to strengthen the Ministry by
his great name and reputation, and, it was alleged at the
time, to please the Queen, who had the highest reliance
on his judgment, wisdom, and unselfish patriotism.
There was a suspicion among the most obstinate of the
old sticklers for Protection, that the new Premier had
leanings towards Free Trade in the abstract, if not in
the particular article of corn; but when the Duke of
Buckingham, who, as Marquis of Chandos had declared
that he "expected to hear no more about the Corn
Laws," was offered and accepted the place of Lord
Privy Seal, even these gentlemen were satisfied with the
composition of the new Ministry, and prepared to yield
it unqualified support.

The League resolved to redouble all its previous
efforts. It saw that Sir Robert Peel was impressionable,
that he was no bigot, and that if convinced by degrees
on smaller matters, he might, with time and patience on

the part of the commercial reformers, be convinced on
larger ones. They removed their head-quarters from
Manchester to London, converted the *Anti-Bread-Tax
Circular* into a weekly London journal, to be called
the "League," and edited by their first lecturer, Mr.
Paulton; raised a subscription of upwards of £50,000 to
carry on the propaganda; and arranged for a series of
public meetings, to be held once a week during the
sittings of Parliament, at which all its great orators were
to speak. The original £50,000 not being sufficient for
their operations, a further sum of £100,000 was raised
without difficulty; and the *Times*, occasionally hostile,
and generally luke-warm in the cause, was compelled to
admit, in the words of the great American philosopher,
Ralph Wardo Emerson, that the League was "*a great fact.*"

One of the first measures adopted by the League on
their removal to the metropolis, was to secure, if possible,
the aid of one or more of the great London daily journals
to disseminate their opinions and advocate their cause.
The hostility of the *Times* had been too marked to lead
them to encourage hope in that quarter; but the *Morning
Chronicle* had always been friendly, if not enthusiastic,
and to that powerful journal they naturally directed their
attention. Their overtures were favourably received;
the *Chronicle* became the avowed organ of the Free
Trade party, and the leaders of the League were
constant and friendly visitors to the office. In the dis-
tribution of work that was the consequence, it fell to
the lot of Mr. Black to write, or cause others to write, the
leading or editorial articles that were to influence and
ripen public opinion, to support friends, to controvert

opponents, and to carry, as it were, the flag of the true principle, high unfurled above the roar and crush of the political battle.    It fell to my lot to collect from all the newspapers of the land the reports of Free Trade meetings, the opinions of provincial journals, and all the facts and speeches bearing upon the cause, that were sown broad-cast over the political literature of the time, and marshal them daily into the columns of the *Morning Chronicle*, under the head of "Free Trade and Commercial Reform."    The performance of this labour brought me into daily and nightly contact with the leaders of the League, and enabled me to form the friendship of Mr. Cobden, Mr. W. J. Fox, and other leading spirits of the party, and the acquaintance of many others scarcely less distinguished.

It soon became evident, under the immense pressure of public opinion that was brought to bear not only on the one great subject of the Corn Laws, but on that of Free Trade generally, that Sir Robert Peel was losing faith in the principles of his party.    The Duke of Buckingham very soon became alarmed, and resigned his place in the Ministry.    The ultra-Protectionists in the press began to hint their doubts of the Prime Minister's stability of judgment, and some accused him, though darkly and timidly, of approaching treachery to the cause on the full tide of which he was wafted into office.    Remaining stanch to his old opinions on Corn and Corn Laws, he cautiously marched in the direction of Free Trade on all other questions except those of corn and sugar, and made it quite clear to the leading spirits of the League that his mind was running in the grooves of progress, and would continue to run in them unstopped at last, and when he had reached them by the sacred articles which were the " be all and end all " of the Protectionist party. He brought forward early in the session a modified scheme of a sliding scale on the importation of foreign corn, which was vigorously opposed by Mr. Cobden and Lord John Russell. Since the rejection of his own scheme of a fixed duty of eight shillings per quarter, Lord John had been approaching more and more closely to the principles of the League ; and on this occasion, though he did not go wholly with the Free Traders, he proposed as an amendment that a fixed duty, not a sliding scale, was the proper solution of the difficulty. On a division he was defeated by 349 votes against 226, or a majority of 123. The League and its friends in Parliament were not to be deterred, even by this majority, from further propelling the little snow-ball of Free Trade, soon destined, as it ran, and grew, and received accretion on all sides of its course, to become an avalanche ; and Mr. Charles Villiers introduced his amendment in a powerful speech, powerfully supported by Mr. Cobden, in favour of Free Trade, pure and simple. The debate lasted five nights. On a division, the Free Traders were in what might be considered a hopeless minority— 90 against 393. But discouraging as this result might well have been considered, Mr. Villiers and the League were *not* alarmed, and still held on, bating no jot of heart or hope, strong in the truth and justice of their cause ; and perhaps fortified a little by the side movements in favour of commercial freedom, which the Protectionist Minister was making in spite of his party, in spite of his ancient self, and in obedience to the impulses of a clear, capacious mind, that loved truth for its own sake, and would follow in due, though perhaps in slow time, wherever it might lead him.

These anticipations were soon justified, as in March, 1842, Sir Robert developed to the House his new scheme of finance, the principal features of which were a reform of the tariff, the abrogation of many onerous duties that obstructed trade, and the imposition of a property and income tax to provide the revenue relinquished, as not worth the trouble of collection. Among the articles which the Ministers proposed to admit into Great Britain, free of the old protection and prohibition duties, were live cattle and meat from foreign parts. This was alarming to the farmers, who imagined that a Minister who had gone so far would go still farther, and that corn would be the next article that would come under his reforming scythe. Early in the session of 1843, in a debate on Lord Howick's motion, for a Committee of the whole House to inquire into the distressed state of the nation, Sir James Graham, the Home Secretary, gave another warning, and administered another fright to the ultra-Protectionists, by declaring that Free Trade was the right and only right principle. "By most men," he said, "the principles of Free Trade were now acknowledged to be the principles of common sense. The time had gone by when this country could exist solely as an agricultural country. We were essentially a commercial people. As long as Great Britain remained the mistress of the seas, she *must* be the emporium of the commerce of the world; and he felt perfectly satisfied that agricultural prosperity in this country, if deprived of the support of manufacturing prosperity, could not and would not long exist." This was highly encouraging to the League, both in and out of Parliament. During this debate an incident of a less pleasant kind occurred. A crazy fanatic of the name of Macnaughten had not very long before shot dead, near Charing Cross, Mr. Drummond, the private secretary of Sir Robert Peel, mistaking that gentleman for the Prime Minister. The circumstance had excited great feeling and commiseration, not alone for the family of the murdered man, but for the living statesman for whom the blow was intended : and Sir Robert Peel was naturally sensitive to the dangers of his position. On the fifth and last night of the debate raised on Lord Howick's motion, Mr. Cobden, in an eloquent speech in vindication of himself and the Anti-Corn-Law League, had somewhat unnecessarily, if not ungraciously, gone out of his way to state that the Ministry was Sir Robert Peel, and Sir Robert Peel alone, that all his colleagues were nonentities compared with him, and that conse-quently on him personally " devolved the *responsibility* for the continued distress of the country." Sir Robert Peel was perhaps suffering from indigestion, or was otherwise out of the even balance of his usually calm system when this remark was made, and rose in a state of excitement that was alien to his gentle and unimpressionable nature, to call the attention of the House to Mr. Cobden's attempt to fix an individual responsibility upon him ; and plainly insinuated that Mr. Cobden had marked him out as a victim for assassination ! Mr. Cobden indignantly

repelled the odious interpretation of his words, but the
feeling of the House was with Sir Robert, who, amid the
shouts of his party declared that "no responsibility
which Mr. Cobden could fix upon him, or induce others
to fix upon him, should deter him from the performance
of his duty." Mr. Cobden was equally surprised and
pained at the rash charge and its ungenerous repetition,
for it was more of a charge than an insinuation; but he
had the satisfaction of hearing, though not for some time
afterwards, that Sir Robert regretted the mistake into
which he had been betrayed, and would willingly have
expunged it from the record of his life. Ultimately, and
on another occasion, he made the *amende honorable*,
and amply atoned for the injustice he had done.

Mr. Cobden had been for two years in Parliament
before his colleague, Mr. Bright, was enabled to find a
seat in the legislature. The opportunity at last offered,
and in July, 1843, after a previous and unsuccessful
attempt at the same place, Mr. Bright was returned for
the City of Durham. At this time the League was
represented in the Commons by five members, Mr.
Villiers, Mr. Cobden, Mr. Bright, Mr. Milner Gibson,
and Mr. W. J. Fox. A strong and gradually augment-
ing phalanx of Free Traders and Liberals, at the head of
which was Mr. Charles Villiers, supported their views,
Mr. Villiers, in right of his long services, taking the
lead in all the parliamentary discussions which the
League desired to provoke. Mr. Bright soon made his
mark in the House, displaying an eloquence more im-
passioned than that of Mr. Cobden, but at the same time
equally logical and convincing. Mr. Bright always

used the simplest, yet the strongest language, put the right word in the right place, and hammered down his arguments with ringing blows of the sturdiest English, plain, unpretending, and forcible as the language of John Bunyan or Daniel Defoe.

The leading spirits of the League, including the four members of Parliament, Mr. George Wilson, the chairman, Mr. Paulton, the editor of the " League," and many Manchester manufacturers who aided the cause with their money and their powers of management and organization, though unable to serve it by their oratory, were in the habit of dining together two or three times a week during the Parliamentary Session at rooms which they had hired in one of the streets not far from the *Morning Chronicle* office, and leading from the Strand to the Thames. I was often a guest on these occasions, and remember that once, in the course of conversation with Mr. Cobden, I remarked, that as good an argument could be made in justification of a legislative and parliamentary monopoly of tailors and shoemakers, as for that of agriculturists. " Quite as good," replied Mr. Cobden; "you should work the idea out. It might form a political fable, and be the means of driving an idea into heads that might not otherwise be converted to the true faith."

At the next meeting at which I attended the following fable was produced and read aloud to the company :—

" THE LEGISLATURE OF TAILORS.

" In a certain powerful and populous country, there was a great peculiarity in the mode of government. That peculiarity was, that no man could sit in either House

of Parliament, of which, as in ours, there were two, who
was not a *tailor*. To be a tailor doing a great stroke of
business was to be eligible not only for a seat in the
Legislature, but for all the principal offices of State ; and
in fact the law was so framed, that if any man of talent,
not a tailor, was anxious to procure admission into
Parliament, he was compelled to do his conscience wrong
and hire a tailor's shop for a day, that he might swear at
the moment of his election that he did really and truly
belong to that eminent fraternity. The consequences of
this state of things may be easily anticipated. People
seeing that the tailors made the law, looked up to the
tailors with becoming respect ; and the monarchs of the
country being in the power of the tailors from generation
to generation, conferred honours, dignities, and emoluments, upon them. The tailors having so much power
and consideration, naturally endeavoured to turn both to
their own advantage, and made a law enacting that coats
and breeches, and every species of attire, should not be
sold under a certain large price. They also enacted other
laws for the protection and sole advantage of tailors.
But these were felt as nothing by them, compared to the
cruelty of making all sorts of garments excessively and
unnecessarily dear; great portions of the community,
unable to pay this price, and prevented by law from sending to the tailors of other countries who had no such
powers and privileges, were obliged to wear very coarse
and insufficient raiment ; and many went without it
altogether, and perished from the inclemency of the·
weather. The tailors, however, did not care what suffering the multitudes experienced for the want of covering ;

how many old men and old women shivered in the
wintry blasts ; and how many little children were nipped
in the bud of existence, who might have lived to old age
if clothes had been as cheap and easily to be procured as
they ought to have been. The tailors accused those who
complained of such evils as men of no knowledge of the
true principles of Government—as men of no rectitude—
who wished to overturn the monarchy, bring about a
revolution, destroy religion, and render us dependent
upon foreign nations for our breeches. They refused
loudly to lower the price of their commodities, and maintained, with many specious arguments, that had it not
been for the great price of coats and other garments, the
nation would not have attained any rank or eminence
among the powers of the earth, and would have been
conquered and overrun by the people of neighbouring
states. These false and ridiculous doctrines were so
widely spread, and so zealously inculcated by the tailors,
and by people connected with them, that many well-
meaning men were convinced that the tailors spoke the
truth, and paid willingly the extortionate sums demanded
by them. The cry of the naked multitudes was heard
occasionally ; but when the weather grew warmer, it was
hushed, and the tailors fancied that it was not the warm
weather, but their arguments, that had stilled the multitude, and consoled themselves, during the hot and quiet
days, with the hope that all opposition had died away.
In these times, there arose a man of the name of Eel—
a very fair-spoken, intelligent man—who, though not
born among the tailors, had bought himself into their
fraternity by his wealth, and acquired great ascendancy

amongst them by his plausible character. This man Eel had great tact, undoubted prudence, and a sort of plain, business-like eloquence that had great weight with all the mediocre minds who did not like the labour of thinking for themselves, and who were very well satisfied that so respectable a person should think for them. Now Eel had the misfortune of connecting himself in early life with the tailors, in consequence of the facilities afforded by their corporation of advancing his ambitious views of power and influence over his fellow-men; and although the older he grew, the more sensible he became that the tailors had not acted justly to the community, and had by their selfishness inflicted many evils upon the nation, he had not the courage to renounce his allegiance to them. Now, the nature of the man was acute, or more properly speaking, cunning; and when the tailors chose him for their leader, there arose a great struggle in his mind upon the coats and breeches question. The more he thought upon the matter, and the more he listened to the voice of reason, justice, and common sense, the more convinced he became that the tailors were wrong, and that the people were right. He was, to do him justice, anxious enough that the monopoly of the tailors should be brought to an end, and that the people should be cheaply clothed; but at the same time, he was anxious not to vex his friends, who had brought him into so responsible a position, nor to destroy the great party of the tailors out of the country. In this perplexity, a scheme was devised, that when the thermometer was ten degrees below freezing-point, the poor people might send for clothes to neighbouring states, and not be obliged to buy from the high-priced tailors of their own country. This scheme, however, was not found to work well; for when the shivering people sent for their clothes, the thermometer not unfrequently rose to twenty or thirty degrees above the freezing-point, before the order could be executed; and when at last the clothes came, they were refused admission into the country unless such duty were paid upon them as made them as dear as the home manufacture. This scheme, therefore, did not work, and great agitation sprung up from one end of the country to the other against the tailors. At last a League was formed, the object of which was to put the tailors upon the same level with shoemakers and other artisans, and with the farmers and owners of land, and generally all those who were concerned in the growth of the people's food. The tailors seeing this, endeavoured to raise an outcry against the League. They accused them of selfish and interested views; and if there happened to be a shoemaker, or stocking-weaver, or landlord among them, raised a great hubbub, called them mercenaries and lovers of mammon—reckless and unprincipled men, who cared not for the throne or the altar provided breeches were cheap—though what connection there was between the price of breeches and the throne, they never properly explained. It is not to be supposed that in Parliament, where their influence was strong, they could be kept silent; and Eel, who knew very well that they could not open their mouths without betraying the weakness of their cause, endeavoured to amuse them with other subjects of discussion. They *would* speak, however, and from time to time uttered such absurdities, especially one man of the name of Goodwood, and another of the name of Stow,* that the people, as miserable as they were for want of clothes, could not avoid laughing at the ridiculous things which these two uttered with all the pompousness of truth and sincerity. Thus the matter remained for two or three years—Eel all the while becoming in his heart more and more estranged from the tailors ; but hesitating with an excess of caution which was characteristic of him to do that which he knew to be right, lest the tailors should be too rudely thrown down from the bad pre-eminence they so long occupied."

"Yes," said Mr. Cobden, "there is quite as much to be urged in favour of the one monopoly as of the other. Publish the jest in the *Morning Chronicle,* and I dare say all our friends in the press will quote it."

At one of the great meetings of the League at Covent Garden, Mr. W. J. Fox took up the idea thus broached, and attacked the supporters of the Corn Laws, not in their capacity of aristocrats, but in their capacity of tradesmen and dealers in a particular commodity, which had no more natural right to protection, according to free-trade views, than any other commodity, whether breeches or boots, cabinet work or upholstery. "A man," said he, "is not to be protected if he keeps a chandler's shop, and cheats, because he happens to be a member of the aristocracy. This is what I complain of. They keep a great chandler's shop; and they enhance the price of every article in their store, by means of the legislature which they control. There was a time when every sort of trading was

---

* The Dukes of Richmond and Buckingham.

thought to be inconsistent with the dignity of an aristo-crat. Your feudal baron did not mind robbing with the strong hand; but he would have turned with contempt from robbing by the short weight of a protective duty, &c. But now, when nobles become tradesmen, when dukes become dealers in corn, butter, beeves, grouse, deer, and salmon, and protect themselves, as far as laws can, against other traders who live in foreign coun-tries, I think it is time for the people to cry out, and proclaim that such dealing is unfair."

While Sir Robert Peel was busy in those reforms of the Tariff which prepared the way for the abolition of the Corn Laws—though doubtless he did not quite foresee the end at which, following out his own principles, he was bound to arrive—a subordinate member of his ad-ministration gave him, according to all the reports of the time, a great amount of assistance in preparing the details of his measures. That subordinate was Mr. Wm. Ewart Gladstone, Vice-President of the Board of Trade and Master of the Mint. He was considered at that time, as Sir Robert Peel had been considered five-and-twenty years before him, as the rising hope of the Tory party, and was thus described by Mr. Francis Ross, of the *Morning Chronicle*, in a work entitled " Sir Robert Peel and his Era," published early in 1843, in a sketch of a " Night in the House of Commons :"—

" By the way, there is the rising hope of the Conserva-tives, and Peel's right arm, William Ewart Gladstone, Vice-President of the Board of Trade and Master of the Mint. In person he is of a good stature, and, like Stanley, has a pretty, good-natured, rather pouting mouth, while the upper part of the face, like Stanley's, has a 'knitted,' if not a frowning aspect. But what disappoints me most is the smallness of the head. Under Stanley's careless locks you can see hidden a good solid mass of forehead ; but this noted young man—this philosophic worker-out of Church principles—I want for him a more capacious skull and greater breadth of face. Can such a small head carry all he knows ?

"We must take men as they are, and not as we imagine them. The head is small, but it is well-shaped. You notice that the upper part of the face rather expresses severity; and I am told that old Gladstone, and the family generally, have been noted in Liverpool for what is called a 'crusty' temperament. If this be so, and this young man inherits it, he is an example of the power of principle, for he seems to have his temper singularly under control. His voice, too, is sweet and plaintive : he has amazing clearness of speech and volubility of utterance, but with a tendency to run into a mellifluous monotony, which he will probably correct.

"Are his abilities as great as they say, or is he an example of being ' cried up ? '

"Oh, no man can doubt that his abilities are great. I do not refer to his books on Church and State, with which he first established his reputation, but to his conduct in the House. He proved ' a friend in need ' to Peel in conducting the tedious business and details of the New Tariff : in fact everything devolved on the Prime Minister and his Vice-President of the Board of Trade ; and though Peel's great business facility and long practice in addressing the House enabled him to expound, state, and

defend the principles and details of the Tariff with more
fulness, force, and weight, it was universally acknowledged that young Gladstone shone in the department of
' Facts and Figures,' and displayed a capacity for official
business of the very first order."

The two young men who were the hopes of the Tory
party—in 1818 and 1843—were destined for other purposes. The "hope" of 1818—the reliance of the protectionists—granted Free Trade and temporarily shattered
the fortunes of the party which trusted him; and the
Tory "hope" of 1843 became the most distinguished of
the Liberal ministers of modern times, and the Liberal
premier of a brilliant Liberal administration, which held
power from 1868 to 1874; and fell by its own hand,
rather than by the assaults of its adversaries.

In the year 1841, Thomas Moore, the popular author
of the "Irish Melodies," "Lalla Rookh," and of political
squibs innumerable, was engaged by the *Morning Chronicle*
to contribute a poem per week on topics of the day to that
journal. A similar offer had been made by Mr. Perry,
more than half a century previously, to Robert Burns,
but was declined by the illustrious ploughman, lest acceptance should have brought him into disfavour with the
Board of Excise, with which he stood in the relation of
employed to the employer, and the members of which,
being ultra-Tories, were not likely to tolerate the publication of liberal rhymes in a London journal by a subordinate in their service, and least of all by Burns, on
whose poetical gifts, when expended on politics, they did
not look with favourable eyes. But Thomas Moore was
under no such obligation of silence, and accepted the offer

with eagerness. He stipulated, however, that his name
should not appear to these effusions, and that each as it
appeared should occupy the same place, namely, at the
head of the first column of the third, or opening page.
Thomas Moore was a Free Trader before the days of
Messrs. Cobden and Bright, and had done good service
to the cause in a more graceful way than Ebenezer
Elliott, but quite as effectually. Thomas Moore wielded
the lancet, Ebenezer Elliott the sledge-hammer, but both
drew blood. Moore foresaw, very speedily after the accession of Sir Robert Peel to power, that the man who
had reformed the Tariff of Customs' Duties was on the
high road to Free Trade, and that the Corn Laws were
doomed. Under this impression he wrote, in February,
1842, the following verses, that appeared in the place
reserved for him in the *Morning Chronicle* of the 23rd of
that month :—

"A THRENODY ON THE APPROACHING DEATH OF OLD MOTHER
CORN-LAW.

> " I see, I see, it is coming fast,
> Our dear old Corn-Law's doom is cast !
> That ancient Lady, of high degree,
> Is as near her end as she well can be ;
> And much will all vulgar eaters of bread
> Rejoice, when they see her fairly dead.
> For never, from ancient Medea * down
> To the late Mrs. Brownrigg, of bad renown,
> Has any old dame been known, they aver,
> Who could starve and carve poor folks like her.

---

* This lady, as is well known, was in the agricultural line. See, for an
account of her farming operations, "Ovid, Metamorph.," vii., 285. Her skill
in "carving" is thus briefly described by the same poet—

> "—— stricto Medea recludit
> Ense senis jugulum——."

" But, dear old damsel, they wrong her sadly,
'Twas all by law she behaved so badly ;
And God forbid, whate'er the event,
That free-born Britons should e'er repent
Wrongs done by Act of Parliament.

" But *is* it, indeed, then come to this,
After all our course of high-bread bliss ?
Poor, *dear* old Corn-Law !—prop of Peers,
And glory of Squires, through countless years,
Must all thy structure of Pounds and Pence,
Like another Babylon, vanish hence ?
Must towering Prices and Rents sublime,
Thus topple, like turrets touch'd by time,—
And all, for what ? that each shirtless oaf,
May bolt, for breakfast, a larger loaf ? !
For this one vulgar purpose alone
Is all this inelegant mischief done.
For this poor Knatchbull—hard privation—
Must lower a peg his ' social station ! '
For this even *lords* (distressing thought)
Will soon to short *commons* all be brought :
Will fall with their wheat, so much per quarter,
And get to look blue as Bucky's garter.
And stars will grow pale, as prices fail,
And fees in tail will be cut off for sale,
And all will sink, by a sliding scale,—
As ' slips o'er its slime the sleek slug-snail,'—*
Nor leave one Corn-lord, high and hale,
Though they flourish now, to tell the tale ! "

Mr. Moore collected the stray verses, which for two
years he continued to contribute to the *Morning Chronicle*,
but this either escaped his researches, or, for some reason
or other, he did not see fit to include it with the others in

---

* A line borrowed, with but little alteration, from one of the Lake poets,
the original being as follows:—

" Slow sliding o'er its slime the slippery, sleek, slug-snail."

the one volume edition of his Poems, published in 1843 by
Messrs. Longman and Co.   Another of the poems which
he contributed to the *Chronicle* at this time, has in like
manner dropped out from or been refused admission into
his collected works, and is as follows, now reprinted from
his own MS. :—

### "APOLLO AT OXFORD.

" 'Twill charm all lovers of song to be told,
   That their friend, Apollo, now grown rather old,
   And a good deal, of late, from the world retired,
   Since his Patent for Inspiration expired,
   Is now, on a visit, from Pindus come down,
   And may daily be met with *incog.* about town.

" Of late, though he once much loved notoriety,
   Apollo but seldom goes into society ;—
   A very wise policy, ev'n in a God,
   When he finds that his Godship's beginning to nod ;
   And 'tis pity the hint isn't yet found out
   By *another* Immortal that's going about—
   Though it doesn't, perhaps, exactly follow
   That Mars should have *quite* as much brains as Apollo.

" Poor Apollo,—his luck in the art obstetrical
   Is hardly much better than 'tis in the metrical.
   He once,—as attending the Muses his trade is,—
   Was Accoucheur-General to all the Nine Ladies.
   But now a young Muse, to be well put to bed,
   Sends for Longman, Murray, or Moxon, instead :
   And, as for the offspring, though midwives flatter,
   And foes in disguise with praise bespatter,
   Depend on't, the God has no hand in the matter.

" No wonder the God, thus wrong'd, should sigh,
   And think poor Poesy's day gone by,—
   Nay, ev'n to the Muses a line should drop,
   Advising those damsels to shut up shop.
   But, no,—his glory had not yet set,
   There was light and life in his Future yet ;

And—what seemed most in the marvellous line,—
From Oxford bards 'twas all to shine !
Yes, Oxford,—spite of her famed Decree,
In the year Sixteen Hundred and Eighty-Three,
When her big-wig sages, of every degree,
And her *then* Professors of Poetry,
Pronounced John Milton's name to be
Not fit for Christian society !—*
Yes, Oxford now would for all atone,
And, perhaps oblige us with the loan
Of a bran-new Milton of her own.

" Such was the hope of better days
For college politics, college lays,
That o'er the God their illusion shed,
As he lay, one foggy morn, in bed,
Perusing *The Sun*, by a farthing taper,—
(That being Apollo's favourite paper)         ,
And, lord, how it made his old heart caper !
Up jumped he, brisk as in younger days,
Threw an old surtout around his rays,
And for Oxford instantly ordered a chaise.

" Poor credulous God, how he came to believe
In Oxonian poets, I cannot conceive.
*One* reverend bard they can boast, but, alack,
A Milman's as rare as a swan, in black.

" What befell the God afterwards, every one knows,
And should only be told in mournful prose ;
For, ne'er hath Immortal, of rhyming renown,
Experienced, on earth, such a *prose* set-down ;
Nor will poor Apollo, if spared to us yet,
Through his whole eternity e'er forget,
The shock that came o'er his ambrosial frame,
When, listening to catch some high-toned name,
Some sounding link of that chain sublime,
Which lengthens its music through all time,

---

* In some Latin verses written in commemoration of this Decree, the
following line occurs :—

" Miltonum, terris cœloque inamabile nomen."

He heard no name but—what shall I say ?
How picture Apollo's face that day,
Or breathe into any initiate ear
The inglorious names he was doomed to hear ?
They were only *two*—but *such* a Two !
It seem'd as from each an arrow flew,
To pierce his Godship through and through ;
And each had a label pinned thereto,
As if with deadlier aim to barb it,—
On *one* was ' WILLIAMS,' on t'other ' GARBETT !

" O'er the rest of the story we draw a veil,—
Let shocked Posterity finish the Tale."

# NEWSPAPER WORK. ANGUS BETHUNE REACH.

———+———

It was one of my duties to open all the letters addressed to the editor, to consign such as were silly, worthless, or irrelevant to the waste-paper basket, to mark for publication such as were well written on points of general interest, which contained valuable information, and which made suggestions that were worthy of consideration, or which preferred well-founded complaints of grievances that it was of public importance to redress. Whenever any subject, political, literary, or social, was prominently before the public, the letter-writers, always active, pertinaceous, and buzzing about the newspapers like flies at a horse's head in hot weather, redoubled their useless and provoking energies. None but those who have had some experience in the matter can imagine the vast heaps of drivelling inanity and offensive silliness sent in the form of letters to an influential journal, and which the writers, though their lucubrations are ill-spelt, ungrammatical, incoherent, and ill-reasoned, each and all think good enough for publication. On any great public question, such as Free Trade and the Repeal of the Corn Laws, or any important and stirring debate in Parliament, the

letter-writers, as far as my experience went, had very
little to say ; but on small social questions they generally
burst forth like one of the plagues of Egypt.  A cheating
case at whist at one of the clubs produced letters that
might be counted by the thousand ; and the famous dispute of Lord Cardigan, then Lord Brudenell, with one of
his brother officers, about wine in a black bottle at the
regimental mess at which he presided as colonel, produced,
literally and without exaggeration, a cart-load of waste
paper during the three weeks that the public interest in
the trumpery matter continued unabated.  Sometimes,
however, though rarely, a letter would come from one of
the most prominent men of the time, from Lord John
Russell, from Lord Brougham, from Daniel O'Connell,
whose name for many years appeared oftener in the public
journals, for praise or blame, than that of any contemporary,
or from others equally noted, which, of course, received
immediate attention.   The Rev. Sydney Smith addressed
his famous letter to the Pennsylvanians, through the
medium of the *Morning Chronicle,* and brought it to the
office himself.   It had no caption in heading as originally
written ; and I asked him, in printing-office *parlance,* how
the letter should be headed. "Head it, '*Pay me my money,*'"
he replied, "or simply, ' To the Pennsylvanians.' "   The
letter was afterwards republished in his collected works.
Another letter with which about the same time he favoured
the *Chronicle* was addressed to Sir Robert Peel.   There
had been a shocking railway accident, which had excited
much indignation against the practice of railway officials
of locking people in the carriages, so that they could not
easily extricate themselves in case of danger.   So much

discussion had ensued in the newspapers—a discussion in which Mr. Sydney Smith took part—that the subject was mentioned in Parliament. Sir Robert Peel, remembering the hard rubs he had from time to time received from his reverend opponent, took occasion to ridicule one of Sydney Smith's letters, and to attribute the interest he took in the matter to "*personal fear.*" Thereupon the canon of St. Paul's rushed into print with the following characteristic letter, which is here reprinted *verbatim et literatim* from the original MS., without correction of its offences against orthography :—

"To Sir Robert Peel.

" a Cruel attack upon me S^r. Robert to attribute all my interference with the arbitrary proceedings of Rail Roads to personal fear.

"Nothing can be more ungrateful, and unkind: I thought only of you and for you—as many Whigg Gentlemen will bear me testimony who rebuked me for my anxiety. I said to myself and to them our lovely and intrepid Minister may be overthrown on the rail. The Lock'd door may be uppermost he will kick and call on the Speaker, and the Sergeant at arms in vain—nothing will remain of all his graces, his flexibilities, his fascinating facetious fury, his Social Warmth, nothing of his flow of Soul, of his dear heavy pleasantry, of his prevailing Skill to impart disorderly Wishes to the purest heart, nothing will remain of it all but an heap of ashes for the parish Church of Tamworth. he perishes at the moment that he is becoming as powerful in the drawing-room of Court as in the house of parliament, at the Moment when Hullah (not without hopes of ultimate success) is teaching him to sing, and Melinotte to dance.

"I have no doubt of your bravery S$^r$. Robert though you have of mine, but then Consider what different Lives we have led, and what a School of Corage is that Troop of Yeomany at Tamworth, the Tory fencibles : who can doubt of your Corage who has seen you at their head Marching up Pitt Street through Dundas Square on to Liverpool Lane? and looking all the while like those beautiful medals of *Bellona frigida* and *Mars sine Sanguine*, the very horses looking at you as if you were going to take away 3 per cent. of their oats. After such Spectacles as these the account you give of your own Corage cannot be doubted. The only little Circumstance which I cannot entirely reconcile to the possession of this very high attribute in so eminent a degree, is that you should have selected for your uncourteous attacks Enemies who cannot resent and a place where there can be no reply.

"I am, Sr, yr. obt. St.

"SYDNEY SMITH."

"June 20th, 1842."

In another letter to the *Chronicle*, in which the reverend gentleman had written 'skipping spirit,' the words were printed 'stripping spirit.' He wrote to set the matter right ; but the printer and the printer's reader could make nothing of the words—so all but illegible was the manuscript—but 'stripling spirit.' After this second failure the facetious canon gave up the contest, confessing that the fault was entirely his own; that he had wasted several of the best years of his life at the university; that he knew something of Horace and Homer, but that he could not spell decently; could not write a hand that a printer could read; and could not work out correctly a simple sum in elementary arithmetic.

Prior to the year 1841 the business of newspaper reporting was not to be considered among the fine arts, or one that required much literary ability. The great things needful for a reporter were quickness, facility in short-hand, and the faculty of abridgment so as to omit judiciously from the speech of a long-winded orator, all irrelevant matter, and all needless repetitions, to give if necessary the spirit without the form of a speech, and to be able to finish in print the sentences which too many public speakers are unable to complete when addressing an audience. The reporter was never called upon to describe anything he saw or to indulge in language of his own. His business was to hear and not to see, to reproduce the meaning and the language of others, whether in Parliament, in the Courts of Law, or in public meetings. Some of the best reporters of that and a previous time were short-hand writers only, and had no more pretensions to literature than a scene-shifter had to tragic or to comic power. To obtain a connection with journals of the highest class it was of course an advantage to a man to be something better than a short-hand writer, for the Parliamentary reporters being for the most part engaged by the year, and Parliament being in recess at least half that time, he who in the Parliamentary vacation could review books or write notices of new

pieces or new actors at the theatres, was of greater value
to his employers than he who was but an echo of what he
heard.   But beyond these two spheres of usefulness, the
reporter was seldom or never required to travel.   His
work was almost purely mechanical, and matters of
description were left to a very inferior class of men
known as "penny-a-liners," who were paid by the job,
and often personally unknown to the editors to whose
journals they contributed.   It was their interest to spin
out their reports to the greatest possible length, and to
tell the story of accidents, fires, robberies, murders, and
executions which formed the specialties of their business
with a plethora of words and phrases that was always
wearisome and often abominable.   But a change was
approaching.   In the year 1841, a young Scottish gentleman named Angus Bethune Reach arrived in London
from Inverness, and presented a letter of introduction at
the *Morning Chronicle* office.   He was just of age, and,
finding his native town in the Highlands too small for
the exercise of his literary talents, determined to launch
into the wider sea of London, and try his fortune on the
daily press.   He had had some little experience on the
*Inverness Courier*, and the letter he brought addressed to
myself was from Mr. Robert Carruthers, the accomplished
editor of that journal.   It was a desperate venture on
which he had entered, but he had a strong heart to
surmount strong obstacles.   And his very obstacles did
him good service.   His father, once the leading solicitor
in Inverness, had fallen upon evil days, from the exercise—
it was reported—of a too generous hospitality in the enter-
tainment of distinguished strangers, who arrived in the

"capital of the highlands," and in his old age had found it necessary to break up his home and with his wife to accompany his son to London. It is usually hard work for a young man in the metropolis without other profession than literature to maintain himself; but poor Angus Reach had a threefold burden—to him no burden because his love, his hope, and his consciousness of genius supported him. There was unluckily no vacancy for him on the *Chronicle*. If there had been, he was too young and inexperienced for political work, and for the work of reporting in Parliament (for which there was always a demand in those days when every London morning paper had its own staff of reporters) he was disqualified because he was unable to write short-hand. This disqualification he immediately set himself to remove, and in the meantime, thanks to one sympathising spirit who knew his worth, and had the means in a humble way of pushing him forward—he procured occasional employment—in describing those events of minor importance, but of general interest which the public liked to read, and very speedily played havoc with the small penny-a-liners on whom the *Chronicle* as well as other papers had formerly been compelled to rely. His father, too—Mr. Roderick Reach—a shrewd and able man, with an excellent literary style, found employment as the London correspondent of the *Inverness Courier*, of which he was once the proprietor. Mr. Roderick Reach was among the first to enter into this walk of journalism, which has since been so largely trodden, and by means of the wayfarers in which the public of the provinces are kept so much more fully informed of the minor doings of the notabilities of the metropolis, and of all the gossip and small talk of fashion than the Londoners themselves. There was at last a vacancy in the reporting department of the *Chronicle,* consequent upon the death of the gentleman who attended the Central Criminal Court, and Angus Reach, pre-informed by myself, was the first candidate in the field. The office was not one of great emolument, but it was a certainty; and Reach, to the great joy of himself and family, obtained it. He had now got his foot on the first rung of the literary ladder, and his upward progress was both steady and rapid. A fortunate accident led to his advancement to the Parliamentary gallery, where he acquitted himself with distinction. One of the ordinary staff had been suddenly called upon to leave London on business of importance to remain absent for two or three weeks, but had begged hard to be excused for domestic and other reasons, to the great annoyance of the editor. The difficulty was to procure a substitute during the day, and it so happened that Reach was in the writing room busy in transcribing his notes. His name was suggested and found acceptance. Being asked how long it would take him to get ready, he promptly replied, "half an hour or less." "That's a man to get on!" said Mr. (afterwards Sir John) Easthope, "a true Scotsman, always ready."

This fortunate circumstance raised him at once from a subordinate to a superior station, and secured him the favour of those who had power to advance him still higher.

In the capacity of a narrator of events which largely

interested the public, he was constantly employed; and introduced a style till then unpractised, except in the editorial articles, by means of which he brought before the reader's mind a vivid picture, such as a novelist would paint, of every occurrence that passed under his eye—rapid, correct, graphic, and full of life and animation. Under his influence the reader could but see what he saw, hear what he heard, and share all the emotions and excitements of an actual spectator of the scene. This was an immense advance upon the old reporting style. It immediately found imitators in other journals, and picturesque reporting became thenceforward the fashion, and has so remained to this day, when the picturesque threatens to be swallowed up by the sensational.

The story of men of letters who are not born to the inheritance of fortune, and are compelled to earn their bread by the rewards of literary labour, is generally a sad one. A man can make a shoe, or dig in a garden, or plough in a field, sell cheese or cloth, or follow any other trade or occupation day after day without interruption or fatigue. It costs no more effort of the mind or body to sell a thousand cheeses or a thousand bales of cotton, than to sell one; but far different is the case of the author, successful or unsuccessful. There is always a market for commodities; but if a man by any possibility could write a thousand editorial articles in a week, where would be the market for more than one or two of them? Even popularity has its drawbacks, for if once the cry is raised against a popular author that he writes too much, his popularity is from that moment on the wane. But he

who writes for bread must continue to write for bread or
die, whatever may be the outcry against him for the
crime—so serious in critical eyes—of writing too much·
Happily it is not necessary in the great fight for daily
bread which those who without fortune to aid them, are
bound to fight if they enter the lists of literature, to sign
their names to all that they write, or the reiteration of
some names would be prejudicial to themselves and perhaps distasteful to their readers.    But, in the first
exuberance of youthful success, and the consciousness of
power, this prudent consideration is apt to be disregarded,
and the young aspirant, aspiring too much, never thinks.
how delicate are the tissues of the brain, or that, if he
overwork the fine faculties the exercise of which gives.
him subsistence in the present and promises him fame
in the future, he runs the risk of even worse than death.
And as for signing the name, it is, at the outset of a
literary career, the one thing that the youthful author
most desires.    It is an advertisement, an aid to his.
business if he do his business well, and a proof of the
growing popularity on which he expects to thrive.    This
was especially the case with Angus Reach.    No amount
of work seemed too much for him, and however apparently overburthened, he seldom refused any task that
came in his way in any department of journalism or
literature.    He had not been three years engaged in the
hard and well-nigh exhaustive work of the *Morning.
Chronicle*, which involved the sitting up till long past
midnight and often till daybreak, before his hand was.
seen in half-a-dozen magazines and periodicals.    Every
subject seemed equally familiar to him.    If never exceed--

ingly good, he was never exceedingly bad, but always respectable and up to the required mark. He was as punctual as the clock, and always performed what he promised by the time he promised. Whether he wrote descriptive and always excellent accounts of daily events; whether he reviewed books in any department of literature; whether he criticised a play or an actor, an opera or a *prima donna;* whether he wrote an original article, a sketch, a parody, or a skit; whether he wrote prose or verse, or whether he took the longer flights of fancy and imagination, and the hard work necessary to produce a novel or romance; he was always sure to write something that was interesting, readable, and creditable to his head and heart. It was said of his amazing fertility and facility, by a friend, half in jest and half in earnest—"that if Reach were asked to write a great historical tragedy and given a month for the task, he would undertake it without hesitation, and astonish his employer by bringing it to him cut and dry in less than ten days." The calls upon his purse were heavy, and were rendered still heavier when he took to himself a wife; and he never found himself in a position with all his industry, to refuse a literary job of any kind, or to be able to say that he was fully a week before the world, and could lie fallow for that time without production. If the day could not suffice him he drew upon the night. If the night were not enough, he drew upon the day, drew upon the hours of sleep, exercise, and recreation, and ate his dinner writing. And when sleep claimed the necessary rest for the brain, he bribed sleep away by copious libations of strong tea or coffee, borrowing time as it were at usurious.

interest.    He wrote—besides articles uncountable, and
that have never been collected, and possibly never will
or can be—three good novels, " Clement Lorimer," the
"Book with the Iron Clasps," and the "Buccaneers." He
also made an extended inquiry for the *Morning Chronicle*
into the condition of the working classes in the midland
districts of England, especially of Sheffield and the
neighbourhood ; and one still more extended and interesting, into the condition of the wine-growers and vine-
labourers in the Garonne, which was afterwards republished in a volume entitled " Claret and Olives," and
dedicated to one whom it pleased him to call his " earliest
and kindest literary friend."    For about fourteen years
he carried on this galloping trade, always ready and
willing, always facile, always delighting his readers and
delighting in his work, always needing the rewards of
his work so laboriously but pleasantly earned, but never
thinking—or if thinking never allowing the thought to
stop him—that the pitcher was going too often to the
well, that the mind was not like the widow's cruse,
inexhaustible, and that it had to be continually replen-
ished if it would continue to outpour, and that like
bountiful earth it required now and then to lie fallow for
the sake of its own fertility.    " Let not the strong man
rejoice in his strength."    Here was, if ever, a strong
man, and one who rejoiced in his strength, bold, buoyant,
hopeful, defiant, thinking no evil, and ready for all that
fate or fortune might impose upon him, cultivating the
intellectual at the expense of his physical faculties, and
taking no heed of the body without whose aid the mighty,
the majestic soul is nothing,—at least in this world.

One day—he was only thirty-five years of age, and had been about fourteen years in London—he went into the shop of Colnaghi, the print seller in Pall-Mall, on some business of art criticism for the *Morning Chronicle*. He had not been there many minutes when he suddenly felt a strange sensation in his head as if something had snapped in his brain with a loud report, succeeded by a dizziness, a half swooning, and a general haze, confusion, and mistiness of thought. The sensation passed off in a few minutes and he thought of it no more. But it was the death warning, though he did not know it at the time. Had he taken a holiday, had he climbed the mountain-top, rowed his boat on the river or the lake, taken a voyage to the Antipodes, or set off on a walking excursion through the glens of his native Scotland, or done any-thing but write, he might have repaired the evil which he had done to the delicate organism of the brain, repaired the broken or snapped string of the harp of intellect, and prolonged his useful days. But he treated the warning as of no account; did not, in fact, suspect that it was a warning; had no one to tell him that the alarm-bell had sounded; and went on recklessly, hopefully, triumphantly as before. But not for long. After a couple of months there was a second warning, louder than the first, and he had to retire from the battle-field of his business, a wounded soldier of literature. The *Morning Chronicle* was mindful of his merits and his labours, though all or nearly all were not expended in its service, and paid him his salary as of old, in the hope of his recovery. Months passed. He grew no better, some of his friends thought worse, and his spirit began to chafe at the thought of

accepting unearned money.  His wife in this emergency
came to the rescue and established a Berlin wool and
stationery shop in Albany Street, Regent's Park, and
appealed to her helpless husband's friends for support
and patronage.  One of his literary friends (I will not
mention the name of this prosperous person—now no
more) took so much pity on his former colleague and
partner in many literary enterprises, as to buy all his
stationery, and especially his sealing-wax, of his unfortunate brother.  But the poor shop came to a sudden
end.  A shop like everything else requires time to grow,
and it was expected by poor Reach's nearest and dearest
connections, though not by poor Reach himself, who was
by this time beyond hoping—almost beyond living—that
the shop would grow up, like Jonah's gourd in a night.
The *Morning Chronicle* salary was by this time becoming
a dubious and precarious reliance.  The *Chronicle* was
not over prosperous; and it was not in the bond
to maintain even a good servant beyond a certain
reasonable time and a certain reasonable hope of his
recovery.  There were ominous rumours that the salary
must surcease, collapse, end, and vanish into good wishes.
At this juncture Mr. Shirley Brooks—who himself owed
his connection with the press and with the *Morning
Chronicle* to the good offices of Angus Reach—volunteered
to perform the duties of the sick man in addition to his
own, if the salary of the sick man were continued.  This
noble arrangement lasted for nearly a twelvemonth, and
might have lasted longer, only in the meantime poor
Angus Reach died of softening of the brain, in the early
prime of his manhood, in the very fructification of his

genius ; died of intemperance in work and of ignorance of the fact that the body is the soul's labourer, and that if the labourer be neglected or badly used, the work must suffer or stop.  In the case of poor Angus Reach the work stopped, and literature lost one who in happier circumstances might have added to it a great name, and written it on enduring stone or brass ; not as John Keats said in his melancholy epitaph on himself—" in water."

# THE CONFEDERATION OF GAUL.

In the summer of 1838, a Polish gentleman, who had
been introduced to me some time previously by Thomas
Campbell, the poet, well-known for the zeal with which he
advocated the cause of Polish Independence, called at the
*Morning Chronicle* office, and asked me to present him to
Mr. Black. He had become possessed of the copy of a remarkable Document, which had been deposited among the
secret archives of the Russian Court at St. Petersburg, and
the author of which had been munificently rewarded by the
Czar Nicholas. The French Revolution of 1830, followed
by that of the Belgians, and by the great revolt of the
Poles against Russia, had greatly displeased and alarmed
the Czar. Nicholas refused to recognise the King of the
Barricades, as Louis Philippe was then called, refused
also to acknowledge the Independence of Belgium, and
the accession of King Leopold; and put forth all his
strength to crush the Poles in their gallant attempt to
recover their independence. The Polish cause excited
great enthusiasm both in France and England; but the
displeasure of the powerful Czar was chiefly vented
against France, as the *fons et origo* of all the revolu-

tionary excesses of Europe. The Document, based on
adequate knowledge of the Czar's hostility to French
democracy, proposed a plan for the dismemberment of
France, and the creation out of its ruins of several
small states, to be called "The Confederation of Gaul."
My Polish friend was of opinion that the Document
of which he had become possessed was of considerable
pecuniary value, and offered it for sale to the *Morning
Chronicle*. Mr. Black, though of opinion that the document was interesting, if not very important, declined to
purchase it at the very high price which was put upon it.
My Polish acquaintance forthwith resolved to offer it to
the *Times*, and told me two days afterwards that he had
been very courteously received by Mr. Thomas Barnes,
the then editor of that journal, at his house in Soho
Square, who after perusal of his manuscript had coun-
selled him to publish it as a pamphlet at Ridgway's, and
had promised to direct public attention to it in the
leading columns of the *Times*, as soon as it made its
appearance. This advice was acted upon, the pamphlet
was shortly afterwards published, and Mr. Barnes kept
his promise by devoting a leading article of the *Times* to
it, and thus spreading a knowledge of it through all
Europe. The *Morning Chronicle*, which at that time
made it a point to disagree with the *Times* in every thing,
denounced the pamphlet as a forgery, chiefly because no
sane man like the Emperor Nicholas would have rewarded
any one for proposing a scheme so extravagant, and so
offensive. The *Morning Post*, the *Courier*, and the
*Globe*, then called *Cupid*, and supposed to be under
the immediate control of Lord Palmerston, were all at a

loss to decide whether the pamphlet were a forgery or a
joke; not considering that it might be neither, and that
there was nothing to prevent any clever or imaginative
diplomatist, young or old, in the Russian Foreign Office,
from drawing up such a plan, or the Czar from being
pleased with and paying for it.  The style of political
warfare in those not very remote days, differed greatly
from the more courteous methods of our time, when
rival newspapers do not call each other offensive
names, or indeed seldom trouble themselves to indulge
in controversy with each other.  It would excite no
little wonder in the year 1875, if the *Times* were to
publish such a leader as appeared in its impression of
the 26th of July, 1838, in defence of the editor of the
" Confederation of Gaul," and in wild and silly abuse of
all who differed from it in opinion as to the authenticity of
that production.  It is here subjoined as a specimen
of the polemics of a bygone era, and of the amenities
of London journalism when Messrs. Barnes and Bacon
presided over the destinies of the *Times*, and were constantly ridiculed by Daniel O'Connell, as Messrs. "Beans
and Bacon."

" That many impartial and unprejudiced persons may
doubt the genuineness of the Russian diplomatic paper entitled ' *The Confederation of Gaul*,' we can readily believe ;
and although, as we have already stated, we strongly
incline to the contrary opinion, we certainly have no
desire to make converts of those who take a different
view of the document.  Nor should we, now, at least,
trouble ourselves to make the attempt, even if we had

been at first disposed to make it,—for the judgment
pronounced upon it by a portion of the press remarkable
chiefly for its ignorance and impudence, and the manner
in which the coxcombs have delivered that judgment, are
far more calculated than anything we could say to shake
whatever doubts may have been entertained respecting
the existence of such a paper in the Russian archives,
and to induce a conviction of its reality. Two Ministerial evening papers, and one morning print ' in the
same interest,' (*The Morning Chronicle*), insist that the
document is a forgery, and so does a would-be Conservative print of low circulation (*The Morning Post*), and
of still lower character, which is not read anywhere but
in servants' halls, house-keepers' rooms, and butlers'
pantries, nor to any very great extent even in those
quarters, if we may judge by the stamp-returns.

" This kitchen-stuff journal assails the publisher of
the document in the true Mrs. Slipslop style, calling
him an ' impudent varlet,' and we know not how many
other polite names, borrowed from area *railings ;* while,
by a piece of facetiousness, which can be fully appreciated only by those who happen to have been born within
the sound of Bow bells, the name of the author of the
document, though imperfectly given in the original
(' Ivan***,') is guessed to be Ivanhoff. ' The last syllable
of the name,' says this Cockney out of livery, ' is cut
(*h*)*off* in the original (*h*original ?), *ergo* (*h*ergo ?), Ivanhoff
(Hivanhoff?) must be the man ! ' Now, of the authenti-
city of what document, alleged to be Russian (if we
except the label on a pot of bear's grease), can such
a simpleton as this pretend to judge ?

"That abject slave and unprincipled tool of the Ministers, the *Courier*, follows in the wake of the print we have been describing: quotes and adopts, as the production of a 'lively vein,' the very joke we have just cited, and honours us with the title of 'Blunderer.' We are not surprised at this. It would have been very unnatural if the *Courier* had not attacked us, and patted the pre*post*erous joker on the head.

'Blockheads, with reason, wicked wits abhor,
But fool 'gainst fool, is barb'rous civil war.'

As a farther evidence of sagacity, the *Courier* adds— 'at the first glance we recognized the parentage of the work: the author is evidently a Frenchman.' Now, any one who understands the French language, in which the document is written, and will take the trouble to read it, must discover, though not 'at the first glance,' that it could not have been written by a Frenchman. So much for wiseacre the second, who is as positive as wiseacre the first, and with quite as little reason, that the document must be a forgery.

"Our amusing cotemporary, *Cupid*, comes next, and was apparently about to attempt some ground for his opinion that the paper is a forgery, when the manner in which the name of its author is printed (viz., 'Ivan***') caught his eye. *Cupid*, characteristically enough, was at once *in nubibus*. Clapping his hands at the asterisks, the 'old boy' exclaimed, 'Mr. Ivan with the stars—Mr. Ivan with the stars—the fellow is as great an impostor as Mr. Murphy; the whole thing must be an imposition.' And with this 'the god of *soft* persuasion' broke off, much, we suspect, to the surprise of his readers, but evidently perfectly well satisfied with himself *à l'ordinaire*, and looking, we doubt not, as he winged his way to the Foreign-office, as contented and as intellectual as a chubby-cheeked cherub carved on a country tombstone.

"Lastly, we have the morning Ministerial organ, (*The Morning Chronicle*), which 'proceeds the entire swine' for the Government on all occasions, except when its own pounds, shillings, and pence (railroads to wit*) are concerned. Flippant and foolish as its brother blockheads, it has moreover the ill-luck to assign two reasons for its decided conviction that the document is not authentic. The first is, that one of the articles says, ' The King of Spain, Charles V., shall obtain Navarre,' &c.; that the plan is dated 15th of June, 1833, and that at that date Ferdinand was still on the throne of Spain. This foolish quibble is noticed in our columns by the editor of the pamphlet in which the document appears. The second reason is, that in the next article, which restores Le Bresse and Le Bugay to the King of Sardinia, 'the allied Powers recommend the King of Sardinia to give quite a republican Government to this state, whose inhabitants are well known for their attachment to freedom.' It is, according to this print, the height of waggery to put such language into the mouth of the parties to such a scheme, but he forgets that nearly the same language was constantly used by the despotic Powers previous to the settlement of Europe in 1815, and

---

* This was an allusion to the connection of Sir John Easthope with the London and Southampton Railway, of which he was a Director, and with the Havre, Rouen, and Paris Railways, of which he was an energetic promoter.

that the three parties to the Holy Alliance bind
themselves ' agreeably to the words of holy Scripture,
which commands all men to love as brethren, and
remain united in the bonds of true and indissoluble
brotherly love; always to assist one another; *to govern
their subjects as parents; to maintain religion, peace, and
justice.*' Now, suppose the treaty of the Holy Alliance
had been surreptitiously obtained from the Russian
archives, instead of being officially promulgated, what
a wag the *Grunticle* would have thought the man who
declared that the words we have here quoted were to
be found in it !

"Thus much, then, for the value of the judgment of
that part of the press which has been so foolishly forward to pronounce the ' *Confederation of Gaul* ' a forgery.
Some of these scribblers, we observe, intimate that the
gentleman who has given this document to the world is
actuated by no other than selfish and sordid motives.
Can it be that he has paid them to advance his object
and push the sale of his pamphlet by their abuse ? "

The editor of the pamphlet wrote in far better taste
on this subject than Mr. Barnes, though it must be
admitted that the advocacy of Mr. Barnes was warm and
thorough; and to use his own phrase "proceeded the
entire swine" for his client.

## "THE CONFEDERATION OF GAUL.

*" To the Editor of the ' Times.'*

" SIR,

"As you have so boldly stood forward in the
cause of truth, by expressing in your widely circulating

columns your belief of the authenticity of the plan for the partition of France, I think it but right to afford you a further justification for your belief, while at the same time I defend myself by answering the perverse reasoning of a prejudiced morning paper.

" The main question is this, — is the acknowledged extravagance of this plan any reason why it should not have been deposed among the archives of the Russian empire, and why its author should not have been rewarded ? If the writer in the *Morning Chronicle* is of opinion that the Emperor Nicholas is too wise and too unambitious to have been pleased with such a project, I can only say that his ignorance of the character of that Sovereign is unpardonable in a public journalist. Let him remember the sane speech of the Emperor at no very distant period, that if aroused to it he would not leave a stone standing at Warsaw. This was said openly (not deposed in the secret archives), and in the face of Europe, which was filled with indignation at the wickedness and extravagance of the threat.

" As to the pretended anachronism which is to stamp the document as a forgery, every unprejudiced reader will immediately see that it is no anachronism at all. The plan was a mere plan ; it was not a manifesto. It was to be carried into execution, or it was not, at some distant date. There is no expression in it which would lead to the belief that it was written to be immediately acted upon. In June, 1833, when it was dated, the conflicting claims of Don Carlos and the infant Princess Isabella were the universal theme of European politicians. The death of Ferdinand was looked for at no remote period,

and the civil war, which broke out a few months afterwards, was prepared and ready to burst forth at the
slightest signal. Don Carlos had even then taken all
his measures. The document does not call him the
actual King of Spain, but the King of Spain that would
be when that plan should come to be acted on.

" In general I do not conceive the logic of some newspapers, which think it impossible that Russia should
form a plan ' to cut France in pieces like a perigord-pie.'
How many instances we may quote from history in which
powerful princes have cut up countries in pieces as easily
as they would pies, meeting resistance where they did
not expect it—at the bones. I am quite as well aware
as anybody can be, that Russia would have found France
a tougher dish to dissect with her sword than she found
deserted Poland to be, and that she might have so
hacked her weapon in the attempt as to have rendered it
altogether unfit for future service.

" I have the honour to be, Sir,

" Your most obedient servant,

" THE EDITOR.

" July 25."

Mr. Albany Fonblanque, of the *Examiner*, beyond all
comparison the wittiest as well as wisest English journalist
whom this country has produced, had his say upon the
" Confederation of Gaul." The *Times* in its first article
affirmed that the document was of " fearful importance,"
upon which the *Examiner*, of the following Sunday,
declared " For belief in the genuineness of a document
called ' The Confederation of Gaul,' a confederation of
*gulls* was absolutely requisite, which the *Times* has kindly

endeavoured to bring about.\*\*\*\* About the authenticity of this document of 'fearful importance,' we think it unnecessary to say one word; but there will shortly be published a plan for the partition of Great Britain, being a copy of a diplomatic paper taken at St. Petersburg in 1836, from the secret archives of the Russian Court. It is proposed to surrender the Isle of Thanet to the Pope; to give the rest of Kent and the whole of Surrey to Colonel Sibthorp, under the name of the Kingdom of East Anglia, the capital of the same being St. George's Fields; France to be contented with that part of Westminster naturally destined for her, called Petty France; St. James's parish to be a republic; the Seven Dials also to be a republic, and their Diet to be held in the street of that name; Her Majesty Queen Victoria to enjoy for herself the title of Queen of Pimlico, her residence being fixed in the palace of the same, and her dominion to be bounded to the east by the iron railings; to the north by Constitution Hill; to the west by Grosvenor Place, and to the south by Arabella Row. The Emperor of Russia will be contented with the pig-tail statue of George III. in Cockspur Street. Considering the services which the Duke of Wellington, in his long career, has rendered to the peaceful policy of the Holy Alliance, and to all the monarchs who have governed England for eighty years, Strathfieldsaye is to be erected into an independent state, &c."

This little squib made an end of " The Confederation of Gaul," and neither the *Times* nor any other journal returned again to the subject.

# A PROPOSED LITERARY UNION.

In the summer of 1842, an attempt was made—not for the first time—to bring together the literary men of London into a Union or Institute. The object was not the formation of a club, but of an association, in which authors, journalists, and critics might meet daily for mutual support and assistance in the battle of life; that they might establish a hall or college of literature, which should unite the purposes of a writing-room, a reading-room, a library of reference, and a social and professional rendezvous, at which translators, copyists, correctors of the press, and working literary men who had not genius enough to write original works, but who had industry and skill enough to be able to render valuable assistance to those whose time was more valuable, might make known their wants and capabilities, and so obtain chances of employment, that were otherwise unavailable. It was proposed to give the Institute the name of Milton, one who, all things considered, was the greatest professional man of letters whom England had ever produced; one who had held the torch of literature aloft in the darkest of times, and had never sullied the purity of his high vocation by word or deed, or printed opinion; who

had never prostituted his divine gifts to unworthy purposes, or spoken unkindly of the humble. The project
was communicated to several of the leading literary men of
the time, with some of whom I was, and with some of
whom I was not, personally acquainted—soliciting their
advice and co-operation. The first answer received came
from Mr. Charles Dickens :—

> "DEVONSHIRE TERRACE,
> "Twenty-sixth July, 1842.
>
> "MY DEAR SIR,
> "In the *principle* of your note I heartily concur.
> Of the chances that hang about its successful reduction
> into practice, I am somewhat doubtful. These experi-
> ments have been very often tried ; and have almost as
> often failed.
> "Nevertheless I shall be exceedingly glad to talk with
> you upon the subject; and any morning this week that
> may be convenient to you, I shall be happy to see you.
> About one o'clock is usually the best time for such a
> purpose with me, but choose your own time, and I will
> make it mine.
> "Faithfully yours always,
> "CHARLES DICKENS.
> "Charles Mackay, Esquire."

Mr. Thomas Campbell, author of " The Pleasures of
Hope," Dr. Beattie, and others, promised their support.
Mr. John Britton, the eminent antiquary, author of an
attempt to prove that Junius was Colonel Barré, and of
a whole library of topographical, archæological, and architectural works, looked upon the project with much favour,

and exerted himself very zealously in its behalf. A meeting was arranged to take place at the Clarence Club, Waterloo Place, to meet Mr. Campbell, to which was invited, among others, Mr. John Robertson, formerly editor of the *Westminster Review*. He wrote:—

"122, Pall Mall,
"Tuesday.

" MY DEAR SIR,

"Need I say that your note has given me great satisfaction. I hail your elevated and manly views of the literary profession with hope as signs of better days to come.

"Of course I shall be happy to be at the Clarence on Thursday.

"Yours very truly,
"JOHN ROBERTSON.

"To Charles Mackay, Esq."

Notwithstanding much verbal and epistolary encouragement, very little progress was made beyond the drawing up of a plan or prospectus. About eight months after the promulgation of the project, Mr. Robertson again wrote:—

"122, Pall Mall,
"19 March, 1843.

" MY DEAR SIR,

"I intended to have done myself the pleasure of calling on you and Mr. Britton to-day, but could not accomplish it. Carlyle, whom I saw last night, will positively come on Saturday. He is stout against the status clause. Craik also is resolute against it. Could not the following be better: 'To adopt means to strengthen each other in forming and acting on the noblest views of the literary profession.' I have written an additional paragraph for the prospectus, which, together with my outline of the business for Saturday, I am anxious to submit to yourself and Mr. Britton before that day.

" I foresee some difficulties in reference to the position of the lady authors. It will be a great kindness if you will turn the matter over, and give us the benefit of your views. Though inclined to make as little difference as possible, we cannot make them councillors, and elect a lady as well as a masculine secretary.

" Begging you to present my kind compliments to Mr. Britton when showing him this note,

" I remain,

" Yours very truly,

JOHN ROBERTSON.

" To Charles Mackay, Esq."

The difficulty as to the status clause, to which Mr. Robertson alluded, was to define *who* was an author. It might seem at first glance that no such difficulty could well arise; but it lay at the very threshold of the enterprise. Sir Robert Peel found it difficult to define a pound, when he held a sovereign between his finger and thumb, and exhibited it to a wondering House of Commons; but his task was easy compared with that which devolved upon us, when we endeavoured truly and satisfactorily to define what we meant by an author. We knew that an author was one who wrote and published a history, a biography, a romance, a poem, a philosophical or scientific treatise, who compiled a dictionary or wrote a book of travels; but as a claim was put forward for the writer of a sermon, a review, a leading article in the newspapers, or of a casual and anonymous contribution to a periodical, it became necessary to decide whether such a claim could be allowed; or, if allowed, whether the composition and publication of one such literary effort were sufficient, and if not, how many? There also arose, as Mr. Robertson stated it, the question of the authoresses, and whether, if they wished to become members of a Literary Institute, they should not form an Institute exclusively for themselves. By this time Mr. Dickens, from whose co-operation much had been expected, had formally withdrawn :—

"DEVONSHIRE TERRACE,
"Seventeenth February, 1843.

"MY DEAR MACKAY,

"I have such strong reasons to doubt the easy working of your project, and to fear it will end in disappointment, that I 'cannot'—as the honest, and I am sorry to add, very heavy servant in 'High Life Below Stairs,' says,—'make one among you.' Some of these weighty arguments shall be yours, when I see you next.

"Faithfully yours,
"CHARLES DICKENS.

"Charles Mackay, Esquire."

Another serious and ultimately fatal difficulty arose. Suppose an author, whom none could deny to be an author, had published a book or books, of which the tendency, avowed or latent, was immoral, revolutionary, treasonable, or irreligious; or what some of the committee might think as bad or worse than all these—a book that was positively silly and contemptible—was he to be admitted to the Union? And if not, would not the members of the Union virtually have constituted themselves into a court of criticism and judgment, and made themselves a literary Vehmgericht? And would not the exercise of such judgment bring the members into constant collision with all the rising and ambitious young members of the literary class? Another unexpected difficulty arose in the question whether a publisher or bookseller could be admitted, even if he were an author, such as Mr. Moxon, who was both bookseller and poet. These were among the weighty arguments to which Mr. Dickens alluded, and which all received careful and conscientious attention. A conclusion was arrived at, that authors were something like spiders. They could spin silk as well as silkworms; but, unlike the latter, they could not associate peaceably together, or without endeavouring to eat each other up. One of the committee told us a story of a well-intentioned enthusiast, who, being convinced that the web of the spider might be made as available for commerce as that of the silkworm, confined about a thousand spiders in a cage. He looked for his busy workers the next morning; but found that one half of them had been devoured or slain by the other half. At the end of a week only one big, bloated insect was left out of the whole number. And to make the little apologue more applicable to the case in hand, a violent feud broke out amid our deliberations by the curt and insulting refusal of one member of the committtee to have any further to do with the project, unless another com-

mitteeman, whom he named, were forthwith expelled, or
compelled to abdicate his place among us. Added to
this unlucky occurrence, our project, having but half-a-
dozen or a dozen supporters and half a hundred enemies,
fell through; and a certain place, not to be mentioned to
ears polite, received a large paving-stone, in the shape of
our good intentions.

# SIR WALTER SCOTT AND HIS MONUMENT.

It was never my good fortune to see Sir Walter Scott. I was but a youth when he died; and one of my early recollections is, on arriving in London from the Continent in 1832, to have come unexpectedly upon a long line of carriages and a crowd of people in that portion of Jermyn Street which stretches westwards from the Haymarket. I stopped to ask a policeman the cause of the crowd, and he informed me, that " Sir Walter Scott was dying at the St. James's Hotel, and that the string of carriages contained people calling to make inquiries." I made my way through the crowd, and stationed myself opposite the hotel, that I might at least see the windows of the house in which the great man was lying. Not knowing in which room he lay, I asked a second policeman if he knew. He replied that the bed-room was the second floor front; and though I thought at the time it was vain, idle, and foolish of me to do so, I gazed at the windows reverentially. But Scott lay in the back room, according to the memorandum of Dr. Fergusson, communicated to Mr. Lockhart, who has inserted it in his well-known Life of his illustrious father-in-law. " When I saw Sir Walter he was lying in the second floor back room of the St. James's Hotel, in

Jermyn Street, in a state of stupor.   I think I never saw
anything more magnificent than the symmetry of his
colossal bust as he lay on the pillow with his chest and
neck exposed.   During the time he was in Jermyn Street
he was calm, but never collected, and in general either in
a state of stupor or a waking dream.   He never seemed
to know where he was, but imagined himself to be still in
the steam-boat.   The rattling of carriages and the noises
of the street sometimes disturbed this illusion, and then
he fancied himself at the polling-booth of Jedburgh."
This was my nearest bodily approach to the great Sir
Walter, with whose immortal novels and poetry my mind
had been familiar during that sympathetic period of early
youth, when poetry and romance exercise their greatest
fascinations.   As all the world knows, he was taken home
to Scotland, and his beloved Abbotsford, where he died
in September, in the presence of his attached family, and
amid the universal regret and respect of his own and
foreign nations.

   Twelve years afterwards it fell to my lot to be greatly
occupied with the name and fame of Sir Walter Scott,
and to be placed in communication with people who had
known him personally, and with most of the leading spirits
of the day.   The business had reference to the completion
of the beautiful monument which the Edinburgh people
had begun to erect in honour of the greatest man who
ever trod the pavements of their picturesque city.   In the
month of February, 1844, the work had come to a stand-
still for want of funds, and the sum of 3000*l.* was urgently
needed, to carry up to the height intended by the architect
the spire of the Gothic shrine, which enclosed the marble

statue of the poet, and otherwise to complete the monument. The shopkeepers of Edinburgh might well have
subscribed the whole sum needed, if they had remembered
that the works of Scott had brought travellers into their
city, with money in their pockets, from all quarters of the
globe, to do honour to his memory, and visit the scenes
which his genius had hallowed. But the generosity or
justice of Edinburgh had been exhausted. The subscription list had been sent round; balls and entertainments
had been given, and considerable sums from time to time
received from these sources; but the Scottish fountain
had run dry, and it was thought advisable to tap the
richer fountains of London, in support of that local work
which many people thought ought to have been made
national. At this time I was assistant editor of the
*Morning Chronicle* under my excellent and earliest London
friend, John Black, and through the introduction of a
relative in Edinburgh, the late John Alexander Mackay
of Blackcastle, I received a letter from Sir Thomas Dick
Lauder, the leading spirit of the Edinburgh committee,
requesting me to notice the deficiency in the columns of
the *Morning Chronicle*, and, if possible, to procure the aid
of Mr. Loch, M.P., the agent of the Duke of Sutherland,
in organizing a movement in London. An article forthwith appeared in the *Chronicle*, for which a vote of thanks
was tendered to the Editor by the Edinburgh people.
Sir Thomas Dick Lauder subsequently wrote :—

> "BOARD OF MANUFACTURES, EDINBURGH,
> "Feb. 19, 1844.
>
> " DEAR SIR,—
> " Mr. Loch's reply to my letter has just reached

me, and I am sorry to say that, from the intensity of his occupation he cannot undertake to follow up his wishes to be of use in getting up a subscription in London, though I have no doubt that if I speak to him he will do all in his power to help us. If he could do no more than get the Duke of Sutherland to take the chair of a meeting, that of itself would be of use.

"I have now, as acting for the Committee here, formally to request that he will kindly undertake the office of (honorary) secretary to any Committee which he may find it possible to organize. I enclose three letters which you may find of use—two of them to the members for Edinburgh, and one to John Richardson, solicitor, of Fludyer Street, a bosom friend of Scott, and who is generally acquainted with the members of both Houses of Parliament.

"I know your good will to be such that I need not entreat of you not to allow the grass to grow at your heels.

"Believe me ever,

"Dear sir,

"Yours most truly,

"THOS. DICK LAUDER.

"To Charles Mackay, Esq."

I accepted the position which Sir Thomas marked out for me, together with the work attached to it, which I little expected would be so onerous as it became, and applied in all quarters for co-operation. It was up-hill work at first, but still progress was made, and several very influential names were secured for the Committee, including that of my friend and fellow-labourer, Mr. Charles Dickens.   On reporting what had been done, Sir Thomas wrote me in reply :—

"BOARD OF MANUFACTURES, EDINBURGH,
"2nd March, 1844.

"MY DEAR SIR,—

"Accept my kind thanks for your letter of the 29th ult.   I anticipated difficulties, and God knows I have had enough of them myself.   But we need only remember that 'improbus labor omnia vincit.'   Mr. Charles Dickens is a host.   Patrick Maxwell Stewart, a particular friend of mine, will be valuable.   Ask him to get the Duke of Somerset to give you his name.   The Duchess will, I am sure, give a handsome subscription as an old friend of Scott.

"One thing you should do, is to try and get some well-known man connected with a Tory paper, to run in harness with you (connected with a Whig paper), so as to neutralize as far as possible, political feeling.

"I have written to Lord Dalhousie to ask him to give his name to the Committee, and to try, if possible, to get those of the Dukes of Wellington and Buccleugh.

"Try if Loch will get us the Duke of Sutherland. What more can I do to help you?

"Ever, in great haste,
"Yours truly,
"THOS. DICK LAUDER.

"Charles Mackay, Esq."

There were many accessions to the Committee.   Among the eminent literary men were Charles Dickens, Charles

Lever, Thomas Moore, Thomas Babington Macaulay (afterwards Lord Macaulay), W. Harrison Ainsworth, Patrick Fraser Tytler, William Jerdan, George Cruikshank, and Angus Bethune Reach. Sir Peter Laurie, a shrewd and sagacious Scotsman, who had served the offices of alderman, sheriff, and Lord Mayor of London,* and had been mainly instrumental in founding the Union Bank of London, was very dubious, if not desponding, of the results of the appeal, and threw cold water upon it in the following letter :—

"PARK SQUARE,
"February 23, 1844.

" SIR,—

"I go out so early that I fear it will hardly be possible to fix a day before Wednesday which would suit your convenience. I shall be at No. 8, Moorgate Street on that day from one to half-past two, and shall be happy to see you.

"The Scottish monument question has been mooted several times, and with the same want of success. All the directors of our bank subscribed; but the thing cannot be got up here. The Abbotsford subscription in the City was a failure, and between ourselves there is a very

---

* Sir Peter Laurie was originally a saddler, and had by thrift, industry, foresight, and judicious enterprise accumulated a considerable fortune. In 1851, seven years after this time, one of the gentlemen proposed and elected to the office of sheriff of Middlesex, was Mr. D. Nicoll, a tailor and clothier in Regent Street. Sir Peter Laurie expressed an opinion that the election of a tailor would be a degradation of the shrievalty. The observation was reported to an active supporter of Mr. Nicoll, also a Scotsman, who said, "I don't see the objection. If a saddler can be a sheriff, why not a tailor? Indeed, the tailor is the superior of the two. A saddler makes clothes for horses; but a tailor makes clothes for *men*."

strong feeling here that the Edinburgh 'bodies' should
pay for their own monuments, and that the real meaning
of a Scottish subscription is to form a London sub-
committee, with a clever head and hand for honorary
secretary to bleed the Cockneys.   I have been connected
with charities for thirty-five years in London, and cannot
say a great deal for our countrymen in supporting the
metropolitan charities.   Believe me,

" Your faithful servant,

" P. LAURIE.

"Charles Mackay, Esq."

In a subsequent letter Sir Peter wrote :—

" PARK SQUARE,

"March 15.

" MY DEAR SIR,—

 " I shall be happy to join the Committee, which
should be as numerous as possible, though I am still of
opinion that we shall fail in obtaining the funds required.

" Yours faithfully,

" PETER LAURIE.

"Chas. Mackay, Esq."

As Sir Peter Laurie was known to be intimately
acquainted with the Right Hon. John Wilson Croker, a
*Quarterly Reviewer,* and a great admirer—as who was
not?—of the genius of Sir Walter Scott, he was requested
by the committee to communicate with that gentleman,
and solicit his support.   He did so, and the following
letter was the result :—

" WEST MOLESEY,

" 24 Ap., 1844.

" MY DEAR SIR PETER,—

 " In return to your letter about the Edin-

burgh monument, will you allow me to tell you candidly
that I long ago subscribed to a memorial of Sir Walter
Scott as much as I could afford, and I hope not
illiberally, and surely you will forgive me for adding that
I think when the Committee determined to make this
monument of so great a cost and size, and so prominent
a feature in the architectural embellishment of the city of
Edinburgh, that they in some degree absolved his more
distant admirers from concurring in an object so decidedly
local.   I really think the Scottish nation, and particularly
the citizens of the Scottish capital, might feel jealous at
its being supposed that English or Irish assistance was
become a *sine quâ non* for the completion of a work of a
character so peculiarly Scottish, and so exclusively to the
ornament of Edinburgh.

"It seems to me a very handsome though perhaps too
florid a design.   I should have liked something simpler ;
but it will no doubt be fine, and, though not a Scotchman,
I think I should have subscribed my mite if I could hope
ever to see it.—Ever, my dear Sir Peter, very faithfully
yours,

"J. W. CROKER.

"Sir Peter Laurie."

It was proposed by Mr. Jerdan, editor of the *Literary
Gazette*, that if Mr. Croker would subscribe, say 50l., the
Committee would pay his expenses to and from Edinburgh,
to take a look at the monument, but as this was only a
jest it fell to the ground, and nothing more was heard
of Mr. Croker.

I was very anxious that Mr. Lockhart, the editor of

the *Quarterly Review*, should use his great influence,
social and literary, in support of the movement, but found
him very lukewarm, not to say cold.   He objected to the
design of the monument altogether; and said he would
have preferred an equestrian statue, as more appropriate
than the one which had been adopted.   I reminded him
of the custom, tradition, or superstition—I did not know
which to call it,—that equestrian statues ought to
be exclusively reserved for military men, for conquerors,
heroes, kings, emperors, and kaisers, to which he replied
that Scott was a quasi military man, inasmuch as he was
quartermaster of the Edinburgh Volunteer Cavalry, and,
acting in that capacity, had looked exceedingly well on
horseback.   I did not know whether he was serious in
this remark, but was ultimately convinced that Mr.
Lockhart would decidedly have preferred a bronze
equestrian statue in Castle Street, where Scott had for
many years resided, to the shrine which had been erected
in Princes Street.   He asked me as a favour to keep him
informed of the Committee's proceedings, and promised
his aid, though he did not think it advisable, considering
his relation to the family, to appear publicly in the matter.
To a letter informing him what had been done at our last
meeting, I received the following reply :—

"DEAR SIR,—
    "Many thanks for your kind communication in
all its parts.
    "I was not aware till two or three days ago that the
person who had taken so generous an interest in the
monument of Scott was himself a poet.   In short, very

stupidly, I had not guessed that I had been visited by the person whom the name of Mackay ought to have at once suggested to me.

"Yours sincerely,

"J. G. LOCKHART.

"24, Sussex Place,
    "July 15, 1844."

The Earl of Aberdeen, afterwards Prime Minister, who contributed £50, wrote to Mr. Murray :—

"I will most readily join the Committee for the purpose you mention, and I hope that by this means some effectual assistance may be obtained. Our countrymen in the North have not acted very judiciously in this matter, but it would disgrace us all if the monument of Scott should remain incomplete."

The Duke of Sutherland, to whom Mr. Loch refused to apply, answered the official letter which I wrote to him in the kindest and promptest manner. "You have," he said, "made an excellent choice of members for the London Committee. I feel hesitation, however, in accepting your invitation to have my name on the list, as that ought to imply an expectation of assisting and attending, which I shall not be able to do. Otherwise, I approve of the formation of the Committee, and of you as a most fitting secretary for attending to and arranging the proceedings with a view to a successful result. If, however, my name should appear desirable to you, it is at your service."

To this I replied that his Grace's name seemed to me of the highest importance ;. and it was accordingly added to the list. In about a fortnight afterwards the Duke wrote—

"LONDON, May 4, 1844.

" SIR,—

" I hope that you are proceeding with the business of the monument to Sir W. Scott as satisfactorily as you may have expected.  I should have been more willing to have accepted your invitation to be on the list of the Committee if the exceeding number of claims on me would have allowed my subscribing to it in any way that might have been useful in encouraging the progress of the work.  I do not wish to make any unnecessary remarks on the design of the proposed monument ; and therefore it is merely to yourself (having occasion to communicate on the subject) that I must confess that it does not appear to me a judicious one ; but I am unwilling to put obstacles in the way of the wishes of others ; and when it becomes necessary to fill up the subscription list, the inclosed order for £21 is in your hands to be added to it for me.

" I am, sir,

" Very truly,

" Your obedient servant,

" SUTHERLAND."

In a letter dated the 8th of March, Sir Thomas Dick Lauder wrote—" You are getting on like a house on fire, and I augur the most prosperous results." In a subsequent letter he wrote—

> "Board of Manufactures,
> "Royal Institution,
> "Edinburgh, 14th March, 1844.

" My dear Sir,—

" Although it is likely that you may have heard from Mr. George Anson and Lord Dalhousie, I think it right to tell you that the former writes thus to me :— ' Buckingham Palace, March 12, 1844.—My dear Sir Thomas,—I have much pleasure in acquainting you that the Prince will readily lend his name for the object stated in your note to me of the 2nd instant.—Yours, G. E. Anson.' Lord Dalhousie says that ' he will readily give his own name to the Committee for Sir Walter's monument, if it does not involve the gift of time, which he really has not at disposal.' He declines interfering with the Duke of Wellington, and says as to the Duke of Buccleuch, that I had better write to him myself. But this I decline. I forget whether I hinted to you that John Gladstone, Esq., 6, Carlton Gardens, should be applied to for the Committee. A gentleman who so very handsomely sent me unasked £50 for the monument must be so brimful of patriotism, *quoad hoc*, that he will be sure to enter heart and soul into your matter, and he may get you all the most influential names in London.

" Pray let me know if I can do anything more for you,

and rely on my doing all I can, and that with all manner
of promptitude.

"Yours most faithfully,

"THOS. DICK LAUDER.

"Charles Mackay, Esq."


In consequence of the hint thus conveyed, I wrote to
Mr. Gladstone (afterwards Sir John Gladstone, Bart., of
Fasque), the father of Mr. W. E. Gladstone, Chancellor of
the Exchequer in Lord Aberdeen's Administration, and
Prime Minister from 1868 to 1874), and received the
following reply :—

"CARLTON GARDENS,
"4th April, 1844.

"SIR,—

"I have had the honour to receive your letter
of yesterday.  In reply, permit me to assure you that no
one can revere the memory of Sir Walter Scott more
than I do, or can feel more indebted to him than I can
for the gratification I have received from his works ; but
unfortunately I am too old, with both my sight and
hearing so greatly impaired as to place it beyond my
power to render any active services in promoting the
objects of the Committee, to which you ask me to become
a member ; but as you are good enough to suppose the
appearance of my name as a member of it may probably
be of some service, should the other members be also of
that opinion, I willingly consent to your request ; and if
I should happen in my limited circle to have any opportunity for aiding the object, whether as member, or not,
I will not fail to avail myself of it.

"I hope you may be in error in estimating the still

existing deficiency at £3000, as that sum was named as being so at the general meeting lately held in Edinburgh; and I think a considerable amount has since been subscribed.

"I have the honour to be, sir,

"Yours most truly,

"JOHN GLADSTONE.

"Charles Mackay, Esq."

Among the many eminent men who refused to aid the cause, four alone declined without giving their reasons—Sir Robert Peel, the Duke of Richmond, the Duke of Portland, and Lord Francis Egerton, afterwards Earl of Ellesmere. Among those who declined, and gave their reasons, was Mr. G. P. R. James, the novelist:—

"The OAKS, near Walmer, Kent,
"7th March, 1844.

"SIR,—

"I fear that you must think me very negligent in not answering your letter sooner; but I was desirous of considering well before I declined to be upon the Committee, and a severe attack of illness, as well as much business, prevented my giving the subject attention so soon as I would have wished..

"The only objection that I can possibly entertain to putting my name on the Committee for raising the additional sum required to complete the monument to my late revered friend, Sir Walter Scott, is this—that my absence from London, and the very numerous engagements which at present press upon me, would render me perfectly inactive and inefficient in all matters of business; and I think it not right in any one to undertake what he cannot perform.

"I need not say that, under any other circumstances, it would give me high satisfaction to do anything to honour the memory of that great and good man.

"Believe to be, sir,

"Your faithful servant,

"G. P. R. JAMES."

I thought it highly desirable to secure the name of Mr. E. L. Bulwer Lytton, himself an illustrious novelist, with whom I was at the time personally unacquainted, and wrote him the most pressing letter I could frame. To this, in due course, I received the following very emphatic reply, which, though it was disappointing, contained some strong truths, very eloquently worded :—

"KNEBWORTH,
"March 10th, 1844.

"SIR,—·

"I regret that I cannot have the honour of belonging to the London Committee formed to collect funds for erecting a monument at Edinburgh for Sir Walter Scott; but I beg you to accept my acknowledgments for the flattering terms in which you have made the proposal. I entertain strong opinions on this matter, regarding money spent on the monument, when money spent on the living might have saved the struggle and prolonged the days, if not a reproach to the subscribers, at least a mockery of the Dead.

"For the world in general the sole monument Sir Walter Scott needs is his works. If the Scotch wish for a more exclusive monument, the Scotch, in my judgment, should pay for it. It is a gratification to their own national vanity, and I think they belie their national pride, even in accepting, much more in seeking elsewhere, pecuniary aid for an ornament to their capital, and a testimonial to their countryman. I must add further my conviction that the moment the Scotch suffered Sir Walter Scott to leave Abbotsford with his debts unpaid, they lost the only opportunity of rendering practical homage to the man who had brought gold into their country through a thousand channels ; and I have no sympathy with attempts to repair that loss by the erection of a stone gew-gaw.

"In the frankness of these remarks, my apology must be found in my desire to place my refusal to serve on the proposed Committee on its true grounds, and clear myself from the suspicion that I might incur, if more reserved, of wanting due reverence for an illustrious name. So great indeed, on the contrary, is my reverence for that name, that I feel if I were a Scotchman, I would sell the coat off my back rather than ask a man not a Scot to subscribe to the monument at Edinburgh.

"I have the honour to be,
"Sir,
"Your obedient and obliged servant,
"EDWARD BULWER LYTTON.
"To Charles Mackay, Esq."

The opinions so excellently phrased by Mr. Bulwer

Lytton were not confined to that gentleman, as I learned from many sources, and especially from the following letter from Mr. Dickens, whom I had asked to forward a circular to Lord Brougham :—

> "DEVONSHIRE TERRACE,
> "Seventh March, 1844.

"MY DEAR MACKAY,—

"I find (so far as I can judge from the few friends I have talked with) that there is an idea abroad that the Edinburgh people, or Scotch people, at all events, should finish their own monument, and that some prejudice is created by the incompleteness of the testimonials to their two great men, Scott and Burns. I would, therefore, prefer to leave men to their own opinions in reference to joining the Committee, and have sent Brougham's letter by post to him, without making any addition to it.

> "Faithfully yours,
> "CHARLES DICKENS.

"Charles Mackay, Esq."

Lord Brougham made no reply to the communication, but, amid many failures and refusals, there was one accession recorded by Sir Thomas Dick Lauder, in his letter of the 14th of March, which was felt to be a tower of strength to the Committee—that of his Royal Highness, Prince Albert, who consented to be "Patron," on the understanding that he could not, and was not to be asked to, attend the meetings of the Committee. As finally constituted, the Committee stood thus :—Patron, H.R.H. Prince Albert; Members—The Duke of Sutherland, the Duke of Buccleugh, the Marquis of Northampton, the Earl of Aberdeen, the Earl of Dalhousie, the Earl of Dunmore, Lieut.-General Sir George Murray, T. B. Macaulay, Esq., M.P., the Right Hon. Holt Mackenzie, the Hon. C. A. Murray, W. H. Ainsworth, Esq., John Auldjo, Esq., Adam Black, Esq., Lord Provost of Edinburgh, The Chisholm, M.P., B. B. Cabbell, Esq., George Cruikshank, Esq., Charles Dickens, Esq., John Dickenson, Esq., Francis Grant, Esq. (now Sir Francis Grant), John Gladstone, Esq., James Hall, Esq., Wm. Jerdan, Esq., R. S. Lauder, Esq., Charles Lever, Esq., James Loch, Esq., M.P., Sir Peter Laurie, James Matheson, Esq. (now Sir James Matheson, Bart.,) Roderick Impey Murchison, Esq., Daniel Maclise, Esq., Thomas Moore, Esq., John Richardson, Esq., Clarkson Stanfield, Esq., Patrick Maxwell Stewart, Esq., M.P., Patrick Fraser Tytler, Esq., Charles Mackay, Esq. (Honorary Secretary), and Angus B. Reach, Esq. (Assistant Secretary). As Mr. Gladstone had expressed a wish to be informed of the doings of a Committee to which he had given his name, but which the infirmities of age prevented him from attending, Mr. Angus Reach communicated to him, after each meeting, the heads of the business transacted. In reply to one of these missives, he wrote :—

"CARLTON GARDENS,
"19th April, 1844.

" SIR,—

"I have your note of yesterday. Begging for subscriptions in any case is an uphill and thankless business. You have got a highly respectable, as well as wealthy Committee ; all, I cannot doubt, highly zealous in

the cause they have espoused. Permit me to suggest as
an easy and speedy way to bring their labours to a close,
that they should each agree to add fifty per cent. to their
previous subscriptions. If this is agreed to, I am willing
to add £25 to mine or to double it if necessary. In
Edinburgh, I believe, they have made their full share of
effort ; let the Scotch in London—that city which is the
patron of mental power and the seat of the arts—not be
left behind.

" I have the honour to be,

" Sir,

" Your most obedient servant,

" JOHN GLADSTONE.

" Charles Mackay, Esq."

Notwithstanding the influential character of the Committee, and the subscriptions of every member, the
money came in but slowly, and there seemed a prospect
that the effort to give effectual aid would fail, as Sir
Peter Laurie had predicted. Mr. Gladstone's recommendation met with no favour. But a brilliant idea was
suggested by Sir Thomas Dick Lauder, who wrote :—" It
has struck me that a grand Waverley Ball might be got
up in London for behoof of the monument ; a fancy ball
of course, and the characters to be entirely from the
Scott poems and novels. I have accordingly written to
Patrick Maxwell Stewart to get his sister, my old friend,
the Duchess of Somerset, to set it agoing ; but I have
not had time to get his answer. I am sure we could get
the Queen to patronise it, and a most brilliant thing it

would be ; and if properly managed might be made most
productive."

I communicated the idea of Sir Thomas to the most
active and zealous member of the Committee, the Hon.
Charles A. Murray, who at that time held an appointment in her Majesty's Household. He entered into the
project with energy and spirit, and speedily procured the
patronage of the Queen and Prince Albert. This done,
success was assured. The Duchess of Somerset, as expected, entered heartily into the project; and all the
Duchesses, Marchionesses, Countesses, Viscountesses,
Baronesses—all the fashion of the town made it an
object of ambition to be present at a gathering so
splendidly supported and for an object so laudable. The
ball took place on the 8th of July, at Willis's Rooms,
and was in every respect a brilliant success. Mr. Murray,
writing on the 9th, said : " I calculate we shall net £900
or little short of it by last night's ball; but I will desire
Mr. Willis to send you a regular report, and desire him
to pay in the money received." Writing on the 10th, he
said : " By the enclosed abstract you will see that our
receipts from the ball will be nearly £1,100 net. Pray
write an official letter to the Edinburgh Committee,
inquiring the exact amount of the present deficiency,
without stating to them what we have collected here,
and learn also the sum total of the subscriptions at the
different bankers, so that at our next meeting we may be
able to complete our work in a business-like manner."

The letter was written, and the reply was, that at least
£3,000 was necessary in all to carry up the monument to
the height intended, to rail it round, and to provide the

statuettes of the prominent characters in Scott's novels and poems, which were to be placed in the niches of the structure, according to the architect's design. The London Committee ultimately decided to close their labours. Though the ball was a decided success, the subscription was a comparative failure, and amounted to only £269. There was some doubt as to whether the Edinburgh Committee had or had it not in contemplation to expend some portion of the money raised in London upon the statuettes, rather than upon the completion of the main design. Upon this subject Mr. Murray wrote :—

"WINDSOR CASTLE,
"July 24, 1844.

" MY DEAR SIR,—

"Since I last wrote to you I have spoken on the subject of our Scott Monument Fund to the Duke of Buccleuch and Lord Aberdeen ; they seem to be of an opinion (in which I coincide) that as our appeals in London were made and our contributions raised for the express purpose of completing the monument according to the design exhibited to us, and by us to the subscribers, we ought to withhold at present the remainder of the Fund now in Messrs. Drummonds' hands, and to refuse to apply it to meeting fanciful or superadded expenses incurred without our sanction and without our being informed of the purposes to which the Edinburgh Committee propose to apply it.

"The two gentlemen above named, whose opinions are certainly entitled to as much weight as any on our list, hold that you, as secretary, should write to the Edinburgh secretary to inform him of the view here taken, and that you will probably not obtain authority from the Committee to pay over the remaining fund, until the Edinburgh Committee show that they have adequate means to complete or nearly to complete the additions that they have made to the original undertaking, the necessity or propriety of which we do not at all recognise.

"Very truly yours,

"CH. A. MURRAY.

"C. Mackay, Esq."

The Edinburgh Committee explained that the money which we had raised would be expended on the main design, and not on the statuettes or other accessories; and on this understanding the cheque was forwarded, and the London Committee rested from its labours.

This, however, was not to be the last of the Scott Monument. More than a quarter of a century afterwards, the statues and statuettes of the niches being still unprovided, I was appealed to, to act as chairman of a London Committee, to do what Edinburgh should have done long before. In consenting to occupy this position, I resolved that I would not be a party to any appeal to the public for funds; for I was more than ever of the opinion of Lord Lytton, that it was not respectful to the memory of Scott, nor creditable to the people of Edinburgh to solicit subscriptions, and that if anything were to be done in London—in default of Edinburgh—it was only to be done by means of another Waverley Ball. A new generation of wealth, beauty, and fashion had arisen

to manhood and womanhood since the date of the first
ball, and it was considered highly probable that the Prince
and Princess of Wales, if properly approached, would lend
the immense weight of their names and influence to the
project.    All the members of the Committee, which was
formed under the active management of Mr. Colin Rae-
Brown, who accepted the post of Honorary Secretary,
were of the same opinion; and Dr. Ramsay, a member
of the Highland Society of London, who had often been
in communication with the Prince on subjects relative to
Scotland and Scotch affairs in London, was deputed to
ask the patronage of his Royal Highness for the proposed
ball.    The Prince and Princess entered heartily into the
idea; the Marquis of Huntley took the post of Honorary
Treasurer, and the Duchess of Buccleuch and other ladies
of the highest rank, acted as patronesses.    The ball took
place at Willis's Rooms, on the 6th of July, 1871; the
year of the centenary celebration of Sir Walter's birthday.    It was expressly stipulated on the part of an illustrious personage, without whose countenance the ball
would not have been a fashionable success, that the
number of tickets issued should not exceed eight hundred,
which was all that the Rooms could comfortably accom-
modate.    In consequence, the net proceeds, after all
expenses were paid, were not equal to those of the first
Waverley Ball, in which the numbers had not been
limited, and only reached £600.    With this sum, and
other funds raised by the Edinburgh Committee, it was
resolved to proceed with the statuettes for the niches, and
commissions were given to the eminent Scottish sculptors,
Messrs. William Brodie, R.S.A., John Hutchison, R.S.A.,

Clark Stanton, A.R.S.A., George A. Lawson, Peter Slater, D. W. Stevenson, Andrew Currie, and Mrs. D. O. Hill. These artists had completed twenty-four of the statuettes by the summer of 1874.

The following description of the parts assumed in the ball by members of the royal family and others appeared next morning in the *Daily News*, from the pen of an eminent Scotsman, who had acquired renown as a war correspondent during the Franco-German War of 1870, and who has subsequently gained fresh laurels in other fields of literary work :—

" Not less fair than the hapless original, but born to a purer life and to a happier fate, the Princess of Wales, as Marie Stuart, moved with a quiet, pensive grace that, while it was all her own, was none the less true to the character she had assumed. The Prince, her husband, strode the floor gallantly as Lord of the Isles—no assumption on his part truly, for the Princes of Wales ever since the union of the crowns are, too, the hereditary Lords of the Isles—his bonnet crowned with heather, the badge prescribed to his clansmen by the first Macdonald, in the  ords, ' Put on your heads, that you distinguish each other from the foe, that which is growing under your feet on the muir;' above the heath the raking feather from the pinion of an eagle of the Hebrides. Prince Arthur was a gay and gallant Prince Charlie ; what unutterable things would George II. and ' butcher' Cumberland have looked could they have seen a child of their race personating the ill-fated hero of the Jacobites !

" But there are no Jacobites now, and in the veins of

our Royal House flows the blood of the Stuarts as well
as of the Guelphs. Buxom Di Vernon with the auburn
tresses and the laughing eye leant on the arm of the
Master of Ravenswood, not yet engulphed in the
treacherous quicksand. In pale ethereal beauty flitted
the White Lady of Avenel; Annot Lyle seemed fair
enough to exorcise the dark spirit from the gloomy
bosom of Alan Macaulay, without the need of recourse
to music. A daughter of the house of Campbell was in
character in every sense as the ' Maid of Lorn.' Here
were Edith Bellenden and ' Bloody Claver'se;' the Fair
Maid of Perth and Lochiel; Brenda Troil and the reckless pirate Cleveland; Rose Bradwardine and Rob Roy
—facile princeps of such rievers and cattle-lifters as
the old Baron of Tullieveolan's birses rose against;
Catherine Seyton and Halbert Glendinning—all these
and many others—items in the population of the many-
scened worlds of fiction which the magic pen created
—dancing in one quadrille or pacing the floor together
in such strange fashion of amity as suggested the
advent of the millennial era when the lion shall lie
down with the lamb.

" A rope had been stretched athwart the centre of the
ball-room, which served to part off the general company
from the special guests and those who were to take part
in the pre-arranged costume dances. What may be called
the unreserved space soonest yet gradually filled in a
great measure with ladies and gentlemen in character
dresses. There were troubadours in plenty—the costume
seemed a favourite one; an Earl of Leicester flashed and
glittered in slashed purple and jewels, Darnley rubbed

shoulders with Rizzio, and close to the orchestra the
'Last Minstrel' stood, in russet brown and long waving
locks of grey. Alice of Woodstock, Jenny Dennison,
Harry Ashton, and Rowena formed one group; a Red
Cross Knight, Sir Walter Raleigh, Edie Ochilree, and
Charles the Bold of Burgundy, in crimson and jewels,
formed another. With those ladies who did not essay
any particular character, 'powder' was much in vogue,
especially with brunettes, but it is a circumstance stimu-
lating foreboding as to ruined complexions that the com-
plement of powder seems to be paint. As regards the
gentlemen, of such as were not in character, a considerable proportion wore the Highland dress, for the most
part of such richness and splendour as materially to
impair the 'Puir Hielanman' theory. Not a few were
in uniform—horse, foot, artillery, and nondescript—and
then came the 'ruck' attired in all the various phases
which that curious remembrancer of the old twopenny
postman, the 'Windsor uniform,' can be tortured into.
Verily the Windsor uniform is an elastic institution.
One of the most noted arrivals in the outer circle was
that of Mr. Lowe, not attired as a fusee seller out of
work, or even with a philactery around his forehead
bearing the motto 'Ex luce lucellum,' but wearing the
sedate Windsor uniform of the pattern affected by
ministers. Inside the rope the scene was even gayer
than outside, for in the reserved space were congregated
those who took part in the special character dances, as
well as the leading guests. From a corner glittered the
cloth of gold and the brilliant tiaras of the Nawab Nazim
of Bengal and his son, the sheen of the stones no whit

weakened by the late denial of a Committee of Inquiry
to their owner; foreign noblemen in dresses and uniforms
not to be named off hand by any insular reporter; the
Turkish Ambassador (Musurus Bey) wearing, like a
staunch Osmanli, the costume of his country; Prince
Teck's blue and gold; the Marchioness of Westminster's
glorious diamond aigrette, which flashed with a dazzling
glitter that was hard to look upon; all these persons and
things lent brilliancy to a scene that changed every instant
like a kaleidoscope."

The hundreth anniversary of the birth of Scott was
celebrated in Edinburgh on the 15th of August, and in other
cities and in the border counties on the 9th of August,
1871. I received an invitation from the Edinburgh Committee to be present on the occasion, which I accepted, and
was furthermore asked to write, and afterwards to recite
an ode in honour of him whom it once—and still is the
fashion to call "the Wizard of the North." This, after
much hesitation, I agreed to do. But the ode though
written was never delivered. The speeches after the
banquet in the Corn Exchange were not only very long,
but very imperfectly heard, and nearly an hour before
the time appointed in the programme for the recitation
of my ode the patience of the vast audience was exhausted, and hundreds of people were making their way
to the doors. Under the circumstances, I went away
with the early goers, and my ode remained unspoken. It
is here inserted—*quantam valeat*—as a tribute to the two
Wizards of the North whose genius in different ages shed
light in such different ways on the history of their
country.

## "THE VISIONS OF MICHAEL SCOTT, THE WIZARD.

*"An Ode for the Scott Centenary.—August* 15, 1871.

### I.

" I, Michael Scott, endowed with power to see
　Up to the dark vistas of futurity,
　And through the veil that shrouds the bygone time,
　With all its sorrow, suffering, and crime,
　Behold two visions open on my sight—
　Hazy and dim the one, the second bright
　With all the purpling hues of life and light.

### II.

" I see the days that were—the days that are—
　Darkened by rapine, cruelty, and war ;
　When over all this beauteous mountain land
　Fraud and oppression rule with iron hand.
　When the weak fall, the victims of the strong,
　When right is crushed by the agressive wrong,
　And good men groan—' Oh Lord, our God, how long?'

### III.

" Because I'm wise—alas ! my wisdom's light
　Is but a taper glimmering in the night ;
　They call me wizard, who, with wicked skill,
　Cleft into three the peak of Eildon Hill—
　Dream that I blight the harvests of the plain,
　Control the summer sun or spring-time rain,
　And rouse or calm the tempests of the main.

### IV.

" They deem I study in a magic book,
　That I can maim or slay by word or look,
　And call the unwilling lightning from the skies,
　Ridden by fiends, to blast mine enemies.
　Poor fools ! they know not, and 'tis vain to tell,
　Sunk in the depths of darkness where they dwell,
　That knowledge comes from Heaven, and not from Hell.

### V.

" Fade from my sight ! go back into the past
   Ye mournful days wherein my lot is cast !
   And let my glad and grateful eyes behold,
   Of the new morn the crimson and the gold,
   When Knowledge, like the ripening rain, shall fall
   Impartial on the great and on the small,
   Cheering, adorning, and sustaining all.

### VI.

" When true Religion's holy light shall shine,
   And every child shall read the Book Divine—
   And wakening Science in her second birth
   Shall turn her piercing eyes o'er Heaven and Earth,
   And work more magic with her wondrous hand,
   In one short day, o'er all the happy land,
   Than Fancy ever dreamed or Wisdom planned.

### VII.

" And the dawning splendour, growing clear,
   Shall the true Wizard and true sage appear,
   In the great light of whose meridian prime,
   Benignant, joyous, tender and sublime.
   All other lights that e'er our Scotland knew,
   Great as they were, the many or the few,
   Shall seem but torches flickering in the blue.

### VIII.

" Lo ! from the vast recesses of his brain
   Emerge the mighty dead to live again ;
   He waves his hand, and lo ! they act their parts,
   And open wide the portals of their hearts.
   Their loves and hates, their inmost hopes and fears,
   All that ennobles, touches, and endears,
   Their grief or joy, their laughter or their tears.

## IX.

" Through glen and strath he walks in generous pride,
  And fills with life the lonely mountain side,
  Peoples the lucent Loch or craggy Ben
  With lovely women and great-hearted men,
  And with a magic key unlocks the gate
  Of Time's dark temple, where he sits elate,
  And lights it up again, in all its state.

## X.

" He takes a lowly maiden from the field,
  And on her brow—no more to be concealed
  While Scotland stands, firm rooted in the sea—
  Places a crown of virtuous modesty,
  Brighter and nobler in its simple sheen
  Than any diadem of king or queen
  That ever glittered since a king hath been.

## XI.

" Where'er he goes men venerate his name,
  Remotest lands re-echo with his fame,
  And his own Scotland, wild and bleak and bare,
  Robed in the light he destined it to wear,
  Becomes the jewel of the northern seas,
  Where throng the pilgrims and the devotees,
  As to a shrine of holiest mysteries.

## XII.

" Then, from the world, his daily magic wrought,
  He hies him home, and shaking off his thought,
  Ploughs in his fields or plants the darling ground,
  Or from his princely hand throws the largess round
  To all who need ; or sitting by the fire
  Becomes the tender husband and the sire—
  A good plain man to love and to admire.

## XIII.

" Alas ! alas ! on that majestic head
  Gather the storms—the lightning bolt is sped—
  Billows of sorrow surge on every side
  With whitening crests to overwhelm his pride.
  But he, in native dignity of soul,
  Rises erect, and sighs ' Let God control ;
  Duty's my fate, my pathway, and my goal.'

## XIV.

" He sees not, feels not, fenced with courage in,
  How fierce the conflict which he may not win ;
  But fights the fight, defiant to the last,
  As firm as Staffa in the northern blast,
  And like its wondrous cave—Titanic piled—
  Receives the raging waters undefiled,
  Or answers back with music weird and wild.

## XV.

" The end is hidden ; but I hear the cry
  As of a mother when her children die ;
  'Tis Scotland weeping for her noblest son.
  His heart at rest, his race of glory run !
  Let her lament ! she may not hope to see,
  In all the countless ages yet to be,
  Another son so great and good as he.

## XVI.

" The sorrow passes like the tearful mist
  In a May morning, when the sun hath kissed
  The mountain tops, and Scotland lifts her head,
  Weeping no longer for her glorious dead,
  And shouts aloud from rugged shore to shore—
  ' The light remains, though not the hand that bore,
  And in *my* heart shall shine for evermore.' "

It will have been seen from the story of the Scott monument in Edinburgh that the Scotch in Scotland have not been very rapid in doing monumental honour to the greatest literary genius which their country has produced.   But the Scotch at home are not nearly so Scotch as the Scotch abroad, or nearly so patriotic or so wealthy. What it has taken between thirty and forty years to do in Edinburgh was in the Scott centenary year, done in New York in one night.   Five or six Scotsmen in that flourishing city met after dinner over a tumbler of the national beverage, and then and there, before the party broke up contributed among them as much money as would suffice to erect in the Central Park a *fac-simile* of the Edinburgh monument.   The city of Edinburgh spent much money in celebration of the marriage of the Prince of Wales.   It did not spend a farthing in celebration of the centenary of the man who did more for Edinburgh than all the kings and princes who ever set foot in it.

# SAMUEL ROGERS.

It was in the year 1840 that I first made the acquaintance of the venerable Samuel Rogers, banker and poet, whose name had been familiar to me from my boyhood, and whose writings along with those of Thomas Campbell had exercised very considerable influence upon my imagination. I was prepared to find Mr. Rogers hideously ugly, for I remembered many of the epigrams and jokes upon his personal appearance, which had been in circulation ever since I began to read, and which his former friend Lord Byron had taken a malicious pleasure in repeating, and which were taken up by a succeeding race of writers, notably by Dr. Maginn and Mr. Theodore Hook, who in their turn were imitated by smaller cynics of society with such little force as was at their command. Byron had written some venomous lines which did not see the light till after his death, which I could not help remembering as I turned from St. James's Street at 10 a.m. to breakfast with him at 22, St. James's Place, a house which his long residence had rendered classic ground,—

> "Nose and chin would shame a knocker,
> Wrinkles that would puzzle Cocker;

Mouth which marks the envious scorner,
With a scorpion in each corner.
Turns its quick tail to sting you,
In the place that most may wring you."

There was much more of the same sort, which it was a pity that a poet of such genius as Byron's, should have soiled his pen, his paper, or his mind by writing. The principal jokes against Rogers turned on the supposed fact that his countenance was deathlike. It was said that he was once refused exit from the catacombs at Paris with the observation by one of the custodians of the place, " *on ne laisse pas passer les morts,*" and that at Byron's funeral he was warned to keep out of the way of the undertakers lest they should seize *him* also and put him in a coffin. But my first look at the poet, then in his seventy-eighth year, was an agreeable surprise, and a protest in my mind against the malignant injustice which had been done him. As a young man he might have been uncomely if not as ugly as his revilers had painted him, but as an old man there was an intellectual charm in his countenance and a fascination in his manner which more than atoned for any deficiency of personal beauty. No man or woman can be positively good looking if bald and toothless, but even the bald and toothless can be intelligent, benevolent, quick-witted, and agreeable in conversation. And Mr. Rogers was all these and more. He received me with the greatest kindness and cordiality, speedily put me at my ease, and increased my pleasure by informing me that he had invited Mr. Campbell, whom I already knew, to meet me. Mr. Campbell kept the breakfast waiting about a quarter of an hour, during

which time Mr. Rogers pointed out some of the pictures
that adorned the wall of his cheerful morning room, looking out upon the Green Park, and a little garden where
Moore and Byron once had, I believe, some sort of a
quarrel and reconciliation. He also took up a piece of
amber, with a fly in it. "There," he said, "that fly, as
Sydney Smith remarks, may have buzzed in the ear of
Adam." Taking up a female hand, exquisitely modelled
by Canova, he said, "You would scarcely believe it, but
that hand is so lovely that I have kissed it a hundred
times." Somehow or other our conversation turned upon
Lord Byron's poetry, of which I expressed my warm
admiration, especially of some passages in "Childe
Harold," "Cain," "Manfred," and the "Bride of
Abydos." I found that Mr. Rogers did not share my
enthusiasm, but met my praises with very emphatic
depreciation. "Byron," he said, "wrote too fast and too
much. Ben Jonson remarked of his friend Shakspeare, in reference to the statement that he had written
no line which dying he would wish to blot, ' Would to
Heaven he had blotted a thousand!' I think it would
have been better for Byron if he had blotted ten
thousand!" There was considerable argument on both
sides, but wishing to close the discussion, I wound up by
saying, "At least, Mr. Rogers, you will admit that there was
*fire* in Byron!" "Oh yes!" he replied, "there was fire,
and plenty of it, but it was ' hell-fire.'" Mr. Campbell
was shortly afterwards announced, and we proceeded to
breakfast, during which Mr. Rogers had nearly all the conversation to himself. Mr. Campbell said but little, and
looked very much as if he were listening for the second or

third time to the stories that his host was telling. But they were all new to me, and I think I may say for myself, that I acted well upon that occasion the not always easy part of a good listener.

The conversation was led by Mr. Rogers to the subject of Pope. " I like," he said, " when I meet with a young author, to know what he thinks of Pope. I test him by that. You, who so greatly admire Byron, what is your opinion of Pope ? " I told him that I did not know which of the two to admire most ; both so different, yet both so excellent. I added that I thought " The Dying Christian to His Soul " was the most perfect gem of poetry in the language, and that it was impossible to add to it, take away from it, or alter it, without damaging its complete and rounded beauty.

" And the ' Essay on Man,' and the ' Essay on Criticism,' " interposed Mr. Campbell ; " perfect in their way, and containing more quotable and oftener quoted lines than any other poems in the whole range of English literature, Shakespeare excepted. Pope rivals Horace in quotability, and that is saying a great deal. There are hundreds of passages in Pope that might be quoted with fine effect by our Parliamentary and other orators, that are quite new, or at all events so new as not to be threadbare. For instance, what can be finer than the picture of the rich man who has outlived his appetite and sense of enjoyment, who in his satiety

> ' Called ' happy dog' the beggar at his door,
> And envied thirst and hunger to the poor ? ' "

" I very early learned to reverence Pope," said Mr.

Rogers. "I perfectly well remember when I was a boy making more than one pilgrimage to No. 5, King's Bench Walk, Temple, where Mr. Murray, afterwards Lord Mansfield, had chambers, and where Pope often called upon him. I was glad to tread over the very steps where the feet of Pope had passed. Do you remember the lines in the ' Ode to Venus,' in the 'Imitations of Horace,' where he declares that at ' sober fifty ' he is too old for love, and calls to the goddess

> ' To number *five* direct your doves,
>   There spread round Murray all your blooming loves ? '

Murray at this time was but thirty-three, Pope being seventeen years his senior."

"I don't know whether Murray, then a rising, and, indeed, famous barrister, had any reputation for gallantry," said Mr. Campbell ; " but whether or not, Pope praised him for something better, though he scarcely praised him in good verse. You know," he said, turning to me, " the famous instance of bathos,

> ' Graced as thou art, with all the power of words,
>   So known, so honoured in the House of Lords.' "

" These lines were well parodied," added Rogers, " by a wit of the time, with very allowable satire and with most excellent alliteration.

> ' Persuasion tips his tongue whene'er he talks,
>   And he has chambers in the King's Bench Walks.' "

" Don't you think," I ventured to inquire, " that

alliteration, when not so overdone as to be tiresome, is a very valuable adjunct to poetic expression, as in that grand passage in Byron descriptive of the battle of Waterloo, where he speaks of the Duke of Brunswick,

> ' Who rushed into the field and foremost fighting fell ? ' "

" ' Foremost fighting fell ' is admirable ; " said Mr. Campbell, " and I have sometimes thought that some future poet might advantageously revive the alliterative blank verse of the author of ' Piers Ploughman.' We are wearing out the old rhymes rapidly, as Pope complained a hundred years ago, when he spoke of the constant iteration of the consonance of ' dove ' and ' love,' ' trees and breezes,' ' eyes and sighs.' "

" I never," said Mr. Rogers, " derived any benefit from the strictures of a critic but once ; and that was on the occasion of an alliteration which I had not premeditated. The second canto of the ' Pleasures of Memory,' as published in the first edition, commenced with the lines—

> ' Sweet Memory, wafted by thy gentle gale,
> Oft up the *tide* of Time, I turn my sail.'

The critic remarked on this passage that it suggested the alliteration

> ' Oft up the tide of Time, I turn my *tail*,'

and added that Time was not a tide, which ebbed and flowe l, but a stream constantly running down into the

Great Ocean of Eternity. I took the hint in my second
edition, and wrote—

' Oft up the *stream* of Time, I turn my sail ; '

thus breaking the alliteration and improving the image."

"In which," said Mr. Campbell, "I think you acted
wisely."

I thought to myself, though I was too young, and
had too much respect for my seniors to say so, that the
author of the "Pleasures of Hope" might have imitated
the author of the "Pleasures of Memory," in taking a
hint, and altered the well-known line,

" Like angel visits, *few* and far between,"

to "*short*" and far between; which would have been
much better. I did not know at the time that the line as
amended was that of an older poet, and that Campbell
had, no doubt, unconsciously conveyed it into his own
poem, and damaged it in the process.

It was on the occasion of this the first of many visits I
was privileged during ten years to pay to Mr. Rogers, that
he gave me what seemed a very cynical, but was possibly
a very prudent, piece of advice. "From your position as
a journalist," he said, "you will in all probability be very
often bored by foolish people who will send you books
of verse, which they will consider poetry (ninety-nine
persons out of a hundred scarcely know the difference),
with a view of extorting your favourable opinion.
Never allow a day to pass without acknowledging
the receipt of the book, thanking them for their

courtesy, and saying that you 'anticipate much pleasure in the perusal.' That will in most cases end the matter; and you will be under no obligation to tell them whether or not the anticipation was realized. But if you allow a week to elapse before acknowledging the receipt, they will imagine you have employed the interval in reading their lucubrations, and will expect you to praise them without stint, and to give reasons for your high opinion of their merits. I have acted upon this plan myself for many years, and have found great comfort and relief from it."

But Mr. Rogers was only a cynic in theory, not in practice, and was always ready to lend a helping hand, either by good counsel or by more sterling and palpable aid, if it were needed, to help young genius, or even young talent, up the steep hill that leads to fame, and may lead to fortune. In my case, when I sent him a volume entitled "The Hope of the World," which I had taken the liberty, in accordance with a practice now going out of date, to "*dedicate*" to him, he wrote as follows :—

"Many, many thanks for your volume, which I found upon my table the other day when I returned home. I need not say how welcome it was! You are one of the very, very few who think before they write—not that any of us think always to the purpose.

"To convince you that I have read you with some attention, I will try to find fault, if one who is faulty himself may do so.

'Who left their bones for vultures.'

A flippant reviewer would say—'Why leave for them what they would leave themselves?'

'To charm in youth to captivate in age.'

Are not the verbs too much alike in sense? Would not elevate do better, or, if no better word be found, would not it be safer to say

'To charm, to elevate, in youth, in age?'

What, I confess, I hate is a distinction without a difference.

"But perhaps you could convince me that they are right, and to be justified, if you were at my elbow.

"And such lines as these—

' Lo ! the first blood that sank into the sod,
Flowed in contention at the shrine of God,'

should strike me blind to all the faults in the world.

"There is a little poem, 'A Grave beneath a Tree,' that is worth all the fine writing that the world has produced.

"Yours very truly,

"S. ROGERS.

"Dec. 24, 1840."

The little poem, which he admired so much, and which Mr. Bates, the editor of "Maclise's Portrait Gallery," from *Fraser's Magazine*, reprinted, with additional notes, in 1873, says that the old man remembered almost to the last, and was wont to speak of in the language of

his letter, scarcely, as the author thinks, merits his
eulogium; but doubtless it appealed to his heart in some
way, and is here appended, with the supply of the
sixth line accidentally omitted in that publication :—

"A GRAVE BENEATH A TREE.

"When my soul flies to the first great Giver,
    Friends of the Bard ! let my dwelling be
By the green bank of that rippling river,
    Under the shade of yon tall beech tree.
Bury me there, ye lovers of song,
    When the prayers for the dead are spoken,
      With my hands on my breast,
      Like a child at rest,
    And my lyre in the grave unbroken."

The line which Mr. Rogers quoted with disapprobation from the "Hope of the World," occurred in a
passage descriptive of the second Crusade :—

"Tell of the sacred crowds as mad as these,
    Who covered earth and swarmed upon the seas ;
When zealous Bernard waved his banner high,
'The Cross,' 'Jerusalem,' 'The Lord,' his cry ;
And of the remnant of that countless host
Who left their bones for vultures on the coast.
Nor once beheld the shores they pined to see,
Bethlehem's green meads or waves of Galilee."

The next time I saw Mr. Rogers after the receipt of
his flattering letter, I did what little I could in defence of the vultures and the bones; stating that I
thought I was right, and that his criticism was somewhat overstrained. "When men lie down to die, in
battle or elsewhere," I said, "there is *flesh* upon their
bones, and that is what the vultures want." "You may

be right," he replied, good-humouredly; "but if I had taken a little more pains, and looked further into your book, I should no doubt have been able to pierce your armour in some more vulnerable point."

Mr. Rogers seldom invited more than four persons to breakfast; and during many years few of the notabilities in literature, art, politics, science, or fashion in London, or distinguished stranger visiting the metropolis, escaped a summons to his hospitable board, at an hour and to a meal which he asserted to be far more favourable to the easy flow of conversation, and to sprightly and rational intercourse, than the more ponderous, and too often unsocial, dinner party. And few who were favoured with invitations were not glad to accept them, and interchange ideas with almost the only remaining relic of a bygone age of literary culture—with one who, when a boy, had knocked at the door of Dr. Johnson, in Bolt Court, in the hope to see the great man, and had run away, recoiling, like Fear in Collins' magnificent Ode, "even at the sound himself had made;"—a man who, until the "Memory," whose pleasures he had, as Lord Holland wrote, sung so well, began to fail, was full of anecdotes of all the remarkable people who had flourished during the previous half century, and who was on terms of intimacy with every living celebrity of his day. He was an excellent story-teller, never missed the point of a joke, and, though he was much addicted to punning, never interrupted the conversation of another to thrust in his own witticism. His good things were not so good in themselves as those of Douglas Jerrold—beyond all comparison the richest, most copious, most rapid, and most

original wit of the nineteenth century—but depended for
effect rather upon the character of the person of whom
they were said, than upon any brilliancy or pungency
of diction.  He was very fond of quoting an epigram
which he had written upon Lord Ward, with whom
he had had a feud of some kind, which is not an unfair
specimen of the calibre of his wit, and the not very
great depth or severity of his invective :—

> " Ward has no heart, they say, but I deny it—
> He *has* a heart, and gets his speeches by it."

It took him, he said, a fortnight to form this couplet, and
polish it so deftly that it could be polished no further.
Writing with great difficulty himself, he disparaged and
undervalued all who wrote with facility; and boasted to me
that he had employed three weeks in writing a short note
to Lord Melbourne, to suggest the bestowal of a pension
on Carey, the translator of Dante.  There was not a
word in it, he said, which he had not studied and weighed,
and examined, so as to assure himself that it could not
be omitted or exchanged for a better.  " Imitate my
example in your writings," he added, in a paternal tone.
" Don't write much ; take time over it ; and aspire to
go down to posterity as a diamond, rather than as a
chaldron of coals, or a heap of bricks and mortar."

Rogers, though by no means insensible to the charms
of female beauty, but on the contrary fond of ladies' society,
never married—a circumstance which he often regretted.
But long after he had turned his eightieth year, he made a
proposal to a young lady of twenty, who rejected him
with the curt reply, that such a union would be too

ridiculous. Long after he had passed his ninetieth year, and when he had almost wholly lost his memory, he remembered, in a dim, faint manner, this particular lady. "When Mr. Rogers was in an almost unconscious state," said Lady Morgan to me, "I called at his house with Miss ——, to whom he had offered marriage, in order to inquire after his health, and leave our cards. His carriage was at the door, and he was about to be lifted into it for an airing. His faithful valet suggested that we should accompany him on his ride, adding that he would surely recognize me, and that he would take it kindly of me. Miss —— objected slightly at first, but we both got into the carriage. After a time I took the old man by the hand, and said, 'You don't know me, Mr. Rogers, do you?' He looked at me with lack-lustre eyes for a while, but gradually a little gleam of intelligence appeared in them, and he said very slowly, 'Yes, I think I know you, but I am not quite sure. Is it Lady Morgan?' I told him he was right. 'Ah, Lady Morgan,' he replied, 'it is very kind of you to come and see me.' He then relapsed into unconsciousness, and so remained for about ten minutes, when I again took his hand, and said, 'And as you know me, Mr. Rogers, perhaps you know this lady also?' Miss —— sat on the seat opposite, and Mr. Rogers, who had not previously observed her, looked at her attentively; and after an effort, as if he were recalling some fast-disappearing train of thought, said slowly, 'Yes, I know her; she has come to marry me.' My companion afterwards told me that she felt as if she could have sunk through the floor of the carriage; but Mr. Rogers relapsed into utter unconsciousness, closed his eyes, and never said another word, or bestowed a look upon either of us, until we deposited him safely at the door of Number Twenty-two, and to the care of his valet."

The reputation which Mr. Rogers enjoyed for cynicism was undeserved. He said unkind things, but he did kind ones in the most gracious manner. If he was sometimes severe upon those who were " up," he was always tender to those who were " down." He never closed his purse-strings against a friend, or refused to help the young and the deserving.

# THOMAS CAMPBELL.

DURING the five years preceding his death, I was in frequent social intercourse with Thomas Campbell, the author of "The Pleasures of Hope," and of the magnificent lyrical poems, "The Battle of the Baltic," "Hohenlinden," and "Ye Mariners of England." The last of these poems appeared originally in the *Morning Chronicle*, and was sent to Mr. Parry from Ratisbon shortly after the declaration of war against Denmark in 1801. During the long intervening period Mr. Campbell had kept up an unpaid connection with his favourite journal, and contributed an occasional epigram or political squib to its columns. There was, however, but little merit in these bye-plays of his fancy; the humour was but weak, and the wit consisted only of indifferent puns. Witness his epistle to Horace Smith from Algiers, which was one of them :—

> " Dear Horace be melted to tears,
>   For I'm melting with heat as I rhyme,
> Though the name of this place is All-jeers,
>   'Tis no joke to fall in with its clime."

There are fourteen stanzas of this calibre, each with a

pun no better than the following, which is worn uncommonly threadbare.

> " The *pain* of my thirst is no *sham*,
>    Though I'm bawling aloud for *champagne*."

Campbell was a keen politician and a thorough Whig of the school of Charles James Fox, and a Free Trader of the school of Richard Cobden. His last contribution to the *Chronicle* does not appear in his collected works ; nor is it included with other similar squibs in his last volume, " The Pilgrims of Glencoe," published in 1842. Some political sensation was created in the clubs and in parliamentary circles, during the height of the Anti-Corn-Law agitation, by the secession from the Liberal party of a Mr. Gordon, the member for Windsor, who, from his great size (he was a man about as large as the Claimant of 1874), was irreverently called Bum Gordon. Mr. Campbell felt sufficiently interested to write on this topic, and sent the following to the *Chronicle :*—

### "TORY LOGIC.

> " Be hushed, ye reformers abusive,
>    We'll see you all damned ere we grant
> Your requests (and our logic's conclusive),
>    We hate the amendments ye want.

> " Is it *timber*, new laws you would bring on ?
>    We've plenty of *wood*, 'twill be seen,
> For you gallows-faced Whigs all to swing on,
>    And a scaffold besides for the Queen.

" Our Corn-Laws that make us so wealthy,
　　Against them how dare you complain ?
Your landlords to make the poor healthy
　　Are temperance teachers in *grain.*

" But the Whig cause is palpably frail,
　　Since Gordon to join us has come,
He had ne'er like O'Connell a tail,
　　But he always was famed for a *bum.*

" Religion you say would delight ye,
　　Uncorked by our clerical screw ;
But we know all about God Almighty
　　A thousand times better than you !

" You atheist Whigs would oblige us,
　　In sceptical darkness to dwell,
And rob us of comforts religious,
　　Even down to a devil in hell.

" ' Death's sleep is eternal' in France,
　　'Twas said by those infidel slaves ;
If the Whigs were all buried, we'd dance
　　Eternally over their graves."

The author originally appended his initials to this
effusion, but sent late at night to the office a missive
by a special messenger to ask the editor to omit them,
for the reason assigned.

" SIR,—I should be obliged to you to omit my initials
when you insert my verses entitled, " Tory Logic," in the
*Chronicle ;* in case Mr. Gordon, on seeing that I had
mentioned *his* bum, should come and kick *mine.*

　　　　　　　　　　　" Yours truly,
　　　　　　　　　　　　　　" THOS. CAMPBELL."

His request was of course acceded to. "Tory Logic" gave general offence, and was the means of depriving the *Chronicle* of at least one subscriber, as appears from the following :—

"UPPER BERKELEY ST.,
"May 17, 1841.

" To THE EDITOR OF THE 'MORNING CHRONICLE.'— By the desire of the Dowager Lady Dunmore I am to inform you that she has discontinued taking your paper in consequence of your admitting into your columns such infamous trash as the enclosed. (Her ladyship enclosed me some lines headed " *Tory Logic*," and begged me to burn them as soon as I had read them.)
"I am, Sir,
"Your obedient servant,
"R. G. D.
(" Newsvender.")

Thomas Moore might have established a reputation by his political squibs had he written nothing else ; but Thomas Campbell, as may be seen from the above, was not fitted to excel in that light, sparkling, and ephemeral department of literature. His genius was of too high and solid an order for these small efforts. His " Pleasures of Hope " was not the poem, though long and still a popular favourite, on which he rested his hopes of fame; neither did his beautiful " Gertrude of Wyoming" seem to him the work that would carry his name to posterity. He rested his hopes of immortality on his splendid war odes, and on " Lochiel's Warning," of which it may be truly said that no change of taste, no variation of literary fashion, no lapse of time, will ever dim the surpassing lustre, or take them out of that inner circle and nucleus of the great galaxy of English literature, where the master-pieces of the master bards are destined to glow in supernal light as long as the English shall remain either a living or a dead language. Campbell's genius was of early growth and maturity. None of his poetical works written when he was above the age of thirty-five, equalled, or even approached in excellence those which he composed in his youthful manhood; and his last work, "The Pilgrims of Glencoe," was a melancholy specimen of decay; mere verse, without a scintillation of the *perfervidum ingenium* of his youthful days.

One of his latest poems, "On getting home a Portrait of a Female Child Six Years Old, by Eugene Latilla," published with "The Pilgrims of Glencoe," but originally contributed to the *Morning Chronicle*, shows how susceptible he was in his later years to the charms of infantile beauty. He saw the portrait exhibited for sale, in a shop-window, and was so struck with admiration of its arch and piquant loveliness, that he gushed into song and into print and purchased the picture at a price he could ill afford. He had it engraved as the frontispiece to his last book, and gave it the place of honour in his chambers at 61, Lincoln's-inn-Fields. Some months later, he was struck by the charms, not this time of a picture, but of a living child, whom he met in St. James's Park, under the charge of a nurse, and with whom he carried on a little innocent flirtation for half the afternoon. He celebrated the occurrence in a poem entitled "Lines on my New Child-Sweetheart," commencing—

> " I hold it a religious duty
> To love and worship children's beauty.
> They've least the taint of earthly clod,
> They're freshest from the hand of God."

The old man, living alone in his melancholy chambers, without wife or child, with no companions but his club friends, yearned for tenderer intercourse, even with a child, and broke out into a pathetic lament—pathetic though sadly prosaic in its phraseology :—

> " Oh beauteous, interesting child,
> Why asked I not thy home and name ?
> My courage failed me—more's the shame.
> But where abides this jewel rare,
> Oh ye that own her, tell me where.
> For sad it makes my heart and sore,
> To think I ne'er must meet her more."

These very mediocre lines are scarcely better than the impromptu of Isaac Watts in his eighth year, when his father threatened to whip him if he persisted in rhyming. Caught *in flagrante delicto*, the father seized young Isaac to inflict the penalty, when the latter cried out in terror and deprecation—

> " Oh, father, do some pity take,
> And I no more will verses make !"

It was on a Saturday afternoon when this little meeting took place, and all the newspaper offices being closed, Mr. Campbell came himself to the editorial rooms of the *Morning Chronicle* on the next day, bringing with him the following advertisement, with an urgent request that it should appear next day :—

"A gentleman, sixty-three years old, who, on Saturday last, between six and seven P.M., met near Buckingham Gate with a most interesting looking child, four years of age, but who forbore from respect for the lady who had her in hand, to ask the girl's name and abode, will be gratefully obliged to those who have the happiness of possessing the child to be informed where she lives, and if he may be allowed to see her again. A letter will reach the advertiser, T. C., at No. 61, Lincoln's-inn-Fields."

The little charmer never re-appeared on his vision. He received calls, he said, from scores of women, all with children, who declared they had been in St. James's Park on the day and hour specified, but who failed to satisfy him that they were not arrant impostors. Some of them were drunk, some exceedingly impudent, and some evidently intent upon extorting money from him. One woman brought a very pretty boy to present to the poet, in hope he would adopt him; but, said Mr. Campbell, "though I was no doubt very foolish in being carried away by my enthusiasm for the beautiful young face of an angelic child, I was not so great a fool as not to know a boy from a girl. I had a deal of trouble with that woman, and had to threaten her with the police and an appearance at Bow Street, before I could get rid of her."

This little episode was but the yearning of a lonely man for the domestic life which he had once enjoyed, and of which hard fate in his later years had deprived him. There was a void in his heart which club companionship and the flattery of society could not fill; and he pined for something to love, something that might recall to him

Q 2

the days of his youth and early prime, when he too could
see children's faces at his hearth, and hear the prattle of
children at his knee.   At last he found the care and companionship—without which his closing years were becoming
wearisome and solitary—in the person of a young niece,
his brother's child, who came from Glasgow to soothe his
declining years, and act as his housekeeper.   He left his
lonely chambers in Lincoln's-inn-Fields, and took a small
house in Victoria Square, close to Buckingham Palace.
But he did not live long in his new abode.   His health
had for years been failing, and with the expectation that
the sea-air would be of temporary benefit, he went to
Boulogne-sur-Mer.   But the anticipated benefit did not
come, and his friend and physician, Dr. William Beattie,
himself a poet, was suddenly summoned from London to
attend him.   He obeyed the call, and reached Boulogne
only to find Mr. Campbell dangerously ill, and to do all
that medical skill, combined with affectionate friendship,
could do, to soothe the last hours of the dying man.   The
poet expired on the 15th of June, 1844, in the sixty-
seventh year of his age.

I had the honour to receive from the executors, Dr.
Beattie, his attached friend, and Mr. Moxon, his publisher,
an invitation to his funeral, which took place in Westminster Abbey, with imposing ceremony.   His pall was
held by six of the most eminent personages of the day:
one of them being Sir Robert Peel, who had recently
resigned office, but who in his fall from power was incom-
parably the greatest man in England of his day; the
others being dukes and earls, whose names I have ceased
to remember.   The ceremonial was marked by two

incidents which were duly recorded in the newspapers of the following morning. The one was the sudden outburst of a thunder-storm, the solemn echoes of which reverberated through the majestic aisle of the abbey, as the officiating clergyman pronounced the deeply impressive words of the funeral service, " Forasmuch as it hath pleased Almighty God of his great mercy to take unto himself the soul of our dear brother here departed, we therefore commit his body to the ground : earth to earth, ashes to ashes, dust to dust, in the sure and certain hope of the resurrection to eternal life, through our Lord Jesus Christ." A thrill of visible emotion seemed to pass like a wave through the crowd of mourners; and Dr. Beattie, next to whom I stood, pressed my arm as if to draw my attention to the appropriateness of the thunder burst, at such a moment, and the beauty as well as sublimity of the incident.

The second incident was equally dramatic. When the solemn service came to a close, one of the mourners, a Polish exile, stepped out of the crowd and sprinkled a handful of earth upon the coffin, saying that it was earth procured from Poland, to mingle with the English earth over the grave of him who had written

" Hope for a season bade the world farewell,
And Freedom shrieked when Kosciusko fell."

Mr. Campbell from his earliest years had been a friend of the Poles, and had never tired in prose or verse, in speech or action, of expressing his indignation at the wicked partition of Poland by the three allied robbers—Russia, Austria, and Prussia. He was mainly instrumental in founding the Polish Association of London ; and to be a Pole and in want, was to have a sure passport to his sympathy, his good offices, and his scanty purse. He was one of the founders of the University of London, and was also Lord Rector of the University of Glasgow, from which, his "Alma-Mater," he received the degree of Doctor of Laws, a title which he never assumed, or placed upon the title pages of his books. Dr. Beattie, to whom he was fond of applying the lines of Pope to Garth—

> " Friend of my life, which didst not thou prolong,
> The world had wanted many an idle song "—

published, in 1849, a life of Campbell, in three volumes, full of the gentle spirit and kindly appreciation of others which was a characteristic of the benevolent and amiable biographer. It would have been better, as Dr. Beattie himself lived to confess, if he had restricted the memoir to one volume, and so saved both labour and money, while producing a work more likely to live than the too voluminous one which his zeal and affection rather than his sober judgment prompted him to write. There is a well-known portrait of Campbell by Sir Thomas Lawrence—a very flattering likeness, but not so true as the excellent drawing by Maclise in Fraser's Portrait Gallery, or the equally excellent bust by Pativa Park, which long adorned Dr. Beattie's dining-room.

———◆———

IT was about the middle of June, 1844, that Mr. Rogers invited me to breakfast at 22, St. James's Place to meet Mr. Wordsworth. I had long wished for a personal introduction to this celebrated poet, and was consequently much disappointed when Mr. Rogers announced, as soon as I arrived, that Mr. Wordsworth was unable to come. The conversation, however, turned upon him all the morning, and especially upon two sonnets which he had written in deprecation of the projected Kendal and Windermere Railway; and upon a long letter upon the same subject which he had just published in the *Morning Post*. In one of the sonnets he indignantly asked if there was "no nook of English ground secure from rash assault," denounced the railway as a "blight" and a "ruthless change," and called upon the "torrents and the winds," if "human hearts were dead" or insensible, to "protest against the wrong." In the second sonnet he declared that the "thirst of gold" ruled o'er Britain like a baneful star, (which, said Mr. Rogers, is rather a confused metaphor, for how can *thirst* be like a *star?*) and called upon the "mountains, vales, and floods," when they heard the whistle of the locomotive, "to share the passion of a just

disdain" of its unwelcome intrusion into the privacy of
the poet.

"I think *Punch's* parody of the sonnet," said Mr.
Rogers, "is much more sensible and to the point than
the original. And as for his letter in the *Morning Post*,
I must regret, as his friend, that he ever wrote it, and
still more that he should have published it." In this
opinion I could not but agree, thinking as I did—and as
I had written—that there was poetry even in the railway,
and that the marvellous triumphs of science in our
age were as susceptible of poetic treatment as any other
subject.

"Yes," said Mr. Rogers, "a good poet, though not to
the taste of our day, and now almost wholly unknown—
Erasmus Darwin—treated of steam in a highly poetical
and prophetic manner, when there was not as yet a railway in the land, or a steam-ship upon the ocean—

> ' Soon shall thy arm, unconquered steam, afar,
> Drag the slow barge or drive the rapid car,
> Or on wide waving wings expanded bear
> The flying chariot through the fields of air."

The last prophecy is not yet fulfilled—who shall be
so daring as to deny that it may be?

The gist of the argument in Mr. Wordsworth's letter
was that the people of Great Britain had no taste for fine
scenery, and that therefore a railway ought not to be
brought through such a district as that of Windermere,
for the purpose of gratifying a taste that was non-existent.
He attempted to prove his assertion by quotations from
the works of Bishop Burnet, and others, who looked

upon the sublime scenery of the Alps with horror, and not with delight; and from some anecdotes of Burns, tending to show that Burns had no eye for the picturesque! He also told a facetious story of a "shrewd and sensible Keswick woman," who said that in her youth such a thing as a "prospect" was never dreamed of. He strenuously maintained that as the taste for scenery was an acquired one, it was not likely that the multitudes would ever possess it! He expressed a horror of any popular amusements on the quiet shores of the lakes, of horse races on the land, or boat races on the water; and concluded his catalogue of the evils likely to result from the railway, by the assertion that "the Sunday in the towns of Bowness and Ambleside, and other parts of the district, would be subject to much additional desecration." "The imperfectly educated classes," he said, "are not likely to derive much good from rare visits to the lakes, paid in this way; and surely on their own account it is not desirable that their visits should be frequent." He added his opinion that "as long as inequalities of private property shall exist, *there must be privileges in recreations and amusements*, and that all cannot be enjoyed by all." "Leave the aristocracy," he went on to say, "in unenvied possession of their privacies, and be assured that, upon the whole, the extremely rich are neither better, nor wiser, nor healthier, nor happier than those who stand far below them in the social scale."

"I do not see," I remarked to Mr. Rogers, "why Mr. Wordsworth should speak for the aristocracy in this matter, for he is not one of them, either by birth or fortune, and is not even a landowner."

"But," said Mr. Rogers, "he is a Tory, and he speaks in the Tory fashion, and has not the advantage that you and I have of being a Whig. It is a pity, however, that he had no friend at his side to prevent him from rushing into print, and Quixote like, attacking a windmill—or something worse. His sonnet was bad enough, but the ridicule attaching to it would have speedily died away. His letter will both revive and perpetuate it, for which I am truly sorry."

"What can be the reason that so great a poet should take so small a view?"

"The reason," replied Mr. Rogers, "is not far to seek. He lives too much alone. He does not associate with his fellow men. He has shut himself up for years among the mountains and the lakes, and worshipped them; he has ended by worshipping himself. He has so continually brooded over his own genius in his darling solitudes, that he has come to consider himself the centre of the universe."

"Is he a vain—a conceited man?"

"I should not call him a vain man, or even a conceited man, by nature or original disposition, but he has become conceited for want of intercourse with his fellows. He sees nobody at Grasmere who is not inferior to himself, and he comes to the conclusion, unconsciously I have no doubt, that everybody, everywhere else, is inferior to him. If he would spend six months every year in London this idea would be rubbed out of him by the wholesome friction of society."

"But is not self-appreciation a good thing?"

"A very good thing in its degree, but not in excess.

In fact, nothing is good in excess ; and excess of solitude
is one of the worst things in which a clever man or a
man of genius can indulge himself.   It either leads to .
madness or to a conceit which is next door to it.   Did I
ever tell you the anecdote of Wordsworth, when he was
called upon to make a speech at the Anniversary Dinner
of the Literary Fund Society ? "

I replied that he had not.

" He sat next to a gentleman at the dinner-table who
told him that Mr. Stephenson, the eminent engineer, was
present, and that Mr. Stephenson was accustomed to say
that his great delight, when superintending the construc-
tion of the Skerrievore lighthouse on the west coast of
Scotland, was in the long summer evenings of those
latitudes to swing in a hammock and read the 'Excursion.'   Mr. Wordsworth was highly pleased, and was
particularly anxious that Mr. Stephenson should be
pointed out to him.   In the course of the evening, the
toast of ' the Poets ' having been proposed and responded
to by some one—I cannot call to mind who, but I think
it was Thomas Campbell—there was a call for Mr.
Wordsworth, who was generally known to be present.
Mr. Wordsworth made no sign, and the cries were redoubled.   At last he rose slowly, and much against his
will.   ' My lords and gentlemen,' he said, ' I cannot make
a speech. ' I never did make a speech, and am afraid I
never shall.   But there is a gentleman here present, Mr.
Stephenson, the great engineer, and if you will call upon
him to speak, he will doubtless tell you something
that will interest you more than anything I could say.
He will tell you how he passed the long summer

evenings, when he was building the Skerrievore light-house ! "

" But is that true ? " I inquired.

" I know not what the truth may be," said Mr. Rogers. " I was not present, but I tell the tale as it was told to me, and can only say for myself that it sounds like the truth, because so accordant with the mingled simplicity and vanity of Wordsworth's character."

" A weak invention of the enemy, I suspect."

" I don't think Wordsworth has any enemies. People may laugh at him now and then, but nobody dislikes him. He only requires to mix a little with the world to be one of the best fellows who ever lived. Who but a very vain main, spoiled by continually reflecting on his own excellencies," continued Mr. Rogers, taking up a volume of Wordsworth's poems from the side-table—well filled with books and writing materials—"would give such titles to his compositions as the following ? " And he read from the Table of Contents, with a running commentary on each :

" *Written with a pencil upon a stone in the wall of the House (an out-house) on the Island at Grasmere.* Who cares whether he wrote with a pen, or a pencil, on a stone, or on a sheet of paper ! "

" *Written with a slate pencil upon a stone, the largest of a heap lying near the deserted quarry upon one of the islands at Rydal.* Can anything be in worse taste ? Nobody wants to know how or where he wrote, but what he wrote ! But the following is still more Wordsworthian as a specimen of the almost childish vanity that is his besetting sin." And Mr. Rogers read the title and the lines with a comic intonation and strong emphasis :—

"LINES WRITTEN ON A BLANK LEAF IN A COPY OF THE AUTHOR'S POEM 'THE EXCURSION,' ON HEARING OF THE DEATH OF THE LATE VICAR OF KENDAL.

> " To public notice, with reluctance strong,
> Did I deliver this unfinished song ;
> Yet for one issue ; and I look
> With self-congratulation on the book,
> Which pious, learned Murfitt saw and read ;—
> Upon MY thoughts his saintly spirit fed :
> He conned the new-born lay with grateful heart,
> Foreboding not how soon he must depart,
> *Unweeting that to him the joy was given,*
> *Which good men take with them from Earth to Heaven.*"

" In other words," said Mr. Rogers, " he was proud of the poem, because the saintly vicar had read Wordsworth's thoughts, and taken them to Heaven along with him."

"I think, after that," said I, " that I must believe the story about Stephenson the engineer. Such vanity amounts to a disease."

" Yes ; and it grows upon him every day, and amuses everybody."

It was not until nearly two years after this conversation at Mr. Rogers's breakfast-table that my long-wished for introduction to Mr. Wordsworth took place. I was returning from London to Glasgow in the summer of 1846, intending to pass through the Lake District on my way, and spend a week at Ambleside and the neighbourhood, when a literary friend, Mr. Thomas Powell, author of a poem entitled " The Blind Wife," asked me to call upon Mr. Wordsworth, and take a message to him from his daughter, Mrs. Quillinan. Mr. Powell had been engaged with Mr. Leigh Hunt and Mr. Wordsworth in modernizing some of Chaucer's Poems. He volunteered to give me a letter of introduction, and asked me to inform Mr. Wordsworth that his daughter had made up her mind to remain in London a week longer, before returning to Grasmere. I undertook the commission with great pleasure, as it gave me the opportunity of making Mr. Wordsworth's acquaintance. I sent up my letter by a messenger from Ambleside, and received an answer to the effect that Mr. Wordsworth would be glad to see me on any day that best suited my convenience. I presented myself at Rydal Mount about noon on the following day, and found the poet walking in his garden, commanding a beautiful view over Grasmere and the hills, or rather mountains, that enclosed and shut in that picturesque little lake. Mr. Wordsworth at this time had turned his seventy-sixth year, and walked somewhat feebly with the aid of a stick. He welcomed me very courteously, and asked me to excuse him for receiving me out of doors, as he preferred the open air, and for walking somewhat slowly, as a few days previously he had strained his foot by stumbling over a molehill. I reminded him that William III. had died from an accident of a similar kind, and expressed my gratification to see that in the present case the result had not been so serious. He suddenly said, I thought somewhat ungraciously,—

"I am told that you write poetry. I never read a line of your poems and don't intend."

I suppose I looked surprised at the apparent rudeness of this, for he went on to say,—

"You must not be offended with me; the truth is, I never read anybody's poetry but my own."

Again I suppose that my face must have expressed what I certainly felt—a slight degree of wonder at a declaration which I thought so very gratuitous.

"You must not be surprised," he added; "for it is not vanity that makes me say this. I am an old man, and little time is left me in the world. I use that little as well as I may, to revise all my poems carefully, and make them as perfect as I can before I take my final departure."

It was quite evident from the frankness of this explanation, that the old gentleman did not mean to wound my self-love while explaining and vindicating his own; and I could but take in good part the confidence he had reposed in me. Desiring to turn the conversation, I stopped a moment in our walk to admire the outline of the picturesque mountain across the lake, and pointing to it, asked him its name.

"Dear me!" he replied, "that's Nab Scaur. Have you never read *my* poems?"

It was on the tip of my tongue to retort, that I never read anybody's poems but my own; but I reflected that he was old enough to be my grandfather, and not only that, but how untrue the statement would have been. So I refrained, and listened attentively as he spoke. "I have described Nab Scaur more than once in my poems. Don't you remember the following?" (And here he recited, in a deep bass voice, a passage of twenty or thirty lines, which was entirely new to me, though I did not like to tell him so.)

"Are you a climber of mountains?" he asked me at the close of his recitation; "because if you are, and can spare the time, you should, now that you are in the neighbourhood, climb to the top of Helvellyn."

I replied that I never saw a mountain without a longing desire to go to the top of it; that I had scaled Ben Lomond three times, Ben Nevis twice, and Goat Fell in Arran half a dozen times, and each time with new delight, and that only two days previously I had mounted to the top of Skiddaw (it was in July), and had been enveloped for three hours in a blinding snow-storm.

"Ah!" he said, "my climbing days have long been over; but, like you, I rejoiced in the sport, the exercise, and the excitement. Are you an angler?"

"No," I said; "I do not go abroad on my mountain rambles to kill anything—neither bird, nor fish, nor quadruped."

"I am glad of that," said he; "there is quite enough of innocent excitement in the free fresh air, the exercise, and the scenery, without the savage excitement of what you justly call 'killing.' I too have been for hours on the mountain tops enveloped in snow and mist, generally alone, and have tasted some of my most refined pleasures in such situations; above the world, literally as well as metaphorically, and happy in the contemplation of such sublime solitudes as only the mountain top can afford."

The mention of Skiddaw turned the conversation upon the vale and town of Keswick, which lie so beautifully under the feet of the climber, as he plods his weary way

to the top of the mountain; and from Keswick to Wordsworth's friend and fellow poet, of what used to be called
"the Lake School," Robert Southey, who had died not
very long previously. I had visited Southey's house,
then empty and in the hands of the painters, preparatory
to the letting of the place to a new tenant, and had stood
in the apartment where he had closed his industrious and
honourable life. Seeing so favourable an opportunity of
putting the question, I asked Mr. Wordsworth if there
was any truth in the current report of the time, that
Southey had died literally of over-work.

"There is no truth in it," said Wordsworth. "He
was a calm and methodical worker, and calm, steady
work never kills. It is only worry and hurry that kill.
Southey wrote a great deal; but he wrote easily and
pleasantly to himself. Besides, only those who have
tried, know what an immense deal of literary work can be
got through comfortably by a man who will work regularly for only four, or even for three hours a day. Take
the case of Sir Walter Scott, for instance. What an im-
mensity of work he got through; and yet he was always
idle at one o'clock in the afternoon, and ready for any
amusement, or for such change of labour as the garden
or the field afforded. Southey was like him in that
respect, and though he worked hard, he always contrived
to enjoy abundance of leisure. Scott died of pecuniary
trouble, not of work. Southey died of grief for the loss
of his wife."

Mr. Laman Blanchard, the assistant of Mr. Albany
Fonblanque in the editorship of the *Examiner* newspaper, had not long before this conversation died under

very painful circumstances in an aberration of mind, caused by the death of a wife to whom he was devotedly attached, and I recalled the fact to Mr. Wordsworth's memory. It seemed to impress him painfully.

"Yes," he said; "it was grief, not labour, that laid its heaviest burthen upon poor Southey, as it seems to have done upon your friend."

I told him I was not intimately acquainted with Laman Blanchard, but that I had met him once at breakfast at Mr. Rogers's.

"Aye, Mr. Rogers!" he remarked. "*He* at all events will not die either of hard work or of sorrow. Nothing will touch *him* in that way. He has a good income, a good stomach, and a heart that is tender enough in a small way; but that no disappointment can either break or seriously affect. I shouldn't wonder if he lived to be a hundred."

At this moment an elderly lady was wheeled in a garden-chair by another elderly lady very close to the spot where we were talking. I wore at the time a Scotch bonnet, known as a Glengarry; and the lady in the chair no sooner caught sight of me, than she struck up in rather a shrill, but not unpleasant voice, the old song, commencing :—

> "A Highland lad my love was born,
> The lowland laws he held in scorn;"

and sang a couple of stanzas of it.

"Come away, Mr. Laman Blanchard," said Mr. Wordsworth; "that's my poor sister—an unpleasant sight—come away."

I reminded him gently that I was not Laman Blanchard, but he replied, "Oh! never mind, it's all the same to her; come away."

"Who is that man?" cried the lady, pointing to me.

"Only Mr. Laman Blanchard, my dear," he replied. "Let us turn down here," he added, *sotto voce*, taking my arm and leading me down a bye-path. "She does not like the presence of strangers, and I would not pain her for for the world."

I afterwards learned that this poor lady was the once celebrated poetess, Miss Wordsworth, some of whose exquisite little poems were quite equal to her brother's best, and that the general opinion of the neighbourhood was that her mind had gradually become affected by solitude. She had nobody to talk to—no one with whom she could interchange ideas; for Mr. Wordsworth was wrapped up in himself, and did not, as he wrote in one of his poems,—

> " Much or oft delight,
> To season his fire-side with personal talk
> Of friends who live within an easy walk,
> Or neighbours, daily, weekly in his sight.
> \*        \*        \*        \*        \*
> Better than such discourse did silence, long,
> Long barren silence square with his desire ;
> To sit without emotion, hope, or aim,
> In the loved presence of his cottage fire,
> And listen to the flapping of the flame,
> Or kettle whispering its faint undersong."

This was all very well for Mrs. Wordsworth, who had taken her solitary husband for better or for worse ; but not well for Miss Wordsworth, who pined for social intercourse, and sought it, rather than not have it at all, with servants and farm labourers, and finally broke down under the weight of too much loneliness.

I spent about three hours in the garden, and was not asked inside; three pleasant hours, however, though I could not but regretfully see that the fires of that once clear and gentle intellect were burning somewhat dimly, and that the end could not be far off. He bade me a kindly farewell, saying "Good-bye, Mr. Laman Blanchard, and if you prolong your stay among the Lakes, remember that I shall be very glad to see you again."

That evening, at the inn at Ambleside, there was an American gentleman in the coffee-room who had a note of introduction to Wordsworth, and was going to deliver it on the morrow. He told me a story he had heard in America of a countryman of his who had lost his way in the vain attempt to discover Rydal Mount; had taken a wrong turn and gone three or four miles beyond or to the side of the point he should have aimed at. Meeting an old woman in a scarlet cloak, who was gathering sticks, he asked her the way to Rydal Mount. She could not tell him; she did not know. "Not know," said the American, "the house of the great Wordsworth?" "No." "What, not the house of the man whose fame brings people here from all parts of the world?" "No," she insisted; "but what was he great in? was he a preacher? or a doctor?" "Greater than any preacher or doctor—he is a poet." "Oh, the poet!" she replied; and why did you not tell me that before? I know who you mean now. I often meet him in the woods, jabbering his pottery (poetry) to hisself. But I'm not afraid of him. He's quite harmless, and almost as sensible as you or me."

"Mal trovato e non vero," I replied. "I have discovered during my stay in the Lake district that Wordsworth is no exception to the old rule ; no one is a hero to his *valet de chambre*, and no one is much thought of in his own neighbourhood, unless he be a duke or an earl, and very rich ; and not always highly thought of even then."

Wordsworth died in 1850, in his eightieth year. He had been fairly rewarded by the Tory party to which he belonged for the honour he had conferred upon the literature of his country : was made distributor of stamps with a salary of £700 per annum ; had besides a pension of £300 a year on the Civil List ; and was poet laureate, a place worth £150 per annum. Wordsworth seems to have accepted this antiquated office on the understanding that it was a reward for past efforts, and not a salary for services to be rendered in adulation of the sovereign or laments for the sovereign's family. His predecessor Southey had thought it his duty to earn his money and his wine by writing birthday odes, funeral songs for Queen Charlotte and the Princess Charlotte of Wales ; triumphal odes in celebration of the visit of George IV. to Scotland and Ireland ; and worse than all, the portentous " Vision of Judgment," in commemoration of the death of George III., which Lord Byron turned into such merciless ridicule. But Wordsworth did not imitate the example. Perhaps at the time the office was conferred upon him, old age had dulled or extinguished his poetic fire ; or perhaps he objected to writing for hire on subjects which did not spring up spontaneously in his own mind, and did not care to pump up a fictitious enthusiasm for either the joys or the sorrows of royalty. However this may be, his laureateship was a silent one. He had an advantage over his predecessor in the fact that, unlike Southey, who succeeded what Scott called " the poetical Pye," who had made the office contemptible, he stepped into the place of a great poet, whom not even the laureateship, and the silly work attached to it, could render ridiculous. It is much to be wished that the office were abolished, and a pension of double or treble is emoluments, awarded to such future Chaucers, Spencers, Miltons, as may arise to write above the heads of an unappreciative public, the immortal verse, that may bring no bread to its authors ; but that may perhaps be the priceless heritage of future ages, and the glory of English literature.

# THE BURNS FESTIVAL AT AYR.

———

HAVING found the labours and the late hours of the *Morning Chronicle* injurious to my health, I left that journal, after a pleasant connection with it, that had extended over nine years. On leaving London for Scotland, to assume the editorship of the *Glasgow Argus*, I had the satisfaction of receiving the following letter from Sir John Easthope, the principal proprietor of the *Chronicle* :—

"19, GRAFTON ST., BOND ST.,
"18 July, 1844.

" DEAR MACKAY,

" Mr. Doyle* had informed me of your desire to leave the *Morning Chronicle* at the end of this month. At this advanced period of the session I am not aware that the suddenness of your determination will produce any very extraordinary inconvenience ; but if it did, the change being for your own advantage, I could not have permitted any such objection to have interposed against your interests. I very cordially hope that all the expectations of advantage you contemplate will be most fully

* Mr. Andrew Doyle, who had married a daughter of Sir John Easthope and succeeded Mr. Black in the editorship of the *Chronicle*.

realised.  I beg you will be assured that my honest
wishes of cordial good will and friendship most truly
follow you to your new engagement.  It will always
give me pleasure to hear of your success, and to evince
the sentiments of friendship which I truly entertain for
you.

> " I remain, dear Mackay, in great truth,
>      " Your well-wisher and sincere friend,
>                       ." JOHN EASTHOPE."

"To CHARLES MACKAY, Esq."


The editorship of the *Argus* was superior in point of
position and of emolument to that of sub-editor of the
*Morning Chronicle,* and the labour was not half so
severe.  Instead of one day's leisure in the week, like a
mechanic, I had four days for such idleness or such change
of work as I desired.  There was the additional advantage—a very great and delightful one to me—of contiguity
to the sublime scenery of the West Highlands, to which
I could resort from Saturday to Monday, away from the
closely crowded and smoky city, to the breezy moorland
and the mountain top—to lake and glen, and rapid
stream—to all the rugged grandeur of Loch Long, and
the softer magnificence of Loch Lomond.

I gave myself a holiday of three months before settling
down to my new duties.  Previously to leaving London,
I had received the following official invitation to attend,
in the town of Ayr, the great festival which had been
arranged in honour of Robert Burns, the immortal poet.
of Scotland :—

"AYR, 2nd July, 1844.

" SIR,

" We have the honour to communicate to you, by directions of the Committee, that a festival in honour of the genius of the poet Burns, and to welcome his sons to the banks of the Doon, is to take place near to the Monument erected to his memory about two miles from this, on Tuesday, the sixth day of August next; and that Lord Eglintoun, the Lord Lieutenant of this county, and Professor Wilson, of the Edinburgh University, are to preside on the occasion.

" At a general meeting it was resolved that you should be invited as a guest, and the Committe fondly hope that the nature of your engagements are such as will enable you to accept their invivation.

" Waiting the favour of your answer,

" We have the honour to be, Sir,

" Your very obedient servants,

" W. BONE, ⎫
" JOHN GRAY, ⎬ *Secs.*
            ⎭

"CHARLES MACKAY, Esq."

" P.S.—On hearing that you are to be present, the Committee will provide proper accommodation for you in Ayr or its immediate neighbourhood."

I gladly accepted the invitation of the Committee, and was very hospitably entertained at the house of Mr. Miller, the Provost of Ayr—a town then, as now, proud of the title given to it by Burns — the town

"Of honest men and bonnie lasses."

Among the visitors from London, representatives of
the press and others, were Mr. Herbert Ingram, proprietor of the *Illustrated London News*, with whom I was
not then acquainted; Mr. Douglas Jerrold, Mr. and
Mrs. S. C. Hall, Mr. Alexander Mackay, author of the
"Western World;" Mr. Patrick Park, the sculptor; and
many others. Mr. Alexander Mackay and Mr. Park had
been my companions in a previous ramble in the West
Highlands, and went to the Burns Festival solely because
I was going, and that we might not be separated before
their return to London. The two great orators engaged
for the occasion were the Earl of Eglintoun, the hero of
the Eglintoun Tournament and Lord Lieutenant of
Ayrshire, who was to occupy the chair; and Professor
Wilson, the redoubtable Christopher North of *Blackwood's Magazine*, who was to be vice-chairman, or, in
Scottish phrase, croupier. The three surviving sons of
Burns—the eldest, Robert, who had been a clerk in one
of the Government offices in Downing Street, and had
just retired from that position on a pension; and Colonel
and Major Burns, who had recently returned from India,
after long service in the army of the East India Company,
were invited to be present. It was the accident that these
gentlemen were all sojourning for a time in the land of
their illustrious father that first suggested the idea of
the Festival. The project was warmly supported by
Lord Eglintoun and the leading literati of Scotland, and
excited great interest in every part of the world, wherever Scotsmen were to be found. In England, whose
people in the large sense of that word take little pride
in their own poets, and scarcely understand the affec-

tionate love and fervent admiration which the Scotch entertain for Burns, the interest was but languid ; and not a single Englishman of any note was present, except Mr. Douglas Jerrold and Mr. S. C. Hall, who attended on professional business for the press. Mr. Charles Dickens, then in the full flush and glory of his early fame, was invited—not for an English but for a Scottish reason—because his name was accidentally connected with that of Burns, for he had married the granddaughter of the George Thompson, for whose musical publications Burns had written so many of his songs, and to whom he had addressed the voluminous correspondence that is usually printed as an appendix to his works. Mr. Dickens, however, was unable to accept the invitation as he was at the time travelling in Italy. Among the Scottish literary men of note who took part in the proceedings were Sir Archibald Alison, the historian, and sheriff of Lanarkshire ; Henry Glassford Bell, the poet, who afterwards succeeded Sir Archibald in the sheriffdom ; Colonel Mure, of Caldwell, the historian ; Professor W. E. Aytoun, of Edinburgh ; and several dignitaries of the Scottish Bench and Bar.

It was my first visit to Ayr, and the banks of the Doon ; and on the day preceding the Festival, Mr. Alexander Mackay, Mr. Patrick Park, and myself, set forth on a tour of inspection of all the objects in the town and neighbourhood associated with the name and fame of the poet whom Scotland most delights to honour. First, there was the town itself, over which his youthful feet had wandered ; then there were the " Brigs of Ayr," the new and the old, which he had celebrated in one of his

best poems ; and most interesting of all, the cottage, or
" clay bigging," where he was born, two miles and a
quarter from the town.   The hut was built by his father's
own hands, and rudely plastered with mud.   On the 25th
January, 1759, the day of his birth, a sudden gust swept
over the country from the sea, and carried away the
gable-wall of the frail erection, to the great alarm of the
inmates, and especially of the mother, who was forthwith
carried, with her babe, through the storm and rain, to a
securer shelter.   The place, after the removal of the
elder Burns, seven years afterwards, became the property
of the Corporation of Shoemakers of Ayr, who little knew,
when they bought the unexpired lease from the struggling
gardener and farmer, that the spot was destined one day
to rival, in the interest of its associations, the old house
at Stratford-upon-Avon, where Shakspeare's eyes first
opened to the light.   The cottage originally consisted of
two rooms, a kitchen, and a *spence*, or sitting-room, with
a recess in the wall for a bed.   The Shoemakers
extended the building, allowing the original rooms to
remain, and let it as a way-side inn.   In after years,
when Death had set the final sanctification upon the
glory of the poet, the little ale-house became a shrine to
which pilgrims and devotees resorted from all parts of
the world, to gratify their curiosity, and pay their homage
to departed genius.   It was still an ale-house in 1844,
as it was in 1870, when I last visited it.   My companions
and I inscribed our names in the Book, inspected the
little niche in the wall where the simple wooden frame
bedstead had been placed, and were informed that a
stable-boy in Ayr had bought it for a few shillings at the

"roup," or auction, of the elder Burns, when he removed, in 1766, to the farm of Mount Oliphant, and had kept it until the death of Burns in 1796, when he parted with it for twenty guineas. From the cottage we proceeded to "Alloway Kirk," the scene of the immortal poem of Tam o' Shanter—enough to stamp the author as a genius of the highest order, if he had written nothing else—written off at a heat in one day, in one burst of glowing and glorious inspiration, and containing within its short compass a specimen of every feeling and emotion which poetry can excite—the tender, the pathetic, the mournful, the grotesque, the witty, the philosophic, the horrible, the natural, the supernatural, and the sublime. Our discourse as we went was of this wonderful poem, which Park maintained was equal to anything in Shakspeare, and showed the poet, if he had lived, to have been capable of the very highest flight in literature.

"But how is it," I remarked, "that Scott, who was as great a poet as Burns, perhaps greater, and whose novels are the glory and pride of his country, has not taken anything like the hold upon the heart of his countrymen that Burns has taken?"

"For many reasons," replied Park. "First of all, Burns died young, when he had scarcely begun to put forth his full powers. Second, Burns was not a faultless monster. He sinned and suffered, and was but too human, and for this reason attracted the sympathy of others who erred, and suffered as he did; and third, he was a man of the people, and a sturdy lover and preacher of independence. He wrote 'A man's a man for a' that,' and was a democrat to the back-bone. Scott was of a

colder, though a greater intellect—he was not of the
people—he was not a sinner like poor Burns, and was
too far above the crowd to attract their affection. The
crowd like a great man all the better for his faults, if the
faults are not mean ones. And no one can say that there
was a particle of meanness in the great soul of Robert
Burns."

"Nor in that of Scott either. But I grant what you
say about Burns. Had he been a rich man and lived in
a palace, acquired a title and associated with the high and
mighty rather than with the poor and lowly, he would
never have become the idol of the Scottish people."

"Aye! aye! a man's a man for a' that. Fancy Sir
Robert Burns, Baronet. Faugh!" said Park, "the
very idea has left a bad taste in my mouth in pronouncing
it, and I'll take a dram of whiskey to remove it," which
he did from a pocket-flask with which he was provided.

We soon reached the grave-yard of Alloway Church,
now a ruin, and not much larger than a moderate sized
barn, capable at most of accommodating a hundred and
fifty or two hundred people. We particularly required
the guide to show us

> " The *winnock bunker* in the East,
> Where sat Auld Nick in shape o' beast."

This *winnock-bunker*, or seat in the window, was very
small, and the arch enemy of mankind was right in the
eye of the poet's imagination to have assumed the
dwarfish shape of a towzie tyke or rough terrier for the
occasion, on which from so confined a space he was to

play up the pipes for the dance of witches. The "bunker" was of stone, or it would long previously have been removed, in common with every particle of the old wood-work of the building, for conversion into snuff-boxes or other relics of the little church, which the genius of Burns had consecrated. Indeed it was asserted in Ayr that wood, purporting to have belonged to Alloway Kirk, had been manufactured into snuff-boxes and trinkets, sufficient in their bulk to have formed all the woodwork existent in the town. In the little cemetery we stopped opposite to the grave of the poet's father, the hero of the beautiful "Cottar's Saturday Night," and read the inscription written by the poet himself.

> " Oh ye, whose cheek the tear of pity stains,
>     Draw near with pious reverence, and attend,
> Here lie the loving husband's dear remains,
>     The tender father and the generous friend :
> The pitying heart that felt for human woe,
>     The dauntless heart that feared no human pride,
> The friend of man, to vice alone a foe,
>     For e'er his failings lean'd to virtue's side."

Were it not for the inappropriate word " stains " in the first line, this composition might be considered faultless.

The Monument to the memory of Burns, erected by public subscription in 1820, at a cost of £3,300, is visible from old Alloway Kirk, and stands on the summit of the eastern bank of the river Doon—the "bonnie Doon" of the well-known song. The edifice is about sixty feet high, and is surrounded by an acre and a rood of garden grounds very tastefully laid out and well kept. A fee of twopence is charged to each visitor for admission, which produces annually as much as pays the salary of the curator and the expense of keeping the ground in order. The interior of the monument is occupied by a circular apartment, in the midst of which is a table with manuscripts, early editions of the poems and personal relics of the poet, among others the Bible which he presented to Highland Mary, the one object of his purest affection, and whom he has immortalised in the tenderest and most mournful love song in the language.

"I think," said Park, with a burst of enthusiasm, "that as soon as I get back to London, I'll model a bust of Burns and present it in marble to the monument. 'Twill be a poor man's tribute to the glory of another poor man. Nasmyth's portrait"—and he pointed to a copy of it as he spoke—"is good, and must have been like what Burns was. I shall take it as my guide, but I will idealize and ennoble it. I'll put my heart into the work!"

Park was one of the warmest hearted and most generous of men that ever lived, and though he could but ill afford the time or the labour, or even the marble for the work, I felt sure that he would carry out his intention. On our way from the monument, to call upon Mrs. Begg, the then surviving sister of the poet, Park returned to the subject. I remarked that in my opinion a bust ought not to be a likeness like a portrait, and that to atone for the absence of colour and of the expression in the eyes there ought to be the idealization and the nobility of which he had himself spoken, so as to suggest the man in the best and highest mood of which he was capable.

" Quite right," said Park ; " if a sculptor cannot make
his subject more or less heroic, he might as well be a
wood-carver or cut figure-heads for ships. When I
model the head of Burns, as I am fully determined to do,
I shall keep him before my mind in the act of composing
one of his best poems, such as ' A Man's a Man for a'
that.' "

" Do you think that poem the best for your purpose ? "
I ventured to inquire. " Is there not a touch of rough-
ness, of contempt, of scorn, and a kind of rollicking self-
assertion about it, rather than of the heroic dignity you
would like to impress upon your marble ? "

" Well, perhaps there is. But, stay, I have it ! I
know something better ! When I set to work, I shall
strive to bring before my imagination how Burns looked
when he was composing the grand patriotic chant,
' Scots wha hae wi' Wallace bled.' Sir Philip Sydney
used to say that the old ballad of Chevy Chace stirred
his heart as with the sound of a trumpet. ' Scots
wha hae ' stirs my heart as with the sound of a thousand
trumpets ! "

Park fulfilled his promise. In less than a twelvemonth
after this conversation he had completed a very noble
marble bust of Burns, which still stands in the place of
honour in the monument. The provost and magistrates
of Ayr entertained the sculptor at dinner, and he was duly
presented with the freedom of the burgh. It is not easy,
as Sydney Smith suggested to Sir Edwin Landseer, to
express in a portrait a sentiment of "hostility to the
Established Church;" and no one would surmise from
inspection of Park's bust that there was any expression

of martial hostility to the English army in the manly
features which he has so successfully portrayed, but no
one can look at it, whether it be a likeness or not, without
feeling that it is a work of genius, and one which any
sculptor might be proud to claim as his own.

We were courteously received by Mrs. Begg and her
daughter, who were living in modest comfort on an annuity
raised by public subscription in Scotland, the United
States, Canada, and India, in honour of the memory of
her brother. In the cottage we found Mr. Douglas
Jerrold and Mr. Herbert Ingram, proprietor of the *Illustrated London News*, then but newly started. It was the
first time I met the last-mentioned gentleman, in connection with whom I was afterwards destined to pass
some of the best years of my life.

The Festival took place on the following day—Tuesday,
the 6th of August—in a large pavilion erected in a
meadow nearly opposite Alloway Kirk, and within sight
of the poet's monument. The pavilion, richly decorated
with flags and other ornaments, was planned for the
accommodation of 2,000 guests, and all the tickets to the
banquet, charged fifteen shillings for the gentlemen and
ten shillings for the ladies, were speedily taken up. For
the gratification of the immense crowds of people that
poured into Ayr from Glasgow, Edinburgh, Dumfries,
Kilmarnock, and every town and village in the west of
Scotland, a great out-of-door procession was arranged, of
which fortunately the beauty and effect were not marred
by unfavourable weather, and the persistent downpour
which too commonly refreshes—and drenches—the west of
Scotland. The procession was composed of the magis-

trates and baillies of many important towns, with depu-
tations of their townspeople, of the Masonic bodies,
amongst whom, when living, Burns stood high in rank
and repute, and who were proud of his brotherhood in
the craft; and of Foresters, Odd Fellows, and many
other societies, preceded by bands of music, and bearing,
many of them, not merely the customary flags and
banners of Great Britain, but the ancient historic flag of
Scotland, under the gleam and glamour of which Bruce
fought and won the battle of Bannockburn. There was
also a grand procession of peasants and farm labourers, assembled in honour of the greatest peasant—next perhaps
to King David of the Jews, a peasant, a poet, a patriot,
and a king—whom any age had produced, and who bore
high erected in the midst of them a gigantic thistle, eight
or nine feet high, and with a profusion of flowers,
which must have been the result of high cultivation.
As this national emblem made its appearance, with the
proud motto, " Nemo me impune lacessit " emblazoned
on a banner streaming over it, the applause of the immense assemblage was loud and unrestrained, and was
repeated again and again as Christopher North took off
his hat in reverence to the symbol as it was borne past.
At two o'clock in the afternoon the banquet was served
in the pavilion, and I had the good fortune, as an invited
guest, to be assigned a seat of honour on the platform,
to the left hand of the distinguished vice-chairman of the
day. I was unable, from the distance and the want of
acoustic facility in the tent, to hear a word said by Lord
Eglinton on the occasion ; but I saw from the newspapers
in due time, that he had made a very eloquent and appre-

ciative speech, and done justice to the genius of the bard whose memory they had all assembled to honour. Professor Wilson's speech, of which I heard every word that he was permitted to deliver, was still more eloquent, and as the literary effort of a literary man, on a great literary occasion, was equal to the Professor's reputation. But he made a great mistake. He took no account of time or space, and painting his picture of the great poet on too extensive a canvas, fairly exhausted the patience of his auditory before he had advanced beyond the threshold of his argument. He dwelt upon the errors of Burns : upon his over passionate youth, and Samson-like enslavement to many Delilahs ; and to the excessive conviviality that brought him into bad company, and over-clouded his day ere the noon had fairly come. The long speech of Lord Eglinton, excellent though it was, had not disposed the audience for a second speech of equal dimensions, and after the Professor had expatiated for about half-an-hour or more on the frailties of the bard, the sounds of impatience, dissent, and disapprobation grew so loud, so prolonged, and so often repeated, that the Professor, seeing the hopelessness of proceeding, sat down with the best part of his speech unspoken. He turned to me, as he resumed his place, and said, "It is a pity they won't hear me out. I only dwelt upon the errors of Burns, that I might lift him out of them in power and glory, as one of the very greatest of Scotsmen who ever conferred honour upon his country." .

"Fortunately," I replied, "you can publish your speech, as you intended to speak it, and so put yourself right."

" Yes," he replied, " I'll shame the fools and print it."

In Mr. Forster's " Life of Charles Dickens " it is reported that Lord Robertson (the famous Peter Robertson of Edinburgh society) had told Mr. Dickens that Professor Wilson had had the bad taste to insult the memory of Burns in the presence of his sons at the Ayrshire Festival. But there was no insult in the case, as the published speech abundantly showed. The Professor had fallen into the error of writing a speech that was too like a literary essay for his favourite *Blackwood,* and had taken no account of the patience of his auditory. And if the place of honour had been assigned to him instead of to Lord Eglinton, and he had been allowed to commence the proceedings, it is both possible and probable that he would have been heard respectfully to the end, and that no misconception would have arisen.

# 1845–6, THE FINAL YEARS OF THE ANTI-CORN-LAW STRUGGLE.

—♦—

THE Reform of the Tariff, the imposition of the Income and Property Tax, and the other free-trade measures of Sir Robert Peel in 1842, emboldened the Anti-Corn-Law League to fresh and greater exertions to secure the total repeal of the Corn Laws. Most people, except the ultra-Protectionist party, saw that the Corn Laws were sooner or later doomed to abolition, and some few went so far as to suspect that Sir Robert Peel's hand would be that which would deal them the death-blow. In 1844, the repeal of the Corn Laws was not only the question of the League and of the Free Traders, but of the Whig and Liberal party, the only dissentients being the semi-Irish and unreasonable Chartists. It was amusing to note how the chiefs of the Protectionist party attempted to draw the masses of the people to their side, on a false scent; how, as was said at the time, they drew red herrings across the path, to bewilder the dogs of public opinion, and let the fox of Food Monopoly escape. Lord John Manners, remembering the beauty of the paternal estate of Belvoir, imagined that if all England were one garden and woodland such as that, the people would be more happy than when condemned to the enervating work and close atmosphere of factories. Full of the idea, he wrote a pamphlet and a poem, deprecating the existence of large towns, describing, in glowing terms, the Arcadian life of a rural population and a rural aristocracy, and praying, as the commencement of a new era, that the legislature would look to the sports of the people, and lay out greens for cricket and leap-frog. Lord Ashley, now Earl of Shaftesbury, was of opinion that the employment of women and children in mines and collieries was the source of all the moral and physical ills which weighed down the multitude; and to this question he directed all the energies of his mind, and made out a case, which caused the sympathetic to weep, and the universal press to resound with his praises. The removal of these evils was *his* panacea for all the rest. Another philanthropist discovered that the people were unworthily treated in the house of prayer; that a rich man would have a fine soft pew in a church by paying for it, but that the poor man and his family had too often to stand during the whole time of religious service; and touched with pity for this popular grievance, he ranged himself on the popular side, and exclaimed, "Away with pews—abolish all distinctions of rank and wealth in the house of God, and Great Britain will not lose her place among the nations; the sun of her prosperity shall not set; and her people once more shall be happy and independent!"

When it was proposed to lay out a park in Manchester—the head-quarters of the troublesome League—for the health and recreation of its hard-working operatives, Sir Robert Peel, who as yet did not quite see his way to

untax the bread of the aforesaid hard-working people,
wrote a letter, in which he "heartily approved of the
wise and benevolent design to provide for those who are
doomed to almost incessant toil, the means of healthful
recreation and harmless enjoyment," and contributed
£1,000 in furtherance of the object. Lord Francis
Egerton, afterwards Earl of Ellesmere, contributed the
like sum. But with all this liberality ostentatiously displayed by great landlords, the reflection forced itself upon
the mind of the Free Traders, that much as they heard
of the growing sympathy of the Tories as a party with
the unhappy, care-eaten multitudes of Great Britain,
their sympathy was always expressed on a very small
scale, and for some comparatively small grievance. These
lights of their party, who were so eloquent upon the fetid
atmosphere of cities—the healthiness and happiness of
the rural districts—the desirableness of public sports,
and a return to the good old times, when the poor man
could enjoy himself upon the green—the atrocity of
allowing a woman and child to work even for good wages
—and the necessity of "healthful recreation and harmless
enjoyment,"—were wonderfully callous or hostile when
any great and comprehensive scheme was brought forward for the improvement of the condition of the people.
They were benevolent in a small way for the sake of
popularity, but they would not be just on a great scale,
because they were trained in narrowness and short-
sightedness, and thought charity more graceful than
justice. If it were proposed to them, as a foundation for
all other improvement, that every child born in the kingdom should be not only entitled to food, but to education,

a clamour of hostile tongues was immediately raised! "He shall be fed out of my spoon, or he shall starve!—he shall be imbued with my religious opinions, or he shall remain ignorant for ever!" was shouted on every side; and the chance of a national scheme of education was lost for another generation. If it were proposed as a remedy for a falling trade, and an unemployed, and there-fore unhappy and degraded population, that the country should turn its national resources to better account, and open its ports for the grain which was rotting in the fields of the old and new world, because the Protectionists would not let it come in; these fine philanthropists thought over the possibility of falling rents and refused. The famished artisan might play at cricket, and his forlorn wife and little ones might breathe the fresh air of the new park laid out for them; but they must wait for bread for the better times which were always promised, but which never came.

But the most amusing instance of well-meaning philanthropy was afforded about this time by the then Duke of Norfolk. The potato crop had failed; there was great distress in the country, and there was a fear, but too well founded, that it would increase as winter approached. There was also a cry for the opening of the ports, so that corn or bread-stuffs, even if only for a temporary purpose, and to check a temporary evil, might be admitted into Great Britain free of duty. The Duke of Norfolk, struck with compassion for the sufferings of the multitude, but not possessing even the glimmering of an idea that a tax upon foreign food for the supposed benefit of the British landowners was a real injury to the hard-

working classes, and that the abolition of such tax would
be a real benefit, announced his remedy—better, in his
opinion, than the cricket and leap-frog of Lord John
Manners, or the parks that found favour with Sir Robert
Peel. At a meeting in Sussex he said—"In consequence
of the badness of the potatoes, they should pay more
attention to the labourer this year than ordinarily.
There was one thing,—it was suggested in a letter by a
lady the other day—a thing which certainly was very
warm and comfortable to the stomachs of the people if it
could be got cheap. He endeavoured, the other day
when he was in London, to buy it. He went to several
places to enquire, and he bought a pound or two of it.
But there was some difficulty attached to it rather than
otherwise. They had not been accustomed to it, and
might not like it. He liked it, however, himself. In
India it was to the people what potatoes were in Ireland.
He meant CURRY POWDER. It might be smiled at at first,
but it was a very warming thing for potatoes and things
of that description. Now, if gentlemen would try it as
he had done, merely *taking a pinch and putting it into hot
water*—he did not mean to say that would make a soup—
a very good one; but *when a man came home and took
this and had nothing better, it would make him warm at his
stomach, and he could go to bed better and more comfortable.*
He might be ridiculed hereafter for what he was saying,
but *he did not care one rap.*"

One universal peal of laughter may be said to have
resounded through the empire on the publication of this
panacea for famine, and though the Duke, to use his own
elegant phraseology, might not have cared "one rap" for

the ridicule he had drawn upon himself and his order,
the Anti-Corn-Law League and the friends of Free Trade
found reason to congratulate themselves that they had
such admirable and serviceable enemies. The Duke of
Norfolk was not the only man of the same high rank and
position who involuntarily aided the cause which he
wished to defeat. The Duke of Richmond, at the same
county meeting, said—" I believe that in parts of Europe
the disease in potatoes has existed. But I hear that in
one country, which is not far distant from our shores by
steam navigation—I allude to Portugal—there never was
a better crop of potatoes ; and if there should be a failure
in this country, there will be no difficulty in bringing
potatoes from that country to this at a price which, though
the labourers cannot pay, we (the landowners) ought and
will."

The Duke of Norfolk showed folly—the Duke of Richmond selfishness ; and with equal innocence of meaning
it, gave a blow to their darling monopoly, than which Mr.
Cobden could not have aimed a better. Why, it was
asked, should it be praiseworthy to take foreign potatoes,
and at the same time patriotic to refuse foreign wheat?
And, more wonderful still, why should the Duke of Richmond prevent the people from *buying* Polish or Russian
wheat, and yet insist on *giving* them Portuguese potatoes
in charity ? The fair conclusion seemed to be that the
Duke realised a handsome profit by his self-imposed con-
tract for supplying the British people with food, seeing
that when they were unable to buy his dear wheat, he
would give them Portuguese potatoes for nothing, rather
than that they should buy corn cheaply from foreign dealers.

Two other dukes rendered themselves conspicuous by denying the existence of the potato disease : proving what is so often proved, that none are so blind as those who will not see, and none so obstinate as those who quarrel with facts that seem to run counter to their interest. One was the Duke of Cambridge, the other the Duke of Rutland. The first was known for his habit of speaking to himself, and his frequent appearance at charity dinners ; the second was not known at all, except as a duke. The first almost pledged his royal word " that the report of a potato famine was a false one," and the second deplored the skyey influences at work in England, which made one person out of every three, what he termed a " croaker." Happy it was for these exalted personages that they were not likely to experience, in their own persons, the evil effects of a scarcity, which was not the less real, because, like hunted ostriches, they hid their lofty heads in holes, and refused to look at it. Unfortunately for the poor, there was no doubt on the mind of any one desirous of discovering the truth, that there was a most lamentable failure of the potato crop throughout the kingdom, and Europe generally; and if there were exaggeration, exaggeration was to have been expected. Serious calamities always appear larger than they are to the timid and the interested ; but in this case too much positive mischief remained indubitable to allow any scope for the efforts of the prejudiced or the heartless, who, on pretence of exaggeration, denied it altogether.

There is an old nursery rhyme, which states that

" The butcher and the baker
Both fell out of a rotten potato."

The aristocratic dealers in those commodities, which supply the trade of the butcher and the baker, were exactly in this predicament in 1845; but it was of no use quarrelling with their fate. They had to resign themselves to it. The potato did them no harm; it only put an end to the food monopoly.

The beginning of the end was at hand. Light had long been gradually breaking into the honest and solid but inert and slow mind of Sir Robert Peel. On the 4th of December, 1845, great political excitement was created in London and all the great cities, by an apparently authoritative announcement in the *Times*, that Sir Robert Peel had not only become a convert to the principles of Free Trade generally, but had resolved to propose, at the opening of Parliament in January, the total, immediate, and unconditional abolition of the Corn Laws; and that Sir Robert in the Commons, and the Duke of Wellington in the Lords, would publicly state the fact, and stake the existence of their administration on the passing of the measure.

Opinion was staggered by the announcement. Some people thought they were imposed upon by an elaborate hoax; and the Glasgow Tories denounced it, in plain, uncourteous speech, as a lie; and the Liberals, willing to believe, were yet afraid to give it credence. On the following day the *Times* repeated its assertion in two separate articles, so emphatically and seriously, that even the dismayed Protectionists could doubt no longer. It was generally believed that Ministers, after long hesitation, had resolved upon this course; and that it would lead to resignation of office by those members of the Cabinet who were either too ignorant to understand the urgency of the case, or too vain of their consistency in error to lend their aid to that paramount measure. Sir Robert Peel did well for his country by the act. There was no other course left open for him. He knew that the potato had destroyed the Corn Law; that his legislation had been even rottener than the unlucky esculent that smote it to the ground; and that if he did not make a virtue of necessity—one year—one little year, but full of trouble, anxiety, and distress—would have swept him from power and his party with him. But there were yet difficulties in the way. On the day that the *Times* made its memorable announcement, the Duke of Wellington and Sir Robert Peel were if not in very cordial, at all events, in substantial agreement as to the necessity of the course to be pursued. The Duke, however, if current reports were to be believed, was immediately assailed by the stanch Protectionists; by the real "croakers" of the Richmond, Rutland, and Norfolk school; and so wrought upon by them as to change his resolution, and inform his colleagues at a second Cabinet Council that he had seen cause to alter his purpose, and that he reverted to the position he had previously occupied of hostility to any change in the law. Upon this Sir Robert Peel declared that he could no longer carry on the Government; and on Saturday he proceeded to Osborne House on a visit to her Majesty. Lord John Russell was in Edinburgh at the time, and was to have been entertained in Glasgow on Friday the 12th at a grand civic banquet, and to receive the freedom of the municipality under the auspices of my friend, Mr. James Lumsden, an active politician, one of the proprietors of the *Argus*, and Lord Provost of the city. On Monday, the 8th, about ten o'clock at night, his lordship was about retiring to rest, at his hotel in Edinburgh, when a Queen's messenger, who had been sent express from Osborne, arrived with an autograph letter from her Majesty, requesting his immediate attendance in the Isle of Wight. Lord John, without retiring to rest, took his departure, and wrote from London to Mr. Lumsden, informing him that as he was unexpectedly commanded to attend upon the Queen, he could not then receive the compliment intended for him by the city of Glasgow.

With regard to the resignation of Sir Robert Peel, it was currently reported that the Duke of Wellington was backed by the majority of the Cabinet; and that three members only supported the policy of their chief, viz., Sir James Graham, Lord Wharncliffe, and the Earl of Aberdeen. For a few anxious days the questions were asked, Will Lord John Russell be able to form an administration on the basis of the question raised by Sir Robert Peel? If he forms such an administration, will Sir Robert lend him official or non-official support; and will the opposition of the Duke of Wellington be withdrawn? Will it be possible to carry the question without a dissolution of Parliament? If Lord John Russell refuse to take office, will an ultra-Protectionist Ministry be formed, with all the dukes in it? or will Sir Robert Peel resume office, and rid himself of the Duke of Wellington? As for Sir Robert Peel himself, many ungenerous persons expressed delight in a position in which they saw the fit punishment of his former transgressions and false pre-. tences. They did not think that no man could have made such sacrifices without a bitter struggle. Whatever his own disappointed party might say of him, the people generally gave him credit for honesty and courage, and in the eyes of the impartial world he stood in the high position of one who made the most painful sacrifices that it was possible for a man to make in support of what he believed to be the truth. Like Lord John Russell, he had recanted error; and resolved to the best of his ability to forward the right cause; but unlike Lord John Russell, who pleased his friends and his party by his recantation, Sir Robert Peel displeased both, and alienated from himself nearly all the friends with whom he had ever acted. Speculation was set at rest for a while by the announcement that Lord John Russell had accepted the task of forming an administration, of which the leading object should be the total abolition of the Corn Laws, by the aid of the actual Parliament if possible, or if that were impossible, by an appeal to the country. As the arrangements proceeded it was complained that the administration was not to be composed of the most popular materials that were available, and that somewhat too much of an aristocratic colouring pervaded it. The country would have been glad to have seen less of the Whig family alliance, and sturdier Liberalism in the more important offices. It would have rejoiced to see Mr. Cobden at the Board of Trade, or Mr. Villiers or Mr. Milner Gibson filling some of the many departments in the Ministry to which their services and talents entitled them to aspire. In omitting to strengthen his administration by such aid, Lord John Russell lost a great opportunity. If he had cordially identified himself and his party with the people generally—if he had relied upon the people, and chosen some of his colleagues from amongst their leaders—the people would have carried him safely through the dangers that beset him, and made him a more powerful Minister than his predecessor. But this was not to be. The family alliances that pervaded the proposed Cabinet, and the attempt to exclude Lord Palmerston from the Foreign Office, led to an inglorious collapse. The circumstances were well described in a letter written at the time by Mr. Alexander Mackay, author of the "Western World." He said—"The Russell Cabinet was and is not. It came suddenly upon us, an unexpected event, and has as suddenly vanished—a mere speck in history. The Peel Cabinets, antecedent and subsequent to it, have completely buried it in their common shadow. It blazed for a moment, like an *ignis fatuus*, and then became extinct. With Peel again in power, it is almost impossible now to realise the fact that, within the last fortnight, we have been living under a Whig administration. But so it has been, and the only prominent fact which that administration has left on record, is the melancholy one of its own utter want of vitality. There was pressure without; but, what was far more fatal, there were wounds within, which would not cicatrize. The disease was not one at the extremities—but a disease at the very heart, and, as in all similar cases, dissolution was both instantaneous and complete. Let it not be supposed, in what I here write, that I regard with regret the mere fact of the termination of the Whig Ministry. In every sense it was a desirable consummation, considering the precise position of affairs. But a desirable end

may be attained by faulty and reprehensible means.   The
Whig Cabinet fell from political fratricide, not from the
successful assaults of its foes.   The death-blow was dealt
by an aristocratic Whig [Earl Grey], whose crotchets
were too much for his patriotism.   It would have been a
noble and gratifying spectacle to all the advocates of a
liberal commercial policy, to have seen the new administration unanimous on the great point at issue between
parties; and then, when they surveyed the difficulties
around them, and became convinced of the utter impossi-
bility of carrying their measures, retiring upon that
understanding, and upon that alone.   There could then
have been but one issue for the country to determine, and
in determining that the whole Free Trade force of the
country would have arrayed itself in a formidable phalanx,
for the reinstatement in power of the retiring Cabinet.
In the meantime a new Government would have been
formed, either with Peel or Buckingham at its head—no
matter which.   With a Whig Government in the back-
ground, on whose unanimity and cordiality Free Traders
might have relied, Peel would have been virtually as
unacceptable as Buckingham.   But where now is this
Cabinet?   It no longer presents an unbroken front.   It
is defunct and dispersed, and the Liberals of the country
must try what they can manage to squeeze out of Sir
Robert Peel.   To Earl Grey belongs the honour, and on
him should fall the *odium* of the disruption of Lord John's
Cabinet.   It is a pity that, at this time of day, we should
have to record such things of him, who, as Viscount
Howick, in the House of Commons, took so early, so
unequivocal, and so manly a stand for the total repeal of

the Corn Laws. He is, however, one of those unfortunately impracticable men, who, though clear in judgment, are wrong-headed and obstinate when called on to act. Earl Grey was to have taken upon himself the duties of Colonial Secretary in the new Cabinet, a post which entitled him to advise, but not to dictate. He chose, however, to do the latter, and his obstinacy has cost the Whigs their newly acquired places. He objected to Lord Palmerston as Foreign Secretary, and rent the Cabinet asunder, by insisting that that should be done which could not be done. What is the party, what is the country to think of such conduct as this?"

Upon the failure of the Whigs—considered a very egregious and unnecessary one—Sir Robert Peel was again sent for by the Queen, and consented to resume office; and the Duke of Wellington, knowing how to yield as well as how to conquer, consented to waive his theoretical objections to Free Trade, and assist his bolder colleague in carrying a measure which at last he saw to be inevitable. Lord Stanley was the sole dissentient, and retired from the Colonial Office, to be succeeded by Mr. W. E. Gladstone, then a young statesman, in the thirty-sixth year of his age. In other respects, the changes were unimportant. There yet remained three weeks before the meeting of Parliament, during which time both the Free Traders and the Protectionists prepared themselves vigorously for the work of political agitation: the one party to afford all possible aid to Sir Robert Peel, and the other to use every possible effort to embarrass and thwart him. The Anti-Corn-Law League resolved to raise a further subscription of a quarter of a million sterling to fight the battle of Free Trade, in case Sir Robert Peel should introduce a partial or imperfect measure, and be defeated in the then existing Parliament, if he proposed unconditional repeal. To this munificent sum the Free Traders of Glasgow contributed, as the result of one great public meeting, about 10,000*l.*; Liverpool contributed upwards of 13,000*l.*; the people of the West Riding of Yorkshire, at a meeting in Leeds, contributed 34,000*l.*; and Edinburgh, Dundee, Manchester, Sheffield, Birmingham and other great towns and cities in like magnificent proportion.

At the opening of Parliament, Sir Robert Peel, in a manly and impressive speech, announced his complete adhesion to Free Trade principles, and explained the facts which led to his retirement from office, and his re-acceptance of it, after Lord John Russell's failure to form a Ministry. At the commencement of November, when his mind had already begun to doubt the wisdom of the Corn Laws, and to be more and more assured of the wisdom of every advance in the direction of Free Trade, which he had carried or sanctioned, the failure of the potato crop in Ireland opened his eyes to the consequences of a longer persistence in an erroneous system of legislation. He proposed to his colleagues the opening of the ports and a permanent change in the Corn Laws. He was outvoted in the Council; and the subject was postponed for three weeks. During these three weeks Lord John Russell published a memorable letter to the electors of London, declaring his adhesion to Free Trade in corn, and hurried the solution of the great problem. Sir Robert Peel, on the re-assembling of his colleagues, brought forward his former proposition—was again out-voted—and resigned office. Sir Robert Peel's speech was a touching confession of past error, which earned for him the gratitude and esteem of all sensible and unpre-judiced men. One by one he took up all the arguments that he had formerly used in defence of the Corn Laws, and showed, from the results of his own more enlarged experience, how untenable and how rotten they were, and demolished every vestige of a reason for the longer con-tinuance of the system. Every one of right feeling sym-pathised with him in his noble, yet painful, position; and some good men, who were still opposed to his policy, did justice to the loftiness and purity of his motives, and appreciated the unexampled sacrifices he had made for the cause that he believed to be the right one.

The Duke of Wellington, as was expected, explained in the House of Lords the reasons that had led him, contrary to his first judgment, to lend the aid of his great name to the Prime Minister. He supported Sir Robert Peel, and would support him;—not because he under-stood his policy, but because he had confidence in him, admired his spirit, and would do anything for him—no matter on what side of the Corn Law, or of any other question, if by so doing he could but maintain the Ministry in a firm position. Sir Robert wrote to him in the country, informing 'him of the circumstances, and stating that if he did resume office, he had determined, happen what might—if he stood alone—that, as the Minister of the Crown, he would enable her Majesty to meet her Parliament. The Duke highly applauded his right hon. friend on that occasion, and determined that

he for one would stand by him.  He felt it his duty ;
and thought the formation of a Government in which
her Majesty should have full confidence was of greater
importance than any opinions of any individual upon the
Corn Law or any other law.  He knew, to use his own
words, "that in standing by Sir R. Peel, in the resump-
tion of his Government, he must be a party to the proposition for a material alteration of the Corn Laws.  He felt
that it could not be otherwise.  He knew it, and he did it."

The *Argus* wrote apropos of the Duke's explanation :—
" Sir R. Peel should think himself happy in having such
a friend as the Duke.  It is an inexplicable kind of
friendship, it is true.  The men are very different ; but
in friendship, as in love, one person will sometimes form
a strong attachment for another for the possession of
qualities the most opposite to his own.  A thin man often
likes a corpulent wife ; and a very small lady will not
unfrequently fix her affections upon a dragoon of six feet
six :—so is it with Wellington and Peel.  The man who
does not study—who jumps to conclusions instinctively—
who sees nothing but broad, clear, plain, large facts ;—
who goes straight to his object, right or wrong ;—and
who would snatch a victory rather than negotiate one, is
the stanch, unflinching friend, and ever has been, in
public and private life, of the man who thinks and reasons,
and arrives at his conclusions by logical process—who
sees small facts and the secret springs of large machinery
—who takes a round-about course if a straight one will
not answer—and who would rather resort to diplomacy
than to the strong arm.  Certainly the reason for this
friendship will be a curious problem for the solution of

the future historian or psychologist; but we in the present day have merely to take the fact as it stands, and if we belong to the Free-Trade party, to rejoice in it;—as for our own part we do most cordially."

There was considerable doubt whether Sir Robert Peel would be able to carry any Free-Trade measure through the existing Parliament, though the ministerial and opposition whips of the day both seemed to reckon upon a ministerial majority, ranging between forty and fifty. The fear was that the Opposition in the House of Lords would not be satisfied with any decision of the old Parliament, and without an appeal to the country. The Duke of Richmond emphatically declared that whatever the Commons might do, the Lords would throw out the bill—that for his part he was not " over sensitive," and that " he would use every means, even factious means, if necessary, to defeat it." The papers of the party followed the lead, and became all but rabid in abuse of their former chief. He was called "Jerry Sneak," "Jim Crow," and " Judas Iscariot." His speech was declared to be " Peel rot," to be full of "fraudulent plausibilities," " vulgar egotisms," " nauseous untruth," and " unprecedented effrontery."

Sir Robert's measure, when propounded to the House, dissatisfied the Free-Trade party, inasmuch as he proposed to adjourn its operation for three years, to give the landowners and farmers time to prepare for the change. But it was not only the Free Traders who objected to the delay, but many farmers and landowners, who, being aware that Free Trade sooner or later must inevitably become law, came to the conclusion that, like a surgical

operation, it would be better done quickly than delayed.
Many of the farmers, so far from being frightened as they
were a few months previously at the bare proposal of a
repeal, were of Mr. Cobden's opinion, that it would be
much better for their interests if the repeal were immediate. An extensive agriculturist, Mr. Paget, of Rud-
dington Grange, addressed the landlords of the United
Kingdom, through the columns of the *Mark Lane Express*, endeavouring to prove to them, as Mr. Cobden
had done, that it would be for their advantage to have an
immediate rather than a delayed repeal. The *Mark
Lane Express*, long the farmer's oracle, was of the same
opinion, and so far turned its back on the Protectionists
as to decline giving any further reports of their meetings.
The *Banker's Circular*—long an obstinate Protectionist—
preferred Mr. Cobden's proposal to Sir Robert Peel's.
Marvellous, indeed, were the events of the time;—and
marvellously rapid was the progress of reason. The old
hag of Monopoly, who might long have withstood the
assaults of her enemies, seemed to be dying of spontaneous combustion; and while her opponents were
looking for a fierce and protracted conflict, she doggedly
gave up the struggle and lay down to die.

Lord John Russell, in an excellent speech, in which
he again slew the often slain fallacies of the Protectionists, expressed himself in favour of immediate abolition,
and urgently requested Sir Robert Peel to reconsider
that part of his measure which postponed it for three
years. Mr. Sidney Herbert, afterwards to acquire so
much renown as a minister and statesman, and who at
that time held office under Sir Robert Peel, delivered a

speech which had an electric effect upon the House. In language of so much eloquence, truthfulness, and sincerity, as were sure to win for him the respect and admiration of the country, he confessed his past mistakes and misconceptions. He admitted that a repeal of the Corn Laws would have come more suitably from Lord John Russell than from Sir Robert Peel; and was prepared to have given his cordial support to the noble lord, had he undertaken the settlement of the question. His own opinion had been slowly, reluctantly, deliberately changed, in obedience to a sense of duty; and at a time when public opinion was so much enlightened, he felt it better to yield to reason NOW what might be extorted by violence hereafter. He ridiculed the idea of the "Constitution," or even the Tory party, being in any way involved—denied that Protection was an "institution," and denounced the original enactment of a Corn Law as the greatest error that was ever committed by any government in this country—a denunciation as true and beautifully said as it seemed to be sincere, and which was received in the House with a general burst of acclamation.

But the most important speech delivered during the course of the often adjourned debate was, as was to have been expected, that of Sir Robert Peel himself. The great minister began his masterly oration by reminding the House that the question for them to consider was, not how a party was to be conducted, but how a great public calamity was to be averted; and how the future intercourse of Great Britain with the nations of the earth was to be regulated. He frankly admitted that,

as regarded his party, his measures were bad,—and confessed that it was unfortunate that other hands than
his had not been entrusted with the task of proposing
and carrying them. He believed, however, that there
was impending over the country a calamity which was
perfectly appalling; and whilst there was a hope of
averting it, he did not think it consistent with his duty
as a public man to evade the difficulty which he saw approaching. He had not a word to say against the explanation which Lord John Russell had made a few
nights previously; but he read a letter to her Majesty,
written whilst Lord John Russell was engaged in the
task of endeavouring to form an administration, from
which it appeared that he had offered not only his individual aid, but his whole influence, to her Majesty and
her new advisers, in carrying out the Free Trade principles
which Lord John Russell was to have proposed. His
own impression was, that if Lord John Russell had
undertaken the Government the cause of Free Trade
would have been successful; and he much regretted that
the noble Lord had not done so. He quoted letters from
Ireland to show the awful nature of the pending calamity
in that country, and put it to the friends of Protection,
whether it would not have been a wise course to have
opened the ports, and whether, if they had been once
opened, it would have been in the power of any Parliament or any Ministry ever again to have closed them.
He admitted to the party which had honoured him with
its support, that it was entitled to withhold from him its
confidence. But he asked whether it was likely that he
should have voluntarily sacrificed its support, unless he

had been influenced by strong motives of public duty? Be the consequences to himself what they might, he would avow that his party could not rob him of the conviction, that the advice which he had given to his Sovereign and the Parliament was consistent with all the duty which he owed to that party. In fact, he avowed, that he would ever remember with pride the advice he had given on the 1st of November that the ports should be opened, and conjured the House to drop its personalities, and consider only whether the measure proposed was right, irrespective altogether of their opinion of the man or men who proposed it.

At last, on the 28th of February, at three o'clock in the morning, after a debate which lasted through twelve nights, a preliminary victory was won. The House of Commons decided by 337 votes against 240— a majority of 97—in favour of going into committee. By this division the end was clearly foreshadowed. The commerce of Great Britain was virtually set free, and the toiling millions received the certain promise of justice at the hands of a once prejudiced aristocracy. But the end was not yet. The bill had to pass through the perils, not only of the committee, but of the second and third readings—and not only the perils of the Commons, but those that might prove more formidable of the House of Lords. The immediate joy of the Free Trade party throughout the country was great, especially in Manchester and Glasgow; and the number of the *Argus* that announced the victory endeavoured to give expression to the general satisfaction in the following terms :—

"A great revolution has been peacefully achieved; a revolution unstained by bloodshed—having for its object no dethronement of a dynasty, no substitution of one tyranny in the place of another—having no punishment, no harshness, no evil of any kind in its composition—was wrought by discussion alone, and by the inherent and irresistible powers of Truth and Justice. As a nation, we may well be proud of the great example we have, by this act, set the whole of the world, by most or all of the civilised nations of which, there is every reason to believe, it will soon be imitated. Its influence who shall calculate? Who shall say what cruel estrangement between classes in our own country it will remedy? Who shall tell the national jealousies, the sanguinary wars, it shall prevent, and the increase of knowledge, civilisation, wealth, and happiness of which it shall be the prolific parent? France, that has looked with admiring eyes upon the preparations for the deed, will approve it with joy, now that it is done, and prepare, by the convictions of her most eminent statesmen, to do as much for her own people at no distant period. The full knowledge which the thinking men of Germany possessed, when the first announcement of Sir Robert Peel's conversion reached them, that his proposal could have but one result, and that, success, has prepared them for it; and events have already shown that the Zollverein has not escaped the influence of these opinions, and that it will shortly become a corporation of Free Traders. The packet that on Wednesday next will carry the tidings over the Atlantic will be a messenger of peace and goodwill to millions of our brethren, and turn their thoughts from war into peace; while, amongst our own people, the poor, unhappy labourers of Dorsetshire and Wiltshire will share the joy of busy Birmingham and princely Manchester, and all the neighbouring hives of enterprise and industry; the largest landowners of Great Britain will rejoice that their order is no longer in collision with the necessities and the justice of the time. The Queen, who so gracefully and kindly performs her exalted functions, will have cause of thankfulness that in her reign the cause which she is known to favour has achieved so brilliant and so peaceful a triumph; and even those who now look upon the measure as one pregnant with evil, will share a benefit which they do not yet understand, and which we most sincerely hope they will all live to be thankful for.

" Though the victory is virtually won, the struggle is not at an end. It is deprived, however, of its bitterness. It has been demonstrated to be hopeless; and though, for form's sake, and in consequence of many personal necessities or party entanglements, it must yet be carried on through all the various stages of the bill, it is consoling to reflect that the intensity of the struggle must diminish from day to day; and that, when these measures receive the royal assent, those who now doubt will have become convinced; and those who condemn will have become resigned—and the Lords themselves, if not very hopeful, at all events will have learned not to despond."

The joyous anticipations of this article have been all fulfilled as regards the British people; but not as regards France, Germany, and the United States, which still, in

spite of our triumphant example, cling with more or less
of pertinacy to the old ideas and fallacies of Protection.
But even these are yielding—slowly it may be, but
surely—to the unanswerable logic of the Free Trade
philosophy.

The original purpose of Sir Robert Peel was to repeal
the Corn Laws gradually, and to impose a sliding scale
for three years.   Mr. Charles Villiers brought forward a
motion for immediate abolition, which was rejected by
265 against 78.   The debate was rendered interesting by
the announcement on the part of Mr. Bright, that
while a remnant of the Corn Laws existed on the statute
book, the League would exist to combat it.   This declaration, which came appropriately from the impetuous Mr.
Bright, somewhat startled his more philosophical and
cautious colleague Mr. Cobden.   But he also agreed in
the policy and expediency of his friend's announcement
—arguing that in the then temper of the Protectionists
there would be no security during the proposed three
years of the sliding scale, that they would not attempt to
render the new system perpetual, and that it was therefore necessary to keep up the machinery of the League
to prevent mischief.   Mr. Bright jumped to this conclusion intuitively.   Mr. Cobden argued himself into it ;
and both were in the right.

During the whole period of the discussions, until the
bill finally passed to the House of Lords, a constant
volley of complaint was fired by the Protectionist press
and Protectionist speakers—that the all but countless
petitions presented in favour of Free Trade were not in
reality signed by a half or a third of the numbers whose

names purported to be appended to them, and that such petitions were frauds upon Parliament. It was conveniently forgotten by the Protectionists that the more truly popular a question is, the more is the right of petition likely to be abused by the frolicsome, the mischievous, and the unthinking. Butcher boys, of whom some of the anti-free-traders made loud complaint, *will*, upon occasions when a petition lies for signature at the corner of a street, try their powers of penmanship; and the waggish *will* sign with names which do not belong to them, and even take liberties with the titles of the peerage, if they happen to have heard of them. But, with all these drawbacks, a petition, signed by ten or twenty thousand persons, is not to be invalidated for such reasons, unless the right of petition be altogether abolished, and the very members who raised objections to such petitions against their own side, would not have had a word to say if all the butcher boys of a town had signed their names thrice to the same petition in their favour.

A little incident occurred about this time in Glasgow, which reflected some discredit upon a once great name, and which proved, moreover, that it was not only members of the Conservative, but of the Liberal party, who were slow to become converts to the principles of Free Trade. In January, before the House of Commons had resolved to go into committee on the bill, a meeting of Glasgow weavers, and of the working classes of the suburban villages of Springburn, Auchenairn, and Bishop Bridge, was held to petition against the Corn Laws. The meeting was chiefly attended by working men;—and the

chairman, one Robert Sinclair, was a weaver of Springburn. The petition, unanimously adopted by them, was
well and even eloquently written, and told some home
truths of the Corn Law system in honest and fearless
language. The petitioners " begged leave to lay before the
Lords Spiritual and Temporal in Parliament assembled,
a simple but honest statement of their severe and pressing grievances, arising from a system of political impolicy
which had been persisted in for a long series of years.
They had, however, the satisfaction to find that the sentiments and opinions in which they expressed themselves
many years past, regarding the cruel and iniquitous
system of taxing the food of man, and throwing barriers
in the way of the free interchange of commodities with
their fellow men in other climes, were now seriously considered by every class in the community. The humble
operative, the middle-class employer, and the high and
titled statesman, had at last found out that they were
right when they told the House in their petitions at repeated times, during the last thirty years, that the corn
and provision laws were a foul blot upon the statute-book
of Great Britain, an outrage upon common sense, a disgrace and a libel upon the intelligent and progressive
progress of the policy of the present age.

" The petitioners were convinced, that to delay any
longer the repeal of the corn and provision laws would
prove ruinous to the commercial and manufacturing
interests of the country, and to all classes of the community, and, more particularly, to the petitioners, who
were then suffering at an inclement season of the year
all the misery and wretchedness which are the con-

comitants of ill-paid toil and high-priced provisions, which have been raised fifty per cent. in consequence of the failure of the potato crop, the staple food of your petitioners for at least eight months in the year. *Hence it is the opinion of your petitioners that no time should be lost in eradicating from the statute-book of this country those laws which are the cause of poverty, starvation, crime, disease, and death amongst them, and consequently ruin and desolation throughout the various ramifications of society.*"

This petition was entrusted for presentation to the Commons by Mr. Denniston, member for Glasgow; and to Lord Brougham—selected for the honour on account of his long services to the liberal cause—for presentation to the Lords. Mr. Denniston, as in duty bound to a portion of his constituents, and agreeing with their opinions, presented and supported the petition. Lord Brougham never even acknowledged the receipt of the document, and never presented it. This want of courtesy somewhat astonished the weavers of Glasgow, who naturally thought that, with all his eccentricities, Lord Brougham practised that very common rule of answering every business letter. Lord Brougham, however, had other notions. He did not practise this rule, but left it to the Duke of Wellington, Sir Robert Peel, Sir James Graham, and all the gentlemen of Great Britain, who invariably act upon it. The chairman of the meeting having waited a long time, and fearing it might have miscarried, looked with some interest through the newspapers to see whether any allusion was made to it in the House of Lords. He at last discovered a passage in the

Parliamentary reports, in which Lord Brougham stated that he had received a petition from some place (unmentioned) alleging that the Corn Laws were the cause of poverty, starvation, crime, disease, and death ; and that he would RATHER PUT HIS HAND INTO THE FIRE UNTIL IT WAS CONSUMED, THAN TOUCH SUCH A PETITION. As the weavers knew full well that the Corn Laws *were* the causes of those calamities, and that they had said so in their petition, they naturally concluded that it was their petition of which the eccentric lord had so much horror. The chairman accordingly addressed the following letter to him :—

"TO THE RIGHT HONOURABLE LORD BROUGHAM AND VAUX.

"My Lord,

"By the instructions of my constituents, seeing that you have returned no answer to the letter which I transmitted to you, accompanied with a petition for presentation to the Lords Spiritual and Temporal, praying for an immediate repeal of the corn and provision laws, now whether your lordship has received the said petition or not I am at a loss to know, as I have got no immediate answer from you, which I think, in common courtesy betwixt man and man, I should have received. However, my constituents and I obtained information through the press, that your lordship found fault with the humble manner in which the language of our petition was couched ; and that your lordship had stated before the right honourable house, that you ' would rather put your hand in the fire until it was consumed, than touch that foul document,' which, I am led to believe, was our petition, because it contained that sentence which stated that the corn and provision laws were the cause of poverty, starvation, crime, disease, and death. Now, my lord, your humble petitioners had no intention of offending your lordship by any uncouth language, which emanating from working men, ought, I think, to have weighed in the balance of your master mind, which has stamped your lordship as one of the brightest political and literary luminaries of the present age. But allow me, my lord, to state to your lordship, that I am no nice discriminator of the language which ought to be used in stating just grievances, or that necessary punctilio which I ought to use in expressing my sentiments and my sufferings, when addressing myself to one so far removed above my humble sphere in life as your lordship; however this may be, my lord, I will affirm, that, as a working man, I must be the best judge of what I suffer, what I see, and what I feel, from the effects of these heaven-accursed corn and provision laws; and I will attempt to prove to your lordship that poverty, starvation, crime, disease, and death, do really proceed from the effects of these baneful enactments. Dare your lordship deny that the corn laws do not enhance the price of food? and is it not an undeniable fact, that the wages of the class to which I belong have long since been reduced to the starving point of existence by the effects of these laws? Now, my lord, is not poverty one of the great causes of crime, and does not starvation generate disease, and is not disease the precursor of death? I am not, however, my lord, directed to argue these subjects with you, I have only to request your answer; and as your lordship has not thought proper to present our petition, you will very much oblige your very obedient and humble servant by returning our petition to my address, ROBERT SINCLAIR, weaver, Springburn, Glasgow.—Feb. 4, 1846."

Lord Brougham never answered the letter. Upon this occasion the *Argus* observed, "It augured a want of knowledge of the noble lord's character in Mr. Sinclair, to expect that he would perform an act of gentlemanly and ordinary courtesy to a weaver, or indeed to any person whatever not moving in the narrow circle to which his lordship thinks it proper to confine the civilities which are essential between man and man. We trust the working classes will for the future be better advised; and that they will let his lordship alone. He is not their man, nor any body's man; and will never again be of service to their cause or to any other. Some people exist who entertain a respect for the eloquent and honest Henry Brougham of fifteen years ago, but their number is daily diminishing; and not a few of those who remain incline to the belief, that the real Brougham was killed at Penrith, some five years ago, by the upsetting of his carriage, as was announced in all the London papers at the time; and that the person who at present represents himself as the identical Brougham, is a sort of Perkin Warbeck, assuming a title that does not belong to him."

The discussion on the third reading of the Corn Law Abolition Bill commenced on Monday the 11th of May. The opposition was led by the Marquis of Granby, who moved the reading of the Bill that day six months. His

speech was only remarkable for a poor parody on Shakspeare, in which he designated Lord George Bentinck—
who had made himself conspicuous by his hostility
to Sir Robert Peel—as the future leader of the Conservative party, and called upon his faithful adherents to
cry,

"God for the Queen, for England and Lord George!"

The most remarkable speech in favour of the third
reading, was that of Sir James Graham, who adverted to
the progress of opinion in Parliament on the Corn Law
question, as a criterion for the fit appreciation of the
recent measures of Government. The Protectionist
party, he said, seemed to argue the question of Free
Trade as though the producers only were to be consulted,
whereas it was notorious that a larger and more important
class had to be considered. That class was the people,
and their interests were bound up with the abolition of
commercial restrictions. Referring to the Irish question,
he repeated his conviction of the want and misery prevailing in that part of the empire, but avowed his belief
that sufficient reasons, beside the state of Ireland,
justified the adoption of the Free Trade policy of the
Government. He also adverted to the foolish and selfish
fears of the landlords, and defied any change of the law
to make worse the condition of the labourers. The
debate continued for three nights, and at four o'clock on
the morning of the 16th of May, the Bill passed the
Commons by a majority of ninety-eight. On the motion
of the Duke of Wellington—a great power not alone in
himself, but on account of the proxies in his pocket—

the Bill was read a first time in the Lords on the 19th
of May, with but little discussion, its opponents reserving
themselves for the second reading, to open the flood-
gates of their discontent. Such opposition as there was
was confined to the Duke of Richmond.

Although the Duke of Wellington was in his place—
although Lord Ripon, the original author of the Corn
Law of thirty years previously, was in his place also—and
although both these noble personages had changed their
opinions with reference to it, the Duke of Richmond had
not a word to say to them. They were there to answer
—but the Duke of Richmond was not anxious to be
answered. Sir R. Peel was not present—he could not reply
—he could be abused in safety—and he became, therefore, the sole object of attack. His Grace flatly accused
Sir Robert Peel of " dishonour," though he took care
afterwards to make the qualification that he was only
" publicly," not " privately," dishonourable. Lord
Brougham entered his solemn protest against such an
expression, and read the Duke a lesson on his own
political gyrations from one side to the other on
the Reform question. The Duke of Richmond, apparently somewhat nettled, denied that he had ever opposed
the Reform Bill. The Marquis of Londonderry also
entreated him to confine himself to the merits of the
question; and gave him an additional reminder, that
reproaches for change of opinion came with a very
ill grace from one who had changed so often as himself.
The Duke, in his reply, made the gratifying announcement, that he had exhausted all his personalities the
first night, intending for the future to devote himself

entirely to a more legitimate opposition. Lord Ripon expressed his satisfaction at the promise, not only on general grounds, but on his own private account, implying that, if personalities were to be bandied about, he, the author of the obnoxious law, would, if any rule of proportion were observed, come in for a larger share than Sir R. Peel himself—an implication which the House received with much good-humour and considerable merriment.

Prior to the second reading and with the object of strengthening the opposition of their lordships, the Central Society for the Protection of Agriculture, held a meeting at Willis's Rooms, which was graced by the presence of the Dukes of Richmond and Buckingham, Lord Beaumont, Lord George Bentinck, and others equally well known for their strong opinions on the question. "No concession" and "No surrender" were the cries adopted, and the speakers indignantly denied that the tenant-farmers as a body had been convinced by the reasoning of the League, or had ceased to fear that the repeal of the Corn Laws would be the ruin of England. A good deal of indignation was also vented upon Sir Robert Peel, but the speakers took especial care to say nothing harsh of the Duke of Wellington, who, if guilt there were, was at all events equally as guilty as the Prime Minister of changing his opinions and betraying his party. A Mr. Bull, of Cambridgeshire, specially exempted the Duke from blame, though upon what grounds it was difficult to discover. He stated "that the only mode in which the Bill could be carried in the House of Lords would be by *abusing* the influence of the name of the Duke of Wellington —*a name most dear to the whole country, and which none but a base and falling party would venture to make use of for such despicable and unconstitutional purposes.*" A Mr. Allnatt of Berkshire "proclaimed his firm reliance on Lord George Bentinck — THAT GREAT MAN whom Providence itself, *still smiling on them,* seemed to have selected as the champion and firm defence of British agriculture." The most curious assertion, however, that was made during the proceedings, was by a Mr. Healey from Lincolnshire, who said "that the farmers were a century ahead of their landlords, and two centuries ahead of the landlords' stewards." This elicited considerable merriment; but there was more truth in it than the meeting was aware of. Landlords dreaded the repeal of the Corn Laws; but the farmers had so little to fear of injury to their business that not one farm in the whole country was known to have let for a less sum in consequence of the impending change, while very many had let at increased rentals.

The *Standard* newspaper, as the organ of the Protectionists, was enraptured with the meeting, and wrote with uncontrolled delight of the *manly strength and beauty* of the farmers that attended it, asserting, at the same time, their intellectual to be equal to their physical superiority over Free Traders. It did not, however, mention, even by a line of report, that on the very same day a meeting still more significant was held in another part of the country, — a meeting of a totally different character composed of men equally in earnest, and having as great

a stake in the prosperity of the country as those who
assembled under the presidency of the Duke of Richmond. That meeting was held at Manchester, and was
composed of the members of the Chamber of Commerce
of that city; men of all shades of political opinion
—men averse from agitation—men who desired nothing
better than to spend, as they usually did, hundreds of
thousands of pounds per week in wages, but who knew
that the rejection of the Ministerial measure would re-
duce many a busy hive of industry to a bankruptcy of
owners, and the destitution of operatives; and who feared
that even the delay in passing it would be productive of
the most injurious consequences.

The debate in the Lords on the second reading was
animated; and all the speeches delivered in its support
were worthy of the occasion, especially those of Lord
Grey, Lord Dalhousie, Lord Lansdowne, and the
Duke of Wellington. Not a fallacy, not an error, that
had been brought forward, not a fear that had been
expressed, that was not met by one or other of these
speakers, and triumphantly refuted. The speech of
the Duke of Wellington was of a different kind. It
did not go into the arguments of the case, but boldly
and honestly met all difficulties by an assertion in
which the nation acquiesced, that he and his colleagues acted from a sense of imperative duty—and
that he, for his part, so far from regretting what he
had done, would, under similar circumstances, if again
placed in them, act in the same manner. Clear, unequivocal, and manly, the words of the illustrious
Duke not only gave satisfaction and inspired respect

for his character throughout the country, but influenced such of the Peers as were still wavering, and helped to increase the numbers of the final majority.

The second reading was carried by a majority of forty-seven, to the great disgust of such members of the Conservative press as had not seen fit to follow the lead of Peel and Wellington, and had cast in their lot with Lord George Bentinck and his lieutenant, Mr. Disraeli. The *Morning Herald*, now defunct, and the *Standard*, still alive under new auspices and conditions, were particularly wroth. The *Herald* discovered that the Lords in the majority for Free Trade were chiefly of paupers! —lords having no houses — impoverished men, having nothing to lose.

" The majority of the Lords," said that journal "would do well to ' put their house in order '—we mean the House of Lords (for *few of the majority rejoice in the possession of private mansions*)—for the end is not distant. The PAUPER PEERS, by whose votes the industrious classes of Englishmen are to be ruined, have, it is true, *little or nothing to lose*, but they have thrown away that little or nothing. \*\*\*\* The Free Trade lords generally have nothing—true, but they are throwing away that nothing. Name and privilege are properly nothing; but they are the little all of our pauper Peers, and this little all they throw away."

This must have been rare news to such men as the Dukes of Sutherland, Hamilton, Wellington, Bedford, and Devonshire; and Earls Fitzwilliam, Essex, Derby, and other paupers with unencumbered estates of a plum or two a-year. But the *Herald*, not satisfied with taunt-

ing these Peers with their poverty, called out for a reform
in their House, in which cry the writer was joined by his
*confrère* of the *Standard*. The latter journal, which
formerly would have worshipped a lord, had other notions
as soon as a majority of the Lords became converts
to Free Trade—and Fergus O'Connor himself could not
have spoken of them in more disparaging terms, than
were employed in that aristocratic sheet :—

" The struggle," says the *Standard*, " is suspended for
the present. The Corn Bill was read in the House of
Lords, by a majority of 47—*more than we anticipated,
because we thought well of the House of Lords.* We hope
their lordships will accept the apology, *though to be
thought well of by any one cannot be much the object
of their ambition.* The Duke of Wellington, in the
unhappy speech in which he apologised for pressing
the measure on the House, hinted that it is not irrevocable. This is true, *the measure is not irrevocable ;
and as sure as the sun shall rise upon the year* 1850,
*it will have been revoked before that year, but not re-
voked until it shall have occasioned such wide-spread
desolation, and such tremendous danger as this country
has never experienced—a ruin, of which a national bankruptcy will not be the greatest evil !* But though the
Bill will be repealed, what is to repair the tattered
reputation of the Houses of Parliament, as was so
eloquently said by the Earl of Eglinton, at the
close of his splendid speech — ' I would remind your
lordships that though laws may be re-enacted and
statutes repealed, CHARACTER ONCE GONE CAN NEVER
BE REGAINED. I beseech your lordships not to permit

this House *to share in the general degradation which the ill-omened measure before it has brought upon the character of British statesmen, and which, I fear, will cast a foul blot on our time, in the eyes of future generations.'*

" This is the great and the permanent evil inflicted upon the constitution, but even this will bring a compensation—*a Radical Reform of the House of Lords*, and as the effect of that reform, an extinction for ever of the red tape school of politicians, and their dry nurses, the sect of political economists."

It is amusing, more than a quarter of a century after the event, to look back upon these gloomy forebodings and absurd predictions of evil; so triumphantly falsified in every particular; and pleasant at the same time, when the violence of party feeling in those days is compared with the calmer agitations of our own—to reflect on the improvement which time has operated in the conditions of public life and parliamentary controversy.

The third reading of the Bill was carried by a sweeping majority, on the very night in June when the Peel administration was defeated on the Irish Coercion Bill by a majority of 292 against 219. The vote in the Commons led to the resignation of the Peel Ministry, at the very time when its Free Trade policy received the final sanction of the Upper House. With regard to the Free Trade discussions, it was felt as soon as the measure had received the royal assent, that the British people, all things considered, had true reason to rejoice at the character of their institutions, and their efficiency for meeting every question that might arise, when a change so momentous had been effected in a manner so strictly constitutional. Heats and animosities there were; severance of political and private friendship there were also—crimination, and recrimination, and much more than the usual malignity of party-spirit—but, upon the whole, considering the magnitude, no less than the suddenness of the change, and the inappropriateness of the instruments by which it was wrought, there was much less irritation than might have been expected. Two very striking results were especially noticed as worthy of public approval—and, indeed, of national congratulation; firstly, the entireness and cordiality of the support given to Sir Robert Peel by the great Whig and Liberal party whom he supplanted in power; and, secondly, the calm good sense—the rational dignity and the true wisdom with which the House of Lords avoided the error which it would have fallen into, if on a question so peculiar it had placed itself in opposition to the other branch of the Legislature.

The *Glasgow Argus*, in commenting upon the result, expressed itself as follows in a passage that proved to be prophetic :—

" The British nation may indeed be proud of itself. It has set a great example to mankind. It has proved the value of free institutions in a manner more striking than this age or any other has seen; and it has entered upon a new course of policy which will change the face of the world—promote the free intercourse of nations; and give a mighty impetus to the progress of civilisation. The year in which it was accomplished will be memorable in the history of the world, and the reign of the Sovereign—who is known to approve of it from heart and from conviction, and not to accept it coldly as a necessity of state—will be rendered illustrious in all future times by this triumph, even had it no other to shed a glory upon it.

"Never, in fact, has the power of truth to conquer error been more beautifully exhibited than in the origin, progress, and triumph of this cause; and the day is coming, we fervently trust, that even the minority in both Houses will confess to themselves, if not to the public, that their fears were groundless—their calculations built on false data—their reasoning unsound—and all their policy erroneous. The national well-being increasing with the freedom of trade will, it is to be hoped, convince them of their error, and make them participators, not in a ruin of which they have so eloquently and affectingly spoken, but of a prosperity which at present they may think Utopian to imagine, but which they will then be convinced of by the surest of calculations—that of actual experience."

On the 29th of June the resignation of the Peel administration, consequent upon the hostile vote of the Commons on their Irish policy, was announced by the Duke of Wellington in the House of Lords, and by Sir Robert Peel in the House of Commons. Sir Robert made a forcible and eloquent vindication of his conduct, not so much to justify himself to his party, for he knew that such men as Lord George Bentinck, Mr. Disraeli, and others, who had attacked, and continued to attack, him with personal, rather than political, bitterness, would accept no justification which he could make, but to set himself right, once for all, with his country, with men

who soared above party, and, most of all, with posterity.
He contemptuously thrust aside the insinuation that love
of power and place had been the motive of his actions;
declared that the object of his ministry in the repeal of
the Corn Laws was to avert dangers which were imminent,
and to terminate a political conflict which, according to
the belief of himself and his colleagues, was calculated to
place in hostile collision great and powerful classes in the
country.   The maintenance of himself and friends in
power was not a motive, for he knew that whether accompanied by success or failure, the certain issue would be
the downfall of his administration.   Smarting perhaps a
little, under the attacks of the chiefs of the great party,
that he had once led, he ignored altogether the aristocratic
friends who had aided in the accomplishment of the great
work—forgot even the Honourable C. P. Villiers, who was
a pillar of the cause before the name of Mr. Cobden was
ever heard of—and said, in words that have become
historical, " The name that ought to be associated with
the success of these measures is not the name of the
noble lord (Lord John Russell), the organ of the party of
which he is the leader, nor is it mine.   The name which
ought to be, and will be, associated with the success of
those measures, is the name of one who, acting, I believe,
from pure and disinterested motives, has, with untiring
energy, made appeals to our reason, and has enforced
those appeals with an eloquence, the more to be admired,
because it was unaffected and unadorned, the name which
ought chiefly to be associated with the success of these
measures is the name of RICHARD COBDEN."   The pero-
ration of this speech—one of the best he ever delivered—

and prompted, as all good speeches are, by personal
feeling and emotion, was touching in its earnest simplicity. "In relinquishing power," he said, "I shall
leave a name, severely censured, I fear, by many who on
public grounds deeply regret the severance of party ties.
I shall surrender power, severely censured also by others,
who from no interested motives, adhere to the principle
of Protection, considering the maintenance of it to be
essential to the welfare of the country. I shall leave a
name execrated by every monopolist who for less honourable motives clamours for Protection because it conduces
to his own individual benefit; but it may be that I shall
leave a name sometimes remembered with expressions of
goodwill in the abodes of those whose lot it is to labour,
and to earn their daily bread by the sweat of their brow,
when they shall recruit their exhausted strength with
abundant and untaxed food; the sweeter because it is
no longer leavened with the sense of injustice."

This impressive speech was, though not exactly
the last, the last great speech he delivered in the assembly of which he had so long been the ruling spirit.
He became thenceforth an almost historical personage.
His work was done. He had no longer any personal
interest in the strife of politics. He had set himself
above parties in the second, as well as in the first, great
act of his life, and had become a kind of umpire in
struggles in which he no longer cared or deigned to par-
ticipate. His last speech, on the miserable affair of Don
Pacifico, which threatened to involve the honour of Great
Britain in a paltry squabble with Greece about the household furniture and warming pans of a quasi-British subject,

was delivered in the evening of the 28th of June, 1850. On the following day he was thrown from his horse on Constitution Hill, when proceeding homeward to White-hall Gardens, after inscribing his name in Her Majesty's visiting book at Buckingham Palace, and fell heavily upon his side. The injuries he received proved to be fatal, and, amid the universal regret and sympathy of the whole nation—his political opponents not excepted—this great statesman expired on the evening of the 2nd of July. His death was looked upon as a public calamity : he was only in his sixty-second year, and might have looked forward to many years of public usefulness and private happiness, and his clear, calm, though cold, intellect, was unclouded and serene till the moment of his unhappy accident. I wrote within a few months after his death the following humble tribute to his genius and his memory, which, after the lapse of five-and-twenty years, seems to me to be quite as just as it appeared to me to be then, and to have been rendered, if possible, more true by the lapse of time.

### THE DEATH OF SIR ROBERT PEEL.

" Notwithstanding all the animosities which some of his greatest measures excited—animosities which had by no means subsided when he died—his contemporaries were not blind to the eminent virtues of his character, to the greatness and purity of his aims, and to the immense influence of his opinions and acts upon the destinies of Great Britain. Even those who raised the greatest out-cry against him for abandoning his party, admitted, when his ear was altogether deaf to popular censure and applause, his personal integrity, and the greatness of the sacrifice which he made from a sense of imperative duty. Before he was conveyed to the simple burial-place of his family, enmity towards him was extinct in every breast, and a halo of affectionate interest, which might not otherwise have surrounded his name, gathered upon it as soon as people heard of his untimely death. All bitter feelings against the individual were allayed : for no man could look down upon such a grave 'without a compunctious throb'—that he should ever have imputed unworthy motives to one so disinterested, so sagacious, and so unfortunate, as he who slept beneath it. His loss was regarded by millions as a national, and by many thousands as a private and personal, calamity. It administered a shock to the feelings of all classes of the people, which did not speedily subside, and read the world a deeply impressive lesson on the instability of human power and greatness, and on the transitory nature of all the blessings which men most enthusiastically prize, and for which they most ardently struggle.

"It was the peculiar misfortune of this great statesman, when considered simply as an individual, but perhaps it was an advantage for his country when he is considered in his public capacity, that he began life under the auspices of a party, with whom his heart and his intellect had less sympathy the older and more experienced he became. The bulk of the members of that aristocratic party, submitting, perhaps unwillingly, to the leadership of a man of plebeian extraction, and not possessing either his intellect or his conscientiousness, or, as individuals, the responsibility which attached to him, could not change opinions at his command, or by his example ; and the cry of treason which they raised was rendered more virulent by allusions to his birth. Even in the very height of his power and fame, there were not wanting men who submitted to his leadership in despite of themselves : who sneered at, while they followed him ; affected to patronise him, at the very time that their position and fate were in his hands, and who could no more have stirred in politics without him than a ship could have directed its own course. But in every change of opinion, it was not the violent plucking out of the fruit of his mind, and the arbitrary substitution of an alien produce, of which he could be accused. It was the natural ripening of the seeds of a slow but steady conviction, and those who complained of, and were deceived by it, had themselves to blame for their want of penetration in not foreseeing the inevitable result. In his famous speech on the passing of the Catholic Emancipation Act, a measure in which his convictions, as regards the mere theory, do not appear to have been so matured as on the great question of the commercial intercourse of nations, he explained himself in a manner, which, if it did not conciliate the prejudiced of his own party, was not his excuse, but his glory, in the estimation of the practical men of his age and country. ' I have,' said he, ' for years attempted to maintain the exclusion of Roman Catholics from Parliament and the high offices of the State. I do not think it was an unnatural or an unreasonable struggle. I resign it in consequence of the conviction that it can no longer be advantageously maintained, from believing that there are not adequate materials or sufficient instruments for its effectual and permanent continuance. I yield, therefore, to a moral necessity which I cannot control, being unwilling to push resistance to a point which might endanger the establishments that I wish to defend.'

" On the question of the repeal of the Corn Laws, in which he stood in a position to himself painfully similar to that which he occupied on the question of Catholic Emancipation, the part which he acted was even in a higher degree useful to his country. Though he broke up a party, he saved a nation. Though he attracted to his own defenceless head the lightnings of the bitterest political storm that ever raged in this country, he rendered those lightnings harmless against the State. He offered up his feelings, his friendships, his very heart, as a man, when he sacrificed his party; but in knowing that he prevented a violent revolution, in which all the best interests of the country might have been wrecked, he had his reward, both as a man and a citizen.

" Throughout his career he may be said to have acted the pre-eminently useful part of a break-water against the floods of democratic change. The men who commenced the struggle for Catholic Emancipation and for the repeal of the Corn Laws, were men before their time; and, had those great questions been carried without the opposition which they encountered, they might, perhaps, have been carried in vain, or carried only that a future time might see their re-enactment. His resistance ripened public opinion and his own; and when both had simultaneously arrived at maturity, he yielded at the very moment when to refuse would have been madness, and

when to yield was to conquer. His wise resistance until
the point when resistance became foolish, and his wise
concession when not to have conceded would have been
perilous or fatal, enabled him to accomplish for those
great causes what their professed friends could never
have accomplished without his aid. Whilst his political opponents were too often mere men of theory, he
was the man, not of theory, but of practice; a man
who was sometimes upon a wrong track, but who always
steadily kept marching to a right one; a man who
was always pressing forward, but never too hastily;
and who never once, in any change of opinion, changed
without long, patient, earnest, and honest consideration.

"No man knew better than Sir Robert Peel how evanes-
cent and worthless a thing was the applause of the mob;
and, at the same time, no man more ardently longed for
applause than he did. Yet it must be said, that he
looked far beyond the loud voices and the clapping of
hands of to-day. He looked like 'mighty Verulam,'—
a man whose greatness he almost equalled, and whose
virtues he far excelled,—to foreign nations and to posterity, to confirm the verdict of his own time, if it should
happen to be favourable; or to reverse it, if it should
happen to be against him. As regards foreign nations,
his wish was abundantly gratified before he died. His
was the name that represented alike the common-sense,
the business-tact, and the enlightened statesmanship of
England. Europe rang with his fame; and nations who
never heard of his rivals or his enemies were familiar
with his actions, and respected England in his person.
But though he valued the approval of foreign nations—

as the verdict of contemporaries who could judge coolly
and impartially upon matters upon which there was too
much heat among his countrymen at home to permit
them to judge impartially—a fair page in the history of
his country was the dearest object of his ambition; and
although we, his contemporaries, living amid the suffoca-
ting dust of the yet unended conflicts in which he was
a leader, are not entitled to speak for those who shall
come after us, and who shall see more clearly than we
can, we do not run any great risk of committing an error
when we assert, that the unborn historian, who shall
write the full and impartial history of the first half of
the nineteenth century in Great Britain, will find in civil
life no purer or higher reputation to identify with it than
that of Sir Robert Peel.

" As an orator, Sir Robert Peel cannot be placed in the
highest rank. His was not the eloquence that could
arouse the passions of a multitude ; or that, having
aroused them like an angry sea, could say to them,
'Peace, be still.' He could not govern an impulsive
crowd, or awe an impatient senate by his winged words,
or hurl the thunderbolts of oratory, like the Jupiters of
the Forum or the Market Place ; but what he wanted in
this impetuous vigour, he supplied by his logical power,
his patient research, his exhaustive argument, his dis-
arming candour, and his thorough mastery of his subject.
As an orator, he was surpassed by many of his contemporaries, both in and out of parliament ; but as a debater,
he had no superior, and but few equals. To expound
and to persuade were his favourite tasks ; and when he
put forth his strength in either department, it was very
dense ignorance indeed, that could not, or would not, be

enlightened; and very obstinate prejudice that would not be convinced. On some rare occasions in his parliamentary life, he soared beyond the useful cleverness which was the general characteristic of his style of debate, into the higher regions of eloquence and feeling; and some passages in his celebrated oration of 1846, when he retired from office, and took a final farewell of its anxieties and responsibilities, will bear comparison with the most noted displays of British oratory.

"The private and domestic virtues of this great statesman were not much known, until death removed a veil from his secret history, and men could speak out who had hitherto remained silent for fear of flattery or misconception. His own family, and the circle of his more immediate friends, loved him with a depth of affection and respect which could only have been prompted by his virtues and kindliness. He was considered a cold man; but, like many others against whom the same objection is raised, the coldness was in the manner, and not in the matter. He was timid and shy in well-doing, and concealed his real enthusiasm of character under a thin mask, which true and intimate judges could easily draw aside, but which, to the outer and distant public, remained impenetrable.

"He was a kind friend, and an unostentatious but liberal patron of merit in whatever walk of intellectual eminence it was displayed; and, during his later years more especially, he showed an appreciation of literature, and of the claims of literary men—who in their life and conduct respected themselves and their high calling as much as he thought they ought to be respected—which augured favourably of his discrimination, and his power to read

the signs of the times in which he lived. Even in the
midst of the thickest turmoil of politics and of business,
he always found leisure to attend to every reasonable,
and indeed unreasonable, claim upon his time. He was
never in a hurry; he took everything coolly and philoso-
phically—and neglected nothing—not even the imper-
tinent requests of people who had no right to intrude
upon his attention or his privacy. Misery never sued to
him in vain; and his generous conduct towards the
painter Haydon—accidentally disclosed to the world by a
short and grateful record in the diary of the unhappy
man, which was made public at the coroner's inquest
upon his body, and which forced a tribute of admiration
wherever it was made known—was but one instance out
of many in which his secret generosity and kindly feeling were exerted towards the unfortunate. His conduct
towards the poet Southey in a time of affliction, and
towards many others still living, whose names may therefore not be mentioned, was of the same character, and
combined generosity with delicacy.

"A judicious patron of literature and the arts; an
exemplary citizen; an elegant scholar; a good and
humane man, unsullied in his life and morals; and a
statesman who loved truth and his country better than
the applause of men, and who, in times of difficulty and
danger, strengthened the institutions and preserved the
internal peace and security of his native land, when less
judgment and firmness might have imperilled and lost
them all; such, in a few words, is the character of Sir
Robert Peel. His fame will grow purer with the lapse of
time; and shine—where he wished it—among the
brightest names of English history."

# PROFESSOR J. P. NICHOL AND THOMAS DE QUINCEY.

—◆—

Dr. John Pringle Nichol, professor of astronomy in the University of Glasgow, and superintendent of the Observatory, author of the "Architecture of the Heavens," and other works, that helped in their day to render the study of astronomy popular, by ridding it for educational purposes of its abstruseness, and of the mathematic difficulties that the bulk of the public have neither time nor inclination to surmount, was a man of an imaginative and poetical mind, and an admirable lecturer. He was also one of the leaders of the liberal party in Glasgow, but not a violent politician. He tempered his imagination with his reason, and came down from his contemplation of the stars, to look upon the things of this world with a calm and practical judgment. He was a firm believer in that dream of science—a dream here, that may be proved to be a reality hereafter—that all the orbs of heaven are habitable or inhabited worlds, fitted to be the abodes of happy and rational creatures. He was also a firm supporter of what, in that day, was called the "nebular hypothesis," which was, that the nebulæ—those apparently thin fleecy clouds in the remotest depth of space were inchoate worlds, existing in the form of vapour, not yet hardened, but to be hardened in thousands, or it might be millions of years, into substances as solid as the earth or stars; and that the earth and the stars had all originally existed in the same form of chaotic vapour. The idea was of ancient growth, but received new currency from its adoption by Sir William Herschel. Thirty years ago it had a large following of astronomers who believed in it, and possibly a still greater number who held, with Sir David Brewster, that the so-called nebulæ only appeared nebulous because no existing telescopes were of sufficient power to resolve them. Great interest was felt by Professor Nichol in the progress towards completion of the gigantic telescope of the Earl of Rosse for use at his Observatory in Oxmantown, and the intention expressed by his lordship to direct the instrument to the great nebula in Orion as a test of its capabilities of piercing into the as yet unfathomed profundities of the sidereal universe. One of the most intimate of the Professor's friends, in 1845-6, was the celebrated Thomas De Quincey, known to fame as the "Opium-Eater," and known to the present generation, as he will be to future times, as one of the purest writers of the rich and copious English language. He was at this time near upon, or upwards of, eighty years of age, and after a course of abstinence, extending over a considerable period of failing health and energy, had returned to the practice of opium eating, or, to speak more correctly, of laudanum-drinking, with, as he said, the most beneficial effects both upon his mind and body. The Professor had introduced him to me, and he paid

me not unfrequent visits at the office of the *Argus*—
visits which were generally concluded by the request on
his part of the loan of sixpence or a shilling to purchase
laudanum—a whole wine-glassful of which he was
accustomed to drink with as little compunction as if it
had been claret. I had often dined with him, or rather
he with me, glad of the opportunity of listening to perhaps the greatest and most eloquent talker of his time,
whose learning and whose memory were alike, as Dominie
Sampson might have said, "prodigious;" whose mind
was no jumble of heterogeneous knowledge, but a vast
store-house, from which he could draw at will the largest
or the smallest facts of history and philosophy at the
very moment that he wanted them. Though older men
than I was considered him tedious and prolix, from the
length of the monologues in which he indulged, and amid
which it was next to impossible for the listener to squeeze
in a word, either by way of dissent, of approval, or of
inquiry—his orations, for such they might be called, were
to me singularly attractive and instructive. With the
veneration which the young ought always to feel for the
wisdom of the old, I sat respectfully at the feet of this
venerable Gamaliel, and acted towards him the dutiful
part of an attentive listener. An incident occurred on
one occasion, in the summer of 1845, when I was asked
to meet him at dinner at the Observatory, which fixed
itself strongly on my memory. The party consisted but
of four, inclusive of the Professor's wife, and the conversation was general, for the time of the monologue—that
of the dessert—had not arrived. De Quincey's talk ran
upon the great mysteries and discoveries of astronomy,

on which subject, contrary to his usual wont on most topics, he allowed the Professor and myself to take our full share of the conversation. The particular theme of discourse was the nebular hypothesis, in the truth of which De Quincey seemed, as far as I could gather, to be as firm a believer as the Professor, and which I too was content to believe, when two such astronomers as Dr. Herschel and Dr. Nichol lent it their countenance. The hypothesis appealed to my poetical sympathies, and seemed to open a door, through which the poor, weak, and limited philosophy of man might pass into the secret laboratory of Nature, and study the inner processes of creation, taking such countless myriads of years for their completion as to render the very name of earthly Time a shadow of infinite littleness. We were in the midst of dinner and conversation when the servant brought in a letter for the Professor. "Excuse me," he said, "if I open and read it. I know the handwriting. It bears the post-mark of Oxmantown, and comes from the Earl of Rosse." The Professor opened the letter, and as he read it passed his hand nervously amid the hair that clustered on his forehead, and said, in evident excitement, "The dream is ended. . . Farewell for ever to the nebular hypothesis!" Handing the letter to me, he asked me to read it aloud, and I did so. It announced that Lord Rosse had directed his telescope to the great nebula in Orion, and that the nebula, as he had expected, was no fire-mist, no star-dust, or inchoate mass of pregnant vapour, but an immense assemblage of suns and stars—a universe of itself.

"A magnificent discovery!" said De Quincey.

" Most magnificent," said the Professor ; it makes an
end for ever of what is called the nebular hypothesis,
not alone as regards the nebula in Orion, but as regards
all other and even more distant nebulæ which not even
the splendid instrument of Lord Rosse can resolve into
the suns and planets that compose them.. " Lord, what
is man that thou art mindful of him ! "

" Aye ! " said the Opium-Eater, " an undevout astronomer is mad," as Pope says, " but you, my dear Professor,
are sanity itself."

" But what do you say of a sectarian astronomer ? "
I asked, suddenly, remembering the bitterness of spirit
with which a noted member of the Free Church of
Scotland, also an astronomer, had lately assailed the
Established Church and all other sects of Christians who
differed from his own. " Is he not as mad as his undevout
brother ? "

" Quite," replied Mr. De Quincey; " nobody can study
the stars without a profound pity or contempt for the
poor, petty, paltry, religious animosities and unchristian
hatreds of mankind. What a sublime science astronomy
is ! It expands yet dwarfs the intellect of men, and
shows us the more we learn, how little it is possible we
can ever know. The stars always preach to me that I
am a prisoner, that I am condemned, possibly for some
sin I have committed in a previous, but now forgotten,
state of existence, to do penance in this cell, or dungeon
—the earth ; and to wear about me, until my term of
captivity is ended, the penalty of a body."

" The penalty of a body ! " said the Professor. " Do
you not—do we not all—underrate and underestimate

the body, and over-exalt the soul? How can soul display itself? how can it act at all, unless it have a body through which to act? I may have one of the grandest souls that it is possible for a dweller on this earth to be possessed of, and something or somebody may come and give me a crack on the skull, sufficient to injure my brain, though not to kill me outright; and what becomes of my soul? It is there where it was before, lodged in its earthly tabernacle, but the earthly tabernacle is damaged, deteriorated, and will not and cannot allow the soul to display itself in its original brilliancy. A blow on the brain may convert in a moment a man of genius into an idiot or a lunatic?"

"I grant you," said De Quincey. "The degradation of the body is a mistake. The body is as divine as the soul. The stars are bodies."

"Yes," I said; "and as bodies, differing vastly as they do from our bodies, in which our souls dwell for a time, may they not have souls also that dwell in their bodies for myriads of years, and not as our souls in our bodies for threescore or fourscore years and ten; and having souls, is it too wild a fancy to imagine, that they reason, that they think, that they may sorrow, and that they may rejoice, and that star may speak to star, planet to planet, as we three are speaking now; and feel, as we feel, the beauty of life, the divinity and sublimity of knowledge, and be endowed, as we are, with an infinite craving to explore all the wonders of infinitude."

"I have sometimes thought so," said the Professor.

"And I also," added De Quincey. "What right have we, arrogant, presumptuous, conceited little creatures that we are, who crawl upon this huge earth, that sustains and feeds us, to say that we only can think, and that our mother earth is spiritless matter. Suppose the little insects that sometimes infest a beggar's doublet, or his head, were to say that the beggar's body was their world, especially created for their enjoyment, and that the beggar had no mind, no soul, no thought, no reason for his existence, except that they might live upon him. Would not that be the most intolerable conceit? And yet it would not be a whit more contemptible than that of a man who boasts, that not only the particular orb on which he creeps, but all the countless hosts of heaven were created solely to give him light, or perhaps to enable silly astrologers to cast his nativity and tell his paltry fortunes, whether he should marry a dark woman, or a fair one; or whether he should be prosperous or unprosperous as a huckster or a pedlar."

"Yes," said I. "And when we reflect that human eyes have never beheld the radiance of a millionth or a billionth part of the stars that are scattered through the awful infinitude of what we call heaven, and never will, at least as long as we continue to be captives in this prison of the earth, as Mr. De Quincey has truly named it, our pride in ourselves, as of necessity the highest of all intelligent beings, and for whom all the worlds were created, would be contemptible if it were not so lofty, and ludicrous if it were not so magnificently audacious. Though I reject the idea, I admire it; and look upon it as a kind of proof that man after all is other than he seems; and that possibly it may be his destiny, after he has shuffled off this mortal coil, to make the circuit of infinitude, and wear a succession of new and more beautiful bodies than he can wear on earth, with newer and grander faculties, in planet after planet, star after star, for ever, and ever, and ever; learning, loving, and adoring as he goes, and increasing alike in wisdom and in happiness.

"Granting this," said the Professor, " a dream which may not be altogether a dream, can you reconcile it to the logic even of a dream, that your eternity should be eternal only at one end—the future? and that you, or your soul, should not have been eternal in the past? To me it seems that a one-ended eternity is no eternity at all, and is a contradiction in terms."

"I like to imagine," I replied, "that I have always been as I always shall be; but I don't like to dwell upon the thought too continuously, for ,'that way madness lies.' Happy for us that we cannot look into the past much more than into the future."

"But," said Mr. De Quincey, "we *can* see into the past, or into that which seems present, but may be past. For instance, the great nebula in Orion, which the telescope of Lord Rosse has shown to be a congeries of stars, how long does its light take to reach this earth of ours? Some thousands of years, I believe! And is there not another nebula, as yet unresolved, of which the light takes fifty thousand years to travel to us?"

"Yes," said the Professor.

" So that if we look through Lord Rosse's telescope, we clearly see worlds which may no longer be in existence, and which may have perished forty-nine thousand years ago or longer?"

"Not as you put it," replied the Professor, "for I cannot grant that a star can perish, or that anything great or small in all the boundless universe can cease to be. All things change—but nothing dies."

"True," said De Quincey, "but what I mean is that when we see the nebula to-day, or to-morrow, we see it as it existed thousands of years ago, and that in the interval it may have assumed a different shape, condition, arrangement, and constitution, and from solid passed into the fluid, or into the gaseous state, or been whirled down—down—down into the abysses of space, so far beyond its seeming position as to be out of telescopic reach."

"There is no down—down—down in space; and no up—up—up," replied the Professor. "These words are relative and not positive; and are of the earth, earthy; but you are right in the theory that when we look upon a star in the illimitable sky, we look upon it as it was, and not as it may be at this moment."

"I grant," said De Quincey, "that 'up' and 'down' are relative, and not positive words, and that if they apply to things on our small planet, in reference to position on that planet, they cannot apply to the heavenly hosts. But all words, except substantives, such words as horse, cow, or man, bread, wine, beef, &c., are more or less vague. How glibly, for instance, we use the great words infinite and eternal! just as if we could understand any thing that was either."

"I have often thought," said I, "of writing an article to be called 'Quarrels with Words.' Take the word 'morality' for instance; that also is a relative not a positive word; in fact, a word that is modified or wholly changed in its meanings by geography, or by lapse of time. Abraham, three thousand years ago, may have been a strictly moral man; but if he lived in our day, and behaved as he did in his own, he would be considered a very immoral man. If a man in England were to put his good old grandfather to death, as too old to live, and helped to eat him, he would not be considered a moral man, and would assuredly be hung; but if he committed the same act in Fiji, he would strictly conform to the morality of the place, and would be considered as performing a work of grand filial duty in sending to Heaven one who had no longer any chance of enjoyment on the earth."

" Write the article," said De Quincey, " or let me do it. Consider the word virtue. What does virtue mean? Originally it meant manliness; but we scarcely know what it means now. It is one epithet as applied to a man, and another very different epithet when applied to a woman. Indeed, we scarcely ever speak of a virtuous man, and would not be understood in any unvarying and fixed sense if we did; but we all know what we mean by a virtuous woman. Then there is the word education— the abuse of which sometimes very sorely irritates me. Education is the act of drawing out. What do we draw out? And if an educated man is a drawn-out man, how has he been drawn out? What has been drawn out? And has not something been put into him? We talk of a man as having been educated, or drawn out, at such a school or university; whereas, we should say that he was taught something, more or less, at his school or university. We hear now and then of young ladies who have ' finished ' their education. As if the drawing out or education of the faculties of any rational human being could ever be finished as long as he or she remained in possession of his or her senses ! "

" And patriotism," said Professor Nichol; " the love of the particular country in which a man happens to be born. If we are to love our country beyond all other countries, merely because we are natives of it, why should we not love our county beyond all other counties ? And if our county, why not our town or village ? And if our town or village, why not the particular street in which our eyes first opened to the light? And if the street, why not the house ? And if the house, why not the room ? "

" I wish you would write the article," I said to Mr. De Quincey. " I resign all my copyright in the idea to you, and shall look out for it in Maga."

I believe no such article ever appeared, though I expected it during many months. But I learned from Professor Nichol, after De Quincey's death, that many scores of articles which he wrote for *Blackwood* were lost to the world through the spiteful acts of a half-crazy woman. De Quincey was long in sore pecuniary straits, and led a single life, in temporary but not hostile or unfriendly separation from his family, and took obscure lodgings, sometimes in Edinburgh, sometimes in Glasgow, sometimes in London. He was not always able to pay for his lodging, and had to resort occasionally to very ignominious shifts. He lived a long time in the house of one woman in Edinburgh, whom he was never able to pay : a woman of a very sharp tongue and most irascible temper, whose wrath at the last moment of grace which she had allowed him, he had not courage enough to face ; so he ran away, leaving his small chattels and his manuscripts behind him. This woman knew his way of life—knew the hours when he was accustomed to write, and the hours when he went abroad for exercise and fresh air, and the loose manner in which he left his papers unprotected on his writing-table. With great trouble and enormous pertinacity, she tracked him from lodging to lodging, and took advantage of the hours when she knew he was not at home, to procure admission to his rooms under one pretence or another, and very often —a great deal too often—contrived to possess herself of his manuscripts and carry them off. De Quincey put the best face on a bad business, and represented to Professor Nichol that the woman had conceived a violent but hope- less attachment to him, which he could not reciprocate, and that this was the method in which her rage and jealousy displayed themselves !

In one of his homeless intervals Dr. Nichol invited him to stay at the Observatory for a week. De Quincey gratefully accepted the invitation, and remained for six months, untroubled by the avenging Hecate, who had utterly lost the clue to his whereabouts, and secure in the possession of his manuscripts. The last time I saw him was in the streets of Glasgow, when I suddenly came upon him at a turning. " I knew I should meet you," he said. " Three streets distant, I was mysteriously aware that you were somewhere in the neighbourhood, and that our two orbs were approaching each other. Have you never experienced such a presentiment, or thought of some one in a sudden and inexplicable manner, whom you had no particular reason to think about, a person who, for all you knew to the contrary, might be a thousand miles away, and come across him unexpectedly in the streets a few minutes afterwards ? "

I owned that such a circumstance had happened to me more than once, and that in the present instance I had been thinking of him in the street, some time before I met him. If I had been in haste to keep an appointment this admission would have been unlucky, but I was in no particular hurry, and had to stand and listen at the street corner, while he poured forth a full stream of poetical and philosophic talk, in explanation of what he called the possibility of spirit meeting with spirit before body met with body. Like the Ancient Mariner with the wedding guest, in Coleridge's poem, the Opium-eater "fixed me with his glittering eye," while in eloquent language he expressed his belief that every human being was surrounded with a spiritual atmosphere ; that the body was but the nucleus of a comet, and that the soul surrounded it with a light unseen by the physical eye ; that the volume of this luminous atmosphere was in proportion to the intellect, and that the light thus cast before him into space by a man of genius, was vastly greater than that projected by the dull ordinary man or woman, and that the atmosphere which enveloped the fool was so slight as scarcely to be considered an atmosphere at all. Thus he said our atmospheres had met and mingled that morning before we knew that we were near each other, and had communicated to each of us, by means of an apparently spontaneous thought, the intelligence that we were approaching, and would shortly meet. I think he kept me listening to him for fully twenty minutes, during which I could not, though I tried two or three times, launch upon him a single word of assent or dissent. He ended, by requesting the loan of sixpence, for a draught of his beloved laudanum, which having obtained he turned back on the way by which he had come, doubtless to the shop of the chemist with whom he was accustomed to deal, and who, knowing his man, was not afraid to serve him with a potion which would have been fatal to any one else, but which on him only acted as a gentle and a beneficial stimulant.

# THE SUNDAY QUESTION IN SCOTLAND.

In 1844-'45-'46, and '47 the Sunday or "Sabbath" question excited much controversy as well as ill-feeling in Scotland. Sunday in London is a day sufficiently gloomy; but it is cheerfulness itself compared with a Sunday in Glasgow or Edinburgh. But the Scottish Sabbatarians and ultra-Calvinists, not contented with the deadness and dreariness of Glasgow, and the stoppage of all the vehicular traffic of the poor—that of the cabs and omnibuses—endeavoured to prevent the rich from going to church in their own carriages, and to stop all railway and postal communication throughout the land from twelve o'clock on Saturday night to twelve o'clock on Sunday night. This was too much for the bulk of the people to endure, although very numerously attended, and very enthusiastic meetings were got together in support of this very unnecessary stagnation. At one of these meetings, in the City Hall, Glasgow, at which it was computed that between four and five thousand persons were present, a very suggestive incident occurred. The principal orator of the evening was the Rev. Dr. Wardlaw, a well-known and highly esteemed clergyman of venerable age, who resided in the country about five or six miles from his church, and who, not being able to walk the distance to and fro, was accustomed to ride into the city on a strong little pony. The doctor was in the full flow and swing of his eloquence, and had spoken for more than half an hour in denunciation of the grievous sin of Sabbath-breaking, committed not only by the railway companies in carrying, but by the British Government in despatching, the mails for transmission through the country on the day that was sanctified to " the Lord God of Sabaoth, and of the Sabbath." He was eliciting loud and frequent bursts of applause from his sympathising and admiring auditory, when a stentorian voice suddenly called out from the gallery, " Will the reverend doctor be good enough to repeat the Fourth Commandment ?" The question excited a storm of hisses, cheers, and cries of " Order! order!" But the man in the gallery was not to be put down; and at the first pause in the hubbub, said in the same loud voice, " I mean no disrespect to the reverend gentleman, but I must beg that he will repeat the Fourth Commandment for the benefit of some of us who may not perhaps understand it ?" Renewed uproar, and cries of " Order! order!" resounded through the hall, in the midst of which Dr. Wardlaw himself requested silence, and said that he had no objection whatever to repeat the commandment. This he did, with good accent and emphasis, until he came to the words " thine ox and thine ass," when he was interrupted by a loud stamping of feet, and cries of " Hear! hear!" from the gallery, with counter-cries of " Order! order!" from the body of the hall. " With the permission of the

meeting," said the first interrupter of the proceedings,
" I will ask the reverend gentleman whether, in view of
the kind nature and whole spirit of the commandment,
the words ox and ass do not mean all animals and beasts
of burden ; and whether the divine law that applies to an
ass does not apply to a pony ?"

A loud burst of laughter and applause greeted the
question.  Dr. Wardlaw replied unhesitatingly, " I do ;"
and concluded his speech without further interruption.
A series of resolutions was ultimately passed, calling
upon the railway companies to cease running their trains,
and upon the Government to cease despatching letters
upon the " Sabbath." There were many dissentients ; but
the great majority was in favour of Sunday solitude.

Next Sunday it was noticed by some of his congregation
that Dr. Wardlaw did not ride his pony as usual, but
walked to Glasgow from his country residence.  The
same thing was noticed on the second Sunday ; but on
the third the reverend gentleman mounted the back of his
faithful animal as before.  He took occasion to explain to
his congregation that the question so unexpectedly put to
him in the City Hall had sorely exercised and troubled his
mind.  The point was one to which he had not previously
devoted his attention, and which he resolved to study in
all its bearings, and by the light of all possible authority.
While still in doubt, he thought it his duty to walk ; but
now that his perplexities were removed he had recom-
menced, and intended to continue his rides.

" I consulted," said he, " the early Fathers of the
Church.  I consulted the writings of the Genevan divines.
I consulted every authority that was open to me.  I looked

upon the matter with the impartial spirit of a judge, and
I hope with all the devout and conscientious feeling of a
Christian, and came to the conclusion, after earnest prayer
for enlightenment, that the institution of the Lord's Day,
as observed by all Christian Churches and sects whatsoever, applied to mankind only, and was for their benefit;
and that in appointing the first day of the week to be the
Sabbath of the Christians—instead of the seventh day,
which was the Sabbath of the Jews—the intention was to
leave the Sabbath of the brute creation, as it originally
stood.   Upon this principle I resolved to give my pony
ts Sabbath rest on the Saturday, and to ride it, as my
increasing age and infirmities demand, on the first, or
Lord's Day, or Sunday."

It was the universal opinion of Glasgow that the
reverend gentleman deserved his ride for his ingenuity;
but the principle was never applied to the horses in the
case of the driving of cabs and omnibuses, or other
vehicles of the poor.   Neither was it ever enforced in the
case of the rich, though it must be observed, in justice to
the Sabbatarianism of the city, that the rich only used
their carriages to convey them to and from church, and
that if they had employed them for any other purpose they
would have lost caste and social position, and, perhaps,
had to endure a reprimand from the Kirk Session.

Some of the Scottish people not only worshipped the
Sabbath, but they worshipped the Saturday evening, as to
a certain extent partaking of the Sabbatical character,
of which a curious instance fell under my observation.
A then celebrated English vocalist, still living, was
asked on a Saturday, when he had no engagement,

to take a trip down the Clyde to the beautiful island of Arran, and stay over the Sunday. It was represented to him that he could easily return on Monday morning, with ample time to prepare himself for his advertised performances in the City Hall on the Monday night. He willingly agreed, and induced a mutual friend, a well-known advocate of Glasgow, to accompany us. The weather was fair at starting, and remained so, until we reached Greenock, that famous town, where it is said always to rain, except when it snows, when the rain began to fall in torrents, and continued to fall until we arrived at Brodick in Arran. The inn was near to the shore; but it had very imperfect and limited accommodation, for the then Duke of Hamilton, to whom the greater part of the lovely isle belonged, objected to the influx of travellers, and doggedly refused to grant a site for a great hotel, or allow an extension of the existing buildings; and on applying for admission we were told that the place was full, and that even the barn was occupied. What were we to do? The sympathetic hostess told us that if we would walk down to the village and apply at the post-office we might possibly be accommodated. The rain was pouring down, and we had no umbrellas, and the post-office was a mile distant. The vocalist was in great distress. He wore a pair of thin patent-leather boots, and his feet sank into the miry road, above his instep at every step he took. His great trouble was that the cold and damp would affect his voice, and that he would lose his G—one of the notes, on the purity of which he most prided himself. But there was no help for it; and we trudged steadily onward to the post-office, arriving about

eight o'clock in the evening, just as it was beginning to
grow dark.   There was a blazing fire in the parlour, and
we were informed that we could have a room in which
there were three beds, and that we could be supplied with
food and other refreshments, exactly the same as if we
had been at the inn.   The vocalist, cheered by the sight
of the fire, took off his wet boots, rubbed his hands
cheerily at the blaze, and began to try his voice to ascertain if his G had suffered.   He ran up the scale several
times, lingering lovingly at each repetition of the "G,"
which seemed to be unimpaired, when the post-mistress,
who had been cooking some bacon and eggs for us in the
adjoining kitchen, suddenly rushed in with alarm depicted
upon her comely countenance, and said, "Gentlemen!
gentlemen! ye may do what ye like in my hoose; I will
do a' I can for your comfort, and am right glad to see
ye, but ye maunna sing!"

The vocalist, more annoyed than amused, asked "Why
not?"

"Because ye maunna!   Ye may do onything else ye
please in my hoose, but ye maunna sing!"

The vocalist gave a loud long whistle—a kind of stage
whistle in fact—expressive of his surprise, which only
seemed to alarm the landlady still more.   "Aye, gentlemen," she said, "the hoose is your ain, in one respect;
but ye see I'm the mistress o't.   Ye can do just what you
like in it; but ye maunna sing, and ye maunna whistle!"

"But why?" I inquired; "singing and whistling are
harmless, and I am sure our friend would do nothing to
annoy you if he knew it.   Why do you object to singing
and whistling?"

"I dinna object to either of them, of theirselves," said the landlady, "but I object to them the noo. Its aucht o' the clock on Saturday night : only four hours to the Sabbath! and there's a minister in the next room!"

But the agitation of the Sunday question in Scotland had its serious as well as its ludicrous side, and more than justified the witticism of Mr. Albany Fonblanque, which had passed into a proverb, that the Scotch desired the *bitter* and not the *better* observance of the Sabbath. A striking instance of the bitterness, rendered more striking by the rank and social position of the person afflicted, occurred in 1848. Although all the Scottish railway companies were compelled to carry the mails on Sunday, but as none of them were compelled to carry passengers, some of them exercised their own discretion, and absolutely refused to render themselves aiders and abetters of the sin, as they called it, of Sabbath desecration, by permitting a single passenger, however urgent his business, whether of necessity or mercy, to avail himself of a Sunday train. Early one Sunday morning a lady arrived at Perth, the then ultimate limit of railway extension in the north. She had travelled post all night from the far county of Sutherland, and was just in time to catch the train that was on the point of departure for Edinburgh with the mails. She was told that she could not be permitted to travel by the train. She said that she was the Duchess of Sutherland, that she had received intelligence that her father, the Earl of Carlisle, was lying at the point of death in Castle Howard, and that she had travelled from Dunrobin all night on purpose to catch this very train, and begged and entreated that she might be permitted for

Christ's and pity's sake to take her seat and hasten to her father. The officials were very courteous and very sorry; but their orders were imperative. They could not allow the desecration of the Lord's Day; and the train took its departure, leaving the afflicted daughter weeping on the platform. Resuming her journey with her wearied horses, the Duchess took the shortest road towards Edinburgh; and on arrival at the ferry over the Firth of Forth from Burntisland to Leith, was fortunate enough to persuade a more truly Christian man, the captain of the ferry-boat, to light his engine fires, and convey her across on her errand of love and devotion. But her only opportunity of reaching the bed-side of her dying father in time to receive his blessing had been lost at Perth. When she arrived at Castle Howard the Earl had been dead for many hours—his last moments unsoothed by the presence of his child. Thus the railway directors, in their endeavour to be ultra-Christian became unchristian, and were guilty of an act of cruelty which scandalized the whole country. The rank of the sufferer gave their bigotry an amount of publicity and of consequent condemnation that would not have been elicited, though quite as much de-served, in the case of a humbler person. It is probable that many hundreds of instances, equally distressing, may have occurred, that excited no notice. Possibly, however, the guilt—for it *was* guilt—rested with the one too rigid or too stupid station-master, and that if he had been wise or tender-hearted enough to break through the rule of the directors—the directors themselves would have condoned his breach of their law—and have said, " Well done, good and faithful servant ! "

It was alleged at the time by some of the Scottish newspapers, jealous of the character of their countrymen for true Christianity, that the refusal of this particular railway company to convey passengers along with the mails on Sunday, was the act not of the Scottish but of the English shareholders; and that the latter, misunderstanding the true spirit of the Scottish people, thought to make the line popular by making its management fanatical. There was a legal question, and it was a pity it was not raised by so powerful a family, whether the railway had any right to refuse the Duchess a passage. The railway company had monopolized the road, by authority of Parliament, it is true; and by its monopoly only granted in the public interest and for the public good, had ruined and abolished the posting traffic between Perth and Edinburgh. It was urged that a Sabbatarian post-master in the pre-railway days would not have dared to refuse relays of post-horses to a traveller who demanded them, on the plea of his conscience, or his respect for the sanctity of the Sunday; and why, it was urged, should a railway company, who supplanted and superseded the post-master, exercise a tyranny which would not have been tolerated in the humbler official?

WHATEVER may be the case at present, the drama did not flourish in Glasgow during the three years of my residence in that city. The two theatrical magnates of the time were Mr. Miller, the manager of a theatre, built on sufferance upon the green—that was green no longer—and liable to be removed at any time by the fiat of the magistracy, and Mr. Alexander, proprietor and manager of a permanent and handsome building in the heart of Glasgow, and in close proximity to Buchanan Street—the fashionable promenade of the city. Mr. Alexander was himself a clever performer, and enacted every sort of part, from Richard III., King Lear, or Macbeth, down to the ghost or the grave-digger in "Hamlet," or the walking gentleman in a farce. He was of eccentric and irascible temperament, and it used to be the delight of the gallery to provoke him to wrath, and make him forget his part so far as to rush from the stage in the full attire of Hamlet or of Rob Roy, to eject *vi et armis* some irreverent and noisy wag who had interrupted the performance, of malice prepense, in order to bring out the manager's peculiarities. The motto of the city arms is now "Let Glasgow Flourish." The full motto,

derived from the Puritanic times of Peden, Cargill, and
martyrs of the Covenant was "Let Glasgow flourish by
the preaching of the Word." Though the last six words
are now omitted, the preaching of the Word has always
been more to the taste of the multitude than literature,
music, or the drama, and Glasgow in my time was considered the most unremunerative city in the three king-
doms for the magnates of the dramatic art. Nevertheless,
there was always a select audience to be obtained for any
London performer of high standing who honoured the
city with his or her presence. Miss Helen Faucit was
always a welcome guest; and Miss Charlotte Cushman,
during her brief visit, had no occasion to complain of
empty or unappreciative houses. In the autumn of the
year 1846, Mr. Macready was invited by Mr. Alexander
to perform a series of his leading parts in Glasgow, and
great efforts were made in the press, and by social influence, to secure him large and fashionable audiences. Mr.
Macready brought a letter of introduction to me from my
old friend William Jerdan, then and for many years previously and subsequently the editor of the *Literary Gazette*,
and also to Sir Archibald Alison and Mr. H. Glassford Bell,
as representing both the literature and the law of the city.
He also brought letters to some of the leading merchants
and to the Lord Provost, and two or three of the local
magistracy. The Lord Provost, a very excellent, hospitable, and shrewd, though simple-minded person, was a
particular friend of mine, and consulted me as to what
he ought to do to honour the great tragedian. I told him
the best thing he could do was to invite him to dinner,
and ask all the principal people of Glasgow to meet him.

He said I was right, and that he should call upon
Mr. Macready at his hotel, the "Queen's," at the corner
of George Square, near the railway station, and ask
him to name the day that would best suit him for
the purpose. The Lord Provost came to my office
two days afterwards to inform me that he had seen
Mr. Macready, who had promised to dine with him on
any Sunday he might appoint, adding that, as he had
to perform every other night of the week for a whole
month, Sundays were the only possible days on which he
could accept the invitation.

"What am I to do?" inquired the Lord Provost in much
perplexity, and speaking broad Scotch. "I'm no that
strait-laced mysel', and wad just as soon gie him his dinner
on the Sabbath as on ony other day; but then I'm the
Lord Provost, ye ken, and bound to set a good example.
If I were to gie a dinner on the Sabbath, and to a player
too, I should raise such a hullabaloo in a' the pulpits of
the town, against me, as I could na stand against. If I
were na' the Provost I wadna mind; and if the man were
na' a player, it wadna look half so bad against me.
What's to be done?"

"Well," I replied, "I'm not a Lord Provost or a baillie,
and will brave all the terrors of the kirks and the pulpits
without giving them a thought. Suppose I ask Mr.
Macready to dine with me—will you come?"

"Ou, aye!" said the Provost. "I'll come, and bring
my friends. But ye maun let me pay for the dinner and
the wine. I shall bring ten friends, and Macready and
mysel' will just mak' up the dozen. And you'll just
invite as many as your table will hold. Not a word

of contradiction; the dinner shall be at my expense, only ye mustna let ony body ken it. I'd gie the dinner in my ain house if I were na' the Provost."

The dinner was given accordingly, among the company being Sheriffs Alison and Bell, and Mr. Sheridan Knowles the dramatist. In his recently published " Recollections," Mr. Macready says but little of his Glasgow engagement and nothing of this dinner, though more than once in after years he was accustomed to repeat with much glee his remembrances of the Provost on this occasion. The Provost sat next to the tragedian, and when the dessert was served became very communicative, to Mr. Macready's evident amusement, though he never smiled, but sat grave and stiff, and looked as if a laugh would have done him good, had he so far come down from the lofty pedestal of his dignity as to indulge in it.

"I remember," said the Provost, "when I was a lad, and travelling in my father's business, I made the acquaintance of *your* father, who was manager of the theatre at Newcastle-upon-Tyne. He invited me to sup wi' him at his lodgings. It was on a Sabbath—just as this is—and he had no other day to receive his friends in comfort. I was na' a baillie at that time, and went without muckle scruple. There were eight or nine people, and they drank and smoked and talked. At last a game at whist was proposed. I was shocked for a while. All my Scottish notions were outraged, and I thought I wad gang awa; but I did na'. I just lookit on, and wondered a wee at the wickedness around me. Your father and I were the only ones who did not play; but we both lookit on, and watched the game. I had had a full share of gin and water, and so I think had your father, but I was na' fou, nor near it, though I might as Burns says, ' have had just a wee drap in my ee,' and I saw one fellow playing so badly, and losing his money, that when the rubber was ended, and he said he'd play no more, I just, without muckle thought on the matter, resolved to take a hand mysel'. I forgot a' about the Sabbath, and before a' was done I had cleared close upon seventeen pounds by the night's wark ! "

Macready's grim face relaxed, and he put his handker-chief to his mouth to prevent a burst of laughter.

The Lord Provost was one of the most public-spirited of the citizens of Glasgow, a man who " wore his heart upon his sleeve for daws to peck at," but a shrewd hand at a bargain, munificent when munificence was needed, and always ready to do a kind or a generous action.

# EARLY EFFORTS IN THE CAUSE OF THE EDUCATION OF THE PEOPLE.

—◆—

As editor of the leading liberal journal in the west of Scotland, I was for the first time in my life in the position of being able to express my own opinions in my own way on political and social topics—untrammelled by the censorship of any literary or political superior. During my residence in Glasgow, the main topics of public interest in Scotland were the endowment of the College of Maynooth, the recent disruption in the Church of Scotland, the struggles and establishment of the Free Church, the abolition of the Corn Laws, and the attempt on the part of a vigorous minority of rigid Calvinists to prevent all locomotion by railways, and the conveyance of the mails through Scotland on the Sunday—or the day which the Scotch jewishly rather than christianly call "the Sabbath." Upon all these subjects it was my duty, as editor of the *Argus*, to be in the fore front of public opinion; but having full liberty of speech on every topic which I chose to discuss, I made it my particular business, as it was my particular pleasure, to place broadly before the public the, to my mind, greatest question of the age—the systematic and national education of the rising generation through the agency of the State, and at the expense of the public.

The question was a very old one, and one that had never ceased to occupy the minds of great and good men from a very early period of British history. "The reforming of education," wrote the illustrious Milton to his friend, Samuel Hartlib, "is one of the greatest and noblest designs that can be thought on, and for want thereof the nation perishes." And the nation had gone on perishing, from Milton's time to our own, until there was a greater amount of popular ignorance among the lower strata of society, and a consequently greater amount of vice and crime, than among the same classes in any other civilized country. Many eminent men had written, spoken, and agitated in favour of the elementary instruction of the whole people; but the religious difficulty had always blocked the way, and made that partial which ought to have been general. I determined to make this cause prominent in the *Argus*. I began my advocacy of it in 1846, and it was not until 1871, under Mr. Gladstone's administration and the immediate auspices of Mr. W. E. Forster, that something was done by the British Parliament to secure, or endeavour to secure, to every child born within the realm the right of instruction. Mr. Forster's measure is one of those incomplete and halting movements which it is the fashion to compliment as "a step in the right direction;" but it was only one step, when two or three might have been taken, or when perhaps with a little more foresight and a great deal more courage, the goal intended might have been fairly reached. "Steps in the right direction" are not always to be commended, for right although their direction may be, these steps very often, and too commonly, have the effect of discouraging future and better effort, and of making the timid and half-hearted satisfied with a little, when the whole might be obtained. The payment of sixpence in the pound upon a debt is a step in the right direction; but few creditors are satisfied with a step so short; though in politics and social science such small instalments are often received with more gratitude than they deserve. Writers in newspapers, unlike members of Parliament, seldom obtain credit for their efforts in a great cause which has to obtain Parliamentary sanction. They sow the seed and leave the harvest to be gathered by others. They prepare the way for triumph, but do not always obtain a recognition of their services; though perhaps without such services—long continued and widely operative—the great question, whatever it may have been, would have failed to approach Parliament at all. With the view of showing, not so much what has been done, but how much yet remains to be done, before the children of the British Isles can be prepared by education for the performance of the social duties which promise (or threaten) to be thrust upon them in their maturity—when successive Reform Bills shall have widened the bases of political power, I reproduce here the main points of the plan, which in a series of twelve letters, addressed to Lord Morpeth, afterwards Earl of Carlisle, I placed before the people more than a quarter of a century ago. I have the less hesitation in republishing these broad outlines of a scheme, which is not yet, but may become the law at no very distant future—because, notwithstanding the lapse of time, all the arguments adduced and all the statements made are as pertinent to the year 1875 as they were to the year 1846.

## A SCHEME OF NATIONAL EDUCATION.

Knowledge is better than Ignorance; an educated people superior to an uneducated people; and the natural tendency of education is to make the educated better and happier in all the relations of life than those who are uneducated. There have been people who have disputed this, but fortunately few of them are left in our day. Scarcely one has the hardihood to assert that the hewer of wood and the drawer of water should moil and sweat from cradle to grave, and never know the words of blessing, or read them for himself. That race is all but extinct, and, it is to be hoped, will ere long become entirely so.

This being conceded, we come to the inquiry—"Are the people of this country (the people in the widest sense of the word) sufficiently educated now, either physically, morally, intellectually, or religiously?" Our eyes tell us that they are not. Our hearts bear witness to it. In our streets, in our prisons, in our hulks, at every corner, every day and every hour of our lives, we see around us the evidence of wretchedness and vice, which might have been removed, had we been wise, twenty years ago. We look still further and still deeper, and we see a younger race, boys and girls, just budding into manhood and womanhood, as degraded as their fathers and mothers were before them—as ignorant of the value and significance of human life as if they lived in an age of barbarism; the one sex ready to launch into the world with their hand against every man, and the other ready to degrade humanity more than man could ever degrade it. Going deeper still, we see the young children, but with no better prospect before them, and we say to ourselves, " Little or nothing can now be done for their elders, but much can be done for the children. These can be saved. These can be made men and women worthy of the name. These can be made wiser and better than those who preceded them. These can be taught. These can be placed in the way to become happy in time, and happier through eternity." It is useless to go over statistical tables to prove the ignorance of a great portion of our population. The facts are patent—all but the mentally blind can see them—all but the prejudiced and bigoted can see, feel, hear, and understand that the deplorable ignorance of no inconsiderable section of the youth and childhood of Britain is a great and shameful reality, which it behoves us to destroy. The great question then arises, " Whose duty is it to attend to these children ?" We ask that question, and the hubbub immediately begins. A thousand voices are heard in reply. The Church, by law established, shouts with stentorian lungs, " Leave them to me; I will attend to them; it is my peculiar province—my duty—and no one has a right to interfere; I will educate the people." But a voice of indignation might reply, and has replied, to this self-sufficient Church —" The reality is against you; if you had done what you say you can do, the question would never have been asked. But you have done nothing; you cannot do anything; and, unless you hope to proselytize, you would prefer ignorance to instruction. There must be better and more zealous teachers than you, for you have been false to your trust, and are unworthy of future confidence or credence." Another sect exclaims, with louder voice, and with more pride and exultation, if not inflation of vanity and conceit—"I have done better. I have educated; I have raised princely revenues; I have saved thousands from ignorance and its co-existent evils and despairs;—leave them to me." The reply is—"You have done much—you have done more than was expected of you—your zeal is beyond all praise; but you, also, desire more eagerly to make religious proselytes than to teach. For the first object you have done much, for the second you have not done enough; and you cannot do enough were your means increased one hundredfold and your zeal in the same proportion." A score of others repeat the same cry, and may be answered with the same answer. One reply serves all. The greater their zeal and liberality have been, the greater proof is there in the state of circumstances which we see around us, that religious differences render them incompetent to the task; for still the young children perish, and there are not hands enough outstretched to feed them and instruct them. Who, then, shall take this mighty matter in hand, if not the WHOLE PEOPLE, acting through the Government, which *de facto* represents the whole people? We are all involved; the humblest of us has a stake in this great question, and an interest that no child born shall be so neglected as to become a burden to society when it grows into a man or woman, but a help and a blessing. This is, however, the grand point—the point of points—on which will turn the whole solution of our difficulties. Wise and good men, while agreeing in the abstract proposition, that a wise and good State should care for and watch over the education of the whole people, demur to the wisdom and goodness of any possible form of Government, and allege that it is a .Scylla and Charybdis risk which we are running in making any movement whatever. They say that there are so many and such grave dangers in allowing the State to have any concern in the matter, that it is better to endure all the multifarious and terrible evils which we see around us, than to intrust the remedy to such hands. Innumerable fears are started—fears for civil liberty—fears for religious liberty—fears for the national intellect itself, which, it is supposed, will be degraded to the low pitch sufficient to bear the burden of a despotism, if once the State is permitted to become drill-master to the souls of the people. Simple as the question is, apprehension has so bemuddled and bemystified it, that it is not easy to convince the terrorists that their alarms are unfounded; that education is so good and so holy a thing that no Government, however much it might wish to do so, could enslave an educated people, but that its inevitable, its only natural and possible result, is Enlightenment, and that the inevitable result of Enlightenment is Liberty, and of Liberty, Progress.

\*         \*         \*         \*         \*

The opponents of State education fear that, as there are several kinds of education, the State, if once permitted to exercise this great power, may choose a wrong system, and educate us into mental slavery. Men, as we know, may be educated into any belief—even into the belief of some savage nations, that murder is a virtue, and war the only rational and dignified employment of human beings. It is urged by some who feel this keenly, that if the State were allowed to educate our children, we should have no security that it would not educate them into a wrong belief in politics or religion, and thereby destroy both civil and religious liberty. Let us meet this objection fully and fairly. Let us see what it is worth. Let us examine if this giant in the way is not an imaginary giant altogether—a monster of mere unsubstantial vapour, that only requires to be closely looked at to disappear, leaving no trace behind it. In the first place, what do we understand by the word EDUCATION ? If there are any friends of a system of State education, by which the people should be taught the doctrines either of one phase of politics or of one form of religion, I must say, for myself, that I am not of the number—that I never knew one of the number who did not prefer ignorance to universal education, and who, pretending to be a friend of popular enlightenment, was not in reality its enemy. On the contrary, I have invariably found every person who has studied the subject, and taken a real interest in it, opposed to any general or national system of teaching, that could by possibility warp the mind in either of these directions. An education interfering with the rights of conscience is not the kind of education desired by the many philanthropic and earnest men who have advocated the interference of the State to save the

masses of our population from ignorance. What then is
this system? I reply, that it is a system in which politics
shall be left to the fire-side and the free-will of each—
and in which religion, not professedly taught, but not
undervalued, shall be left exclusively to voluntaryism,
and to such agencies as are at present at work. There
will be no interference—there *can* be no interference in
either respect in any system to be supported by the
people of this country. The first' step in a national
system must of course be to provide instruction in
reading, writing, and arithmetic, for every child born
into this country—to be provided, not as a favour, but
as a right. These are the tools of knowledge, and must
be taught. The opponents of the Prussian system sneer
at these indispensable acquirements, and state that their
possession does not suffice to make a virtuous and happy
population. Most assuredly they do not;—but they are
the first steps, without taking which no higher ascent is
possible. Of essential value as the basis of an intellectual education, they are not to be despised even as
moral agents. A man may lie, cheat, and steal behind
a counter when possessed of them; but if he were not
possessed of them, the chances are, that with these seeds
of evils in his nature, his lying, cheating, and stealing
would assume more outrageous, offensive, dangerous, and
anti-social forms. Bad as he might be behind his
counter, he would be worse if he had not the tools of
education to raise him to, or keep him in, that position
of *quasi* respectability; and would, in all probability,
pass his days in violence, or end them on the scaffold.
The records of all our prisons prove this. It is impos-

sible to open a book of statistical returns relative to crime without seeing that out of ten criminals nine are either entirely ignorant of the commonest rudiments of education, or imperfectly acquainted with them. Of 15,000 prisoners in Scotland last year, as stated in Mr. Frederick Hill's report, only 1 in 15 was found able to read and write well; and only 1 in 60 knew anything more than mere reading and writing; while upwards of 3,000 could not read at all, and upwards of 8,000 could not write at all. I cite this as the latest instance, and because the fact relative to the northern part of this kingdom, where education is more diffused than in the southern portion, is rather a favourable sample of the whole nation than otherwise. But upon this it is needless to dwell. Reading, writing, and arithmetic are moral agents. Though insufficient, they are worth something; and that something, little as it is, and sneered at as it may be by the bigoted and prejudiced, it is of importance to secure to all who, under the present system, or rather non-system, have neither the means nor the opportunities of procuring it. In addition to instruction in these elementary branches, a good national system of education should provide for the physical as well as mental training and development of the young. There should be baths, and large airy playgrounds attached to each school, with facilities for athletic and invigorating games—so that the *mens sana in corpore sano* principle should be fully tried. It is a well-known fact, that generally the inhabitants of our prisons are, merely as animals, inferior to those who keep out of prison. In the same valuable report from which I have already quoted—the latest at my hand—Mr. Hill says that the young prisoners are mostly inferior in physical as well as mental development to people generally. He says that this inferiority is "owing, no doubt, to the unfavourable circumstances of their birth and early training, and to frequent exposure to cold and want, often alternating as age advances, with the effects of dissipation. Many who are committed, and liberated while young, probably die before they reach manhood ; but the same general inferiority is observable to a greater or less extent in prisoners of all ages." This point is of great importance ;—it has hitherto been grossly neglected both by and for the young and the old ; and our crowded, reeking, filthy, pestilential lanes, wynds, and alleys, have year by year sent forth their swarms of stunted, vicious, and reckless humanity to fill the land with ignorance, crime, and suffering ; and no effort worthy of the name has hitherto been made to cope with the mighty evil. We have at last awakened to the necessity of sanatory legislation, and in any system of State education the application of sanatory principles to the schools must not be neglected. In addition to these means of mental and physical training for the young of the nation, which the Government, without alarming the jealousies of any class or sect, might be fairly allowed to employ, that of Music should not be forgotten. Its humanising influence is well known by the rich, and felt by the poor. It should not be omitted. Its preventive and reformatory power is of immense value, and should be brought into operation even in the commonest primary and elemental schools. "In Prussia," says Mr. Horace Mann of Mas-

sachusetts, in the interesting report of his Educational
Tour in Germany and other parts of Europe, "all the
teachers are masters, not only of vocal, but instrumental
music. One is as certain to see a violin as a blackboard
in every schoolroom. Generally speaking, the teachers
could play upon the organ also, and some upon the piano-
forte, and other instruments. Music is not only taught
as an accomplishment, but used as a recreation. It is
found a moral means of great efficacy. Its practice pro-
motes health. It disarms anger; softens rough and tur-
bulent natures ; socializes and brings the whole mind, as
it were, into a state of fusion, from which condition the
teacher can mould it into what form he will as it cools
and hardens." The man who really loves music cannot
be a thoroughly bad man ; and he has a heart more open
to all genial, kindly and religious influences than if he did
not love it. It would be easy to dilate upon this subject
were it needful to do so. But it is not needful. The
advantages, the blessings of music are familiar to every
cultivated mind ; and there is no reason why they should
not be extended to the humblest amongst us, until every
man who could read, could sing, or play some instrument, and until the man who could do neither, should be
considered an extraordinary and disgraceful exception to
a common rule. These should be the means of physical
and mental improvement for the young, their religious
training being left where it now is, and, at all events,
with no worse chances than it has at present—to the
home circle, if there be such a circle for the child, or to
the efforts of zealous religionists, who teach in Sunday
schools or from the pulpit ; and who are not likely to

relax in their diligence in this particular branch of teaching, in whatever way the Government may act with reference to intellectual training. In the more advanced schools, there should be the same system, with the addition of geography, astronomy, history, mathematics, and general science, with the same scrupulous avoidance of religious teaching.

\*　　\*　　\*　　\*　　\*

We are not, like the Prussians, a military nation; and will not tolerate a military system in educational matters. We are a nation divided into various sects—a nation with two Established Churches, which form a small majority merely—with Roman Catholicism forming the great majority in one important section of the empire; and Dissent, in all its multiplied varieties, constituting a powerful minority in the other two. We are a free people, jealous of our freedom — a religious people, peculiarly sensitive upon religious matters, and inimical to any, the very slightest, interference with the rights of conscience. We are a people who have a greater reverence for the Bible than any nation under the sun; and at the same time a people who dispute more and differ more upon the doctrinal questions of the Bible than any other in existence; and who, however much we disagree upon interpretations, agree in believing that education, without the aid of the Bible, is of a very questionable value, if not altogether useless. We are a nation, who, by means of voluntary efforts amongst our sects, have done a great deal of educational good; but who, in consequence of our sectarianism, have left a great amount undone. We are a nation at the head of the civilisation of the world, not-withstanding all our faults and shortcomings; and a nation that, knowing this, is but too apt to undervalue any institution, however good and perfect, that comes from a people less powerful, free, and independent than ourselves. What system, then, can we adopt that shall shape itself to all these twists and turns, and yet answer its purpose of providing education for the whole people? I do not deny that the answer is difficult. I do not pretend that I am qualified to give it. I merely state my opinion as the result of earnest study and long considera-tion—to be taken for what it may be worth—and at the least as a contribution that may excite thought in some, and, perhaps, help other minds to a far better solution. Five years ago the answer would have been more difficult to give than it is now. We have, in the interval, got rid of a portion of our religious prejudice. The Established Church does not speak with so much confidence and self-sufficiency upon her exclusive right to teach the people as she did then—and Dissent, though still showing some-thing like a firm front against any teaching of which religious doctrine is not the basis, begins to waver. Both the Church and Dissent see, that if the people are left in ignorance until they agree, there is great risk of their remaining in ignorance for ever. Both have awakened to the truth that each has a mission to fulfil—that each can instruct its own people, and push its zeal to a much greater extent than it does now or ever did, and yet leave a large residuum, whom, if the State care not for, no one will care for. The signs of this abatement of the religious difficulties of the case meet us on every side. Dr. Hook and Dr. Vaughan are not solitary voices speaking in a wilderness, but orators who sway each one his own multitude, and who will, should there be a struggle in the cause, march to aid it at the head of no inconsiderable band of attached adherents. Neither the Church nor Dissent urge any exclusive right over the residuum. The Church did so once—Dissent never did; and although there will yet be, in any system, considerable difficulty in getting at this residuum and teaching it, without exciting the fears or jealousies of one or the other of them, the difficulty will be greatly diminished if the basis of an educational system be declared to be non-interference with any voluntary effort. When I say non-interference, I mean that the State shall not prohibit any existing school whatever ; but I do not mean that the State shall not inspect all schools, whether public or private, and that it shall not require proof from every one engaged in the occupation of teacher that he is duly qualified. There can be no doubt in any reasonable mind, that it is the duty of the State to take the most stringent measures to see that the incompetent and ignorant teacher shall be no longer allowed to follow a vocation so high and so sacred. Here the subject naturally branches off into two parts. First,—How all existing schools and schoolmasters are to be improved without any interference with chartered or natural rights, or voluntary exertion ; and, secondly, —How primary and other schools are to be established and maintained, wherever the absence of other schools and the wants of the population show them to be necessary.

To render existing schools efficient, we require—

A responsible Minister of Education.

A Board of Education.

An efficient Staff of School Inspectors.

A system by which Superintendence and Inspection may be made complete.

A sufficient number of Normal Schools for the training of Schoolmasters. And,

A law rendering any person, male or female, liable to punishment for keeping a school, or teaching in one, without a diploma from the Central or a properly constituted Local Board.

The results of the employment of such means would be the elevation of the character and status of the schoolmaster; the increased responsibility of every person engaged in tuition; and the greater efficiency of all existing seminaries, public or private, endowed or unendowed, proprietary or charitable. There would be no interference with religious or political opinion—the mode of instruction or the rights of private judgment; —no despotism—nothing that could in any way shock or jar upon the feelings of a perfectly free and earnestly religious people.

The second part of the subject, namely, the provision of primary and other schools, lets loose the elements of discord; or rather, would have let them loose some years ago. I think the signs of the times give evidence that *now* the elements will mix somewhat more kindly than before; and that if we are to have some warring—some muttered thunder now and then—it will be but a harmless storm, clearing and purifying the intellectual atmosphere of the country, and enabling us to see and to enjoy a finer landscape than we have yet been accustomed to. Upon this part of the subject it will be sufficient to sketch a plan, reserving the details for future consideration.

The establishment of primary schools should be *compulsory*. The duty of the School Inspector of the district should be to notify to the Government the name of every village, or parish, or portion of a parish, in which a school is required by the wants of the population. This done, the Board of Education should notify to the village, the parish, or the district in which the deficiency exists, that a school must be built, and that a portion of the cost will be defrayed by the Government. If the notification be not attended to, the Board should have power to order the erection of the building, and to assess the district or parish for the *whole* amount.

In these schools, reading, writing, arithmetic, music, &c. should be taught; and to each school should be attached conveniences for physical education. Doctrinal instruction should be excluded from the schools; but, as Dr. Hook proposes, a certificate of attendance at *some* place of Divine worship should be expected from every child receiving instruction, and the failure to bring such a certificate should be considered an offence requiring the earnest and public admonition of the teacher.

These schools should, as far as possible, be made self-supporting; and the parents of every child attending them should pay at a reasonable rate for the instruction afforded, unless in cases where poverty is pleaded and proved, when the child should be admitted without payment. The attendance of children should be made compulsory, as far as compulsion is consistent with the feelings of the people, and the freedom of our institutions. Direct compulsion might perhaps be avoided. Mr. Mann, in his Educational Tour, shows, that in the free State of Saxony direct compulsion is submitted to as a necessary portion of an efficient system; but there are means of indirect compulsion which have much to recommend them. For instance, no man who cannot read and write, whatever his other qualifications might be, should be allowed the exercise of any local or parliamentary franchise; and no man who, after notification of a school inspector, that his child or children is or are of age to receive primary scholastic instruction, should neglect to send them to school, should be deprived of all franchises whatsoever. Another means might be the reading, at all the places of worship in the district, whether at Established or Dissenting churches, of the names of all the recusant fathers who refused to give their children the benefit of the education provided for them. Such a dereliction of duty might also be brought in evidence against the parent, in aggravation of his punishment, if arraigned before a tribunal for any offence against the laws of property or the person. These are merely hints thrown out for those who may be induced to study the possible co-existence and concurrence of compulsion and freedom; but hints as they are, they will serve to show that the task is not quite so hopeless as many at first glance might be inclined to consider it.

Having thus very briefly sketched the outlines of a

plan, I return to the consideration, individually, of all these various requisites of a complete system, taking them in the order in which I have placed them.

Firstly, then, of the Minister of Public Instruction. This minister, from the importance of his functions—far more valuable and holy in an advancing state of society than those of the judge—for he prevents, while the judge only punishes—should in a right system be above the influence of political parties—chosen for his undoubted and universally acknowledged fitness for the office, for the independence of his mind, and for the purity of his character. It is not a necessary consequence of the removability of such a high public servant on every change of Ministry, that the office should become the reward of political exertion or subserviency — but the irremovability of such a minister, through all the mere changes of party, would be a guarantee to the country of his independence, and of his elevation into a serener and purer atmosphere than that which usually surrounds the statesman who is involved in the tactics and struggles of a party: a guarantee not to be obtained in the case of a removable functionary.

The presence of this great officer in one or other House of Parliament should be considered absolutely essential to his continuance in office. To him should be confided all educational and literary subjects—public schools, public libraries, Museums, Athenæums—all the institutions for the education of the infancy, youth, and maturer age of the people, so that in the engrossing struggles of a commercial nation the interests of art, science, and literature should not be overlooked or jostled out of notice by the fights of parties, the fierce scrambles of railway or other projectors, and all the material interests that in a material world are sure to force themselves into prominence. This Minister might be aided by a Board, of which he should be the President—a board constituted of men distinguished in Parliament—in Literature—in Science—in the Church—and in the general Christianity of the nation, without reference to sect, and who, receiving no payment for their services in connection with it, would of necessity be chosen from the ranks of those who would receive honour from their office and confer honour upon it. This Board and its President should form the great Educational Director and Superintendent for the whole nation—making its beneficial influence felt in the remotest corners of the land, and spreading its ramifications to every county, city, town, village, hamlet, and parish — so that the smallest congregation or community of British subjects should be within the sphere of its vigilant and kindly operations—favouring no sect—teaching no doctrine—promulgating no views of its own—but confining its functions to making known the interest of the State in an educated people, and putting in the power of the humblest the opportunities and the means of instruction.

\*　　\*　　\*　　\*　　\*

There is another part of the subject on which no sufficient attention has been bestowed. It is not enough for the interests of a great nation like this, and amid the commercial and manufacturing rivalry which we must expect on every side, that the vice and crime of our swarming cities should be reformed by education. This is but the first step. If we teach our children reading, writing, arithmetic, music, and gymnastic exercises—and improve their minds and bodies to such a degree as to make them sober, industrious, healthful, moral, religious, and intelligent, we shall doubtless have done very much. But though *much*, it will not be *all* that we must do. The wants of society require schools of a higher class for more advanced pupils. Primary schools —secondary schools—and tertiary schools or lyceums, will all be necessary, one after the other, for the improvement of the same individuals before they attain manhood or womanhood. These will be required in order that, in the competition of the nations in this practical age—this century of discovery and invention, and of immense mechanical power, every day developing itself in newer and more startling results and combinations — we may not be outstripped in the race, and left in a poverty from which our more vigorous rivals shall have long before emerged. We have hitherto run in the career of civilization, like the hare in the fable—very fast indeed, and greatly to our own satisfaction, and to the wonder and delight of all beholders. We must not go to sleep, however, upon the idea of our swiftness. The tortoise is behind us, and will not lag or flag, whatever we may do. It may win the race, if we even so much as doze. We must have Schools of Industry as well as primary Schools—we must have Athenæums, Museums, and Libraries, at the national expense — the latter not in London only, or in places inaccessible to three-fourths of our population, but dispersed through-

out the country, on a scale commensurate with the
wants of the people, and aided by the State, in proportion to the voluntary support of the localities for the
immediate benefit of which they are to be established.
"The knowledge required for the scientific pursuit of
mechanics, agriculture, and commerce, must be provided to an extent corresponding with the demand and
the exigencies of the country. Of the necessity of our
immediate attention to this point, abundance of proofs
might be collected. I select a few that come readiest
to my hand. In the evidence given before the Poor-
Law Commissions by Mr. A. G. Escher, of Zurich, an
experienced engineer, who employs many hundreds of
workmen, it is stated, in reply to a question as to the
effects of a deficiency of education in success in
mechanical employments :—

"These effects are most strikingly exhibited in the
Italians, who, though with the advantage of greater
natural capacity than the English, Swiss, Dutch, or
Germans, are still of the lowest class of workmen.
Though they comprehend clearly and quickly any simple
proposition made or explanation given to them, and are
enabled quickly to execute any kind of work when they
have seen it performed once, yet their minds, as I imagine
from want of development by training or school education, seem to have no kind of logic, no power of systematic arrangement, no capacity for collecting any series
of observations, and making sound deductions from the
whole of them. This want of capacity of mental arrangement is shown in their manual operations. An Italian
will execute a simple operation with great dexterity; but

when a number of them is put together, all is confusion. For instance, within a short time after the introduction of cotton-spinning into Naples in 1830, a native spinner would produce as much as the best English workman; and yet up to this time, not one of the Neapolitan operators is advanced far enough to take the superintendence of a single room, the superintendents being all northerns, who, though less gifted by nature, have had a higher degree of order and arrangement imparted to their minds by a superior education."

In reply to the question, whether education would not tend to render the work-people discontented and disorderly, and thus impair their value as operatives, Mr. Escher states:

"My own experience and my conversation with eminent mechanics in different parts of Europe, lead me to an entirely different conclusion. In the present state of manufactures, where so much is done by machinery and tools, and so little done by mere brute labour (and that little diminishing), mental superiority, system, order, punctuality, and good conduct,—qualities all developed and promoted by education—are becoming of the highest consequence. There are now, I consider, few enlightened manufacturers who will dissent from the opinion, that the workshops, peopled with the greatest number of well-informed workmen, will turn out the greatest quantity of the best work, in the best manner. 'The better educated workmen are distinguished, we find, by superior moral habits in every respect.'

"From the accounts which pass through my hands, I invariably find that the best educated of our work people manage to live in the most respectable manner, at the least expense, or make their money go the farthest in obtaining comforts.

" This applies equally to the work people of all nations, that have come under my observations ; the Saxons, the Dutch, and the Swiss, being however decidedly the most saving without stinting themselves in their comforts, or failing in general respectability. With regard to the English, I may say, that the educated workmen are the only ones who save money out of their very large wages.

" By education I may say, that I throughout mean, not merely instruction in the art of reading, writing, and arithmetic, but better general mental development ; the acquisition of better tastes, of mental amusements and enjoyments, which are cheaper while they are more refined."

The report of the Poor Law Commissioners furnishes many other instances equally striking. In the United States the same effects flow from the same causes. In the year 1841, Mr. Horace Mann, the Secretary of the Massachusetts Board of Education, made a careful inquiry into the comparative productiveness of the labour of the educated and uneducated manufacturing operatives in that State. He gives the substance of the information received from the manufacturers, and of the facts observed by himself, as follows :—

" The result of the investigation is the most astonishing superiority in productive power on the part of the educated over the uneducated labourer. The hand is found to be another hand when guided by an intelligent mind. Processes are performed not only more rapidly, but better, when faculties which have been cultivated in early life furnish their assistance. Individuals who, without the aid of knowledge, would have been condemned to perpetual inferiority of condition and subjected to all the evils of want and poverty, rise to competence and independence by the uplifting power of education. In great establishments, and among large bodies of labouring men, where all services are rated according to their pecuniary value, there is it found, as an almost invariable fact, other things being equal, that those who have been blessed with a good common school education, rise to a higher and a higher point in the kinds of labour performed, and also in the rate of wages paid, while the ignorant sink like dregs to the bottom."

In agriculture, the same necessity for the instruction of the labourer in the days of his youth is perhaps more urgent. When our population is increased by ten, fifteen, or twenty millions, as it must be, if it goes on at the present ratio, we shall not be able to afford sustenance for a vast body of unskilled agriculturists. They must grow their own food on the best and most economical principles—or we shall find ourselves in the very thick of a most serious and appalling difficulty. It will not do then to have four millions of waste acres in Ireland, which might be cultivated if the people but knew how to set about the work—nor in Scotland will it answer to allow the bases of the mountains to remain undrained, and to grow heather instead of turnips or oats. It will not do to allow hundreds of thousands of acres to lie waste in England, and a still larger surface of country to be cultivated by men who know not how to drain or to fence, or to manure on scientific principles. The hunger

of our increased millions—were they allowed to remain
in their present ignorance—would be something fearful to
grapple with when the days of adversity came. Lavoisier,
the celebrated chemist, by applying science to agriculture,
although he had not a minute knowledge of the art of
farming, doubled in nine years the produce in grain of
the same piece of land, and quintupled the number of his
flocks. Every farmer and farm-labourer should have the
advantage of the knowledge promulgated by Lavoisier—
and after him, still more successfully, by Liebig—so that
the smallest garden allotment might be made to produce
double what it brings forth at present, and the wild
brown moors become green with fertility. It would be a
cheap national expenditure which should lead to such a
result as this—and whilst the return would be super-
abundant in mere wealth, it would in virtue and happiness be altogether incalculable.

\*     \*     \*     \*     \*     \*

A few words in conclusion with the believers in all and
every variety of religious doctrine. Let them have faith
in themselves, and in their own truths, and cease to look
upon secular education as unfavourable to religion. Let
them cease to talk of thraldom, while they themselves
remain under the unchristian thraldom of sectarian
jealousy. Let them make friends with the human intellect, which is the ally and not the foe of religion and of
religious liberty. Let them assist the government in
providing education for the whole people, and if the
people gain much in civil and material benefits, let them
be assured that they will gain as much or more, religiously
and spiritually. Let them give human nature a chance

of being better in the next generation than it is in the present. Let them rely upon the conviction that knowledge is the source of freedom, morality, and religion—the mother of progress, and the friend of man : and if they should be disappointed in their own lifetime, those who succeed them may perchance see and taste in the fruit what they have beheld in the blossom. One generation is insufficient for the task ; but let us begin it, and we shall arrive so far towards the goal we aim at, as to be rewarded for the past, and encouraged for the future.

A few words also on the question of compulsion. " We will not be compelled to go to church," it has been argued ; " and why should we be compelled to go to school ? " The cases, however, are not parallel. There is conscience to be respected in the one. Conscience has no necessary connection with the other. The man who has a tall chimney pouring forth offensive vapours to poison the atmosphere and injure the health of the community around, might also complain of compulsion, when forced under penalty of prosecution and punishment to remove the nuisance. The disgusting vagrant exposing his nakedness and his sores in the public way, might also complain of compulsion, when removed by the arm of authority, and forced to respect public decency ;—but would any friend of civil liberty sympathise with these ? Is it not a portion of our liberty that we should have power to use compulsion towards those who would break the laws established for the general benefit ? The man who has a family of children, and will persist in bringing them up in idlenesss, vice, and ignorance, when the means of instruction are placed at his very door—given at the cheapest rate if his circumstances are humble—given for nothing if he be too poor to pay anything—is surely as great an offender against the public weal as the man whose offences are merely physical. Yet is all our sympathy to be given to him? Is he not to be compelled directly or indirectly—persuaded, if we *can* persuade him —but forced, if we cannot—to remedy the moral nuisance which he would fasten upon society? An ignorant and degraded father may not know that he is interested in having an educated, moral, and well-disposed offspring—but a wise State knows it, and has a right to coerce such a father, if persuasion fails. It has a clear right to make him conform to a regulation which the welfare of the whole community requires. Compulsion seems a hard word; but, if we have borne the *thing*, why should we complain so much of the *name?* We are compelled to pay taxes—we are compelled to obey the laws—we are compelled to conform to police and sanatory regulations; and in such compulsion there is no outrage upon civil rights or the rights of conscience. Neither would there be any outrage upon them in being compelled to send our children to school;—not necessarily to the State school, but to *some* school—the school of our own choice—the school of our own sect or denomination—the school in the teachers of which we should have most confidence. To rich and poor, to high and low, the same rule would apply. In the case of the former, the law, though existing, would be *de facto* a dead letter. The wealthy—the people in the middle classes of society—the well-disposed of the working classes—do not now, and would not then, require compulsion. All these send their children to school, and for them Government would do all that it could do in helping to raise the social standing of the schoolmaster. But the ignorant—the grossly, the dangerously ignorant—will not send their children to the school merely because we build a schoolhouse in their neighbourhood, and tell them they may come in. To use the eloquent words of Dr. Chalmers in a lecture bearing upon this subject, which he delivered in Edinburgh :—

"Ignorance never will bestir itself by a spontaneous movement of its own for the acquisition of knowledge. Irreligion will never bestir itself by a spontaneous movement of its own for the acquisition of religious knowledge or religious principle. The more the people are sunk in irreligion or ignorance, the more careless they are about either knowledge on the one hand, or religion on the other; and if we trust to a mere attractive power, and say, here is an institute, the door of which is open, where schooling may be had for all your children, or where you may all hear Divine service, it will turn out a miserable failure. If you trust merely to the attractive influence of education on the one hand, upon the people who are not wholly ignorant, but who don't care about knowledge,—and if you trust merely to the attractive power of religion on the other to people who are wholly irreligious, and who don't care about their souls, you will find that it will turn out a miserable abortion. The ecclesiastical labourer may have to preach to empty benches; and the teachers may be destitute of employment,—neither scholars on the one hand, nor hearers on the other, will come of their own accord, either to the schools or the places of worship, you have instituted."

The Reverend Doctor was well acquainted with the poor, and described them truly. He asked "how are we to mend this,—how get the better of this grievous inertness and indifference that is abroad among the people? Why, by what he would call the aggressive principle, which is neither more nor less than this,—they won't come to you for knowledge and religion; but you may go to them, and by the moral suasion you bring to bear on them, you will at length prevail over them, either to send their children to your school for knowledge, or to come themselves for your religion to the services you provide for them." Ministers of religion—teaching religion as well as secular knowledge—may act upon this principle, and will save many from perdition by so doing. But the State cannot and must not act upon it, because it is not its province to interfere with religion, and because religious opinions differ so much amongst us. The State must regulate. Rules are its only " suasion," and such rules for the protection of the good will be operative only against those who do evil—the evil—the great, growing, and intolerable evil of neglecting or refusing to give their children the inestimable benefit of education. To those who merely neglect this duty to themselves, to their offspring, and to the community, and who are careless, but not wicked, a first warning will, in most cases, prove sufficient—a second, a third, as in free Saxony, invariably so. On those who obstinately refuse after repeated and kindly notice, compulsion will be well applied. They will deserve no sympathy, and will not obtain it; and will rank in the estimation of their compeers in the same cruel and degraded class as those who having food to give their children, will not allow them to eat; and who having clothes to cover them, turn them naked into the streets. Let the State say, that no child born into this realm of Britain shall be allowed to perish for want of the mental food of education,—let it provide that food for all who cannot provide it for themselves; and if the Britain of the future be not a more free, a more intelligent, a more moral, a more religious Britain than that of the present and the past, there is no efficacy in education, and the triumphs of civilisation are in vain.

The twelve letters to Lord Morpeth were reprinted as a pamphlet, and contained, in addition to the plan, of which the foregoing is but a brief abstract, a careful and conscientious refutation of the prejudiced misstatements of Mr. Samuel Laing, the well-known traveller and writer, who had made himself prominent as the enemy of State education. Mr. Laing's particular bugbear was Prussia, and his terror was that a national system of education in this country would inevitably Prussianize the English people, and tend to the introduction of a military despotism. Mr. George Combe reviewed the pamphlet in the *Scotsman*, and stamped it with the emphatic approval of that powerful journal. On the subject of Prussia he strengthened my arguments against Mr. Laing by stating the results of his own personal experience.

"The author," he said, "successfully answers Mr. Laing's disparaging remarks against the Prussian system of education; and from some knowledge of the system and its effects, gained by intercourse with all classes of

the German people during a residence in that country of
nearly two years, we offer our testimony in favour of the
author's views, and against the accuracy of the
'Traveller;' much as we esteem the acuteness and
authority of the latter on many other subjects.  In our
opinion, the Prussian system, which, with slight modifi-
cations, has been adopted in nearly the whole of Germany, with the exception of Bohemia and Austria, has
raised the German people from the condition of ignorant
indolent boors, to that of comparatively intelligent and
active men and women.  It has nearly extinguished the
narrow patriotism which rallied round the prince of a
small territory, and regarded the subjects of every
adjoining state as natural enemies ; and in its place has
created a national spirit, embracing all who speak the
German language.  One effect of this change is, that
Germany now presents to France on the one side, and
Russia on the other, the solid form and combined
strength of a *nation*, in place of a rickety assemblage of
rival sovereigns, each ready to sacrifice the general
interest to his petty jealousy of his neighbours.  German
education has engendered moderation and reciprocal
forbearance between the different religious sects,—a love
of freedom and a power of combination among the
people, which have already secured representative consti-
tutions to most of the States, and are steadily labouring
to extort them from Prussia and the few others which
still withhold them ;—it has delivered the masses of the
people from the dominion of the priests, and substituted
the spirit of Christianity and reason in its place ; and it
is now doing battle for the liberty of the press : In short,

a few years more will, in our opinion, suffice to convince
the world that the Prussian system of education has
been one of the greatest boons ever conferred on a
country.

" If Mr. Laing, or any one else, desires to discover the
real effects of the education which has been bestowed on
the German people, we advise him to visit Hesse Homburg, a very small territory, in which public instruction
has been much neglected. He will there find the common
people in that condition of stolidity and ignorance in
which we conceive the Germans of the last century universally to have existed. We conversed with at least
half-a-dozen of grown men, before we could learn from
them whether the majority of the inhabitants of the
town of Homburg, in which they lived, were Roman
Catholics or Protestants ; whether there were in the town
public schools ; by what tenure the land in the neighbourhood was held ; and so forth ; and at last when a
person was found among the people who did know something about these simple matters of detail, it turned out
that he was a native of another state, had served his
three years in the army, and been at school during his
military service !   Contrasted with these uneducated
inhabitants of Homburg, the same class of people in
Prussia, Saxony, Wurtemburg, Bavaria, and Baden,
appear like philosophers and statesmen.   The latter are
intelligent, possess the capacity of observing and thinking
as well as reading, and many of them are companionable
persons.   Among other effects which education has produced on the German mind, is a feeling of astonishment
when they hear that there is no system of national

education in England! This is increased when they are told, farther, that in England, some persons consider that their political freedom will be in danger, if a law should be enacted to punish them for not sending their children to school! One German cabman, to whom we communicated this information, exclaimed—'Why, Sir, they might as well complain of the magistrates for apply-ing the fire-engines without their consent to extinguish a conflagration in their houses.' To the common people of Germany *who have been educated*, this objection appears so wholly irrational, that they cannot comprehend its being urged by any intelligent being!"

Read by the lurid light of the war between Germany and France in 1870, Mr. Combe's observations on what popular education had done for Prussia twenty-four years previously, seems prophetic of what was destined to be, when an educated, was pitched in mortal combat against an uneducated, nation. Compulsion—odious as its name appears—is not so dreadful after all. The giant is not a giant, only a mist and fog, which we can all walk through if disposed to do so.

The educational efforts of Mr. W. E. Forster and the Gladstone administration of 1873 fell far short, it will be seen, of the plan sketched out in 1846, and advanced little further than the elements of reading, writing, and arithmetic—tools of education, but not education itself—and a quasi, but scarcely a real compulsion brought to bear against the neglected poor of the larger cities, but which left the neglected poor of the rural districts almost untouched, and very little cared for.

If it were allowable to speculate upon what might have

been, had certain events occurred, which have not occurred, the lawgivers and administrators of to-day might well ask themselves, whether if such a scheme of popular education as that which was proposed and left unheeded in 1846, had been passed within five years of that date, there would have been the same amount of drunkenness and brutality among the lower strata of the labouring classes of the year 1875, as our judges deplore and punish. It cannot justly be said of the English people that as a race they are inferior to the Germans, or that they are more naturally prone to moral evil than the people of any other country. Yet the lower order of English are grossly intemperate ; they use brutal violence to one another, and to the weak and tender women and children who are dependent on them ; and kick not only their wives but their comrades to death. They no longer think it unfair and cowardly to hit a man when he is down ; and have little or no taste except for the most brutal amusements. The educated Germans of the same class, though they drink a good deal of beer, do not get drunk. When they go to the *bier-garten* to hear the excellent music provided for them, they are able to appreciate and enjoy it, and they take their wives and children along with them. They do not kick women, and if they lift their hands against one another—which is a rare occurrence—they do it in fair fight ; and, more-over, they do not systematically and constantly make use of foul and blasphemous language. They have been taught not only reading, writing, and arithmetic, but vocal music, as mentioned by Mr. Horace Mann. Is it too much to ask whether this teaching of music in their early youth has not softened their manners, disposed them to enjoy rational and elevating amusements, and exercised—with education generally—a refining influence upon their hearts, minds, and language ? If the street arabs, the roughs, the rowdies, born in our great towns and cities twenty or twenty-five years ago, had been subjected to the same training in their early and impressionable days, might they not have grown into better men than such Liverpool roughs as kicked an inoffensive man to death, because he would not give them sixpence, or such kindred ruffians as are every day brought up before the police magistrates for acts of violence that would disgrace savages. Education will not eradicate vice and crime either in Germany or England, or any other part of the world, but it will tend to diminish both; and if it have in the course of two generations rendered the Germans the nation that we now behold them, might it not in the same space of time have done as much for the rude elements of our lower English ? It would be a libel upon England and the English to doubt it, and it is more than time that British statesmanship, to say nothing of Religion and Philanthropy, should open its eyes to the fact that delay in this paramount matter is perilous to the best interests of the nation, and that it is never too late to undertake a long neglected duty.

The secular education of the British people still remains a work to be accomplished if we would retain a place at the head of civilisation—at the head not only of arms and arts, but of manners and morals. Our zealous clergy of all denominations may be trusted, at least, as much as they have been trusted hitherto, to look after the souls of the people and fit them for the expectations of the world to come. It is the business of statesmanship and philanthropy to look a little more after the bodies of the people so as to fit them for work in the world in which they live and in which they have duties to perform towards themselves, towards their neighbours, and towards the State; to abolish the laws that tend to produce pauperism, or that by their stringency in preventing harmless amusement at the only time when hard-working men and women are able to take recreation, force them down into lower strata of animal indulgences which the law cannot reach; to set before them an example of model citizenship, and fit them to be what all recent political movements foreshadow that they must be, the first fountains of all authority, and all possible forms of government. The squabbles of churches and chapels must no longer be allowed to prevent the growth and development of citizenship, for if they do, Great Britain will sink into a lower rank among the nations than she ought to occupy, and will become, like Spain or Turkey, a third or fourth-rate power, overshadowed by Germany and her own colonies, who will occupy in her default the seat of empire which she unwisely abdicated.

# POOR LAWS AND DEER FORESTS;—SHEEP AND GROUSE *VERSUS* MEN AND SOLDIERS.

———+———

At the close of the year 1844, and throughout the year 1845, and part of 1846, there was considerable agitation in Scotland on the subject of the Scottish poor laws, and the necessity for their amendment. In Scotland the able-bodied poor have no legal title to relief. Only the aged and the impotent have a vague and shadowy right to be prevented from dying of famine; and such relief is administered with a doleful niggardliness that might excite the wrath of the hardest hearted overseer, who ever frowned at a pauper in England. The *Times* had devoted much attention to the subject, and Mr. Philip Pusey, M.P. for Berkshire, had travelled through Scotland to investigate it personally in all its details, and had published the results in a pamphlet. Both the writer in the *Times* and Mr. Pusey indulged in many sneers at the people of Scotland generally, and at Scottish landlords and Scottish philosophers particularly. There was nevertheless too much reason for the hard words in which they indulged and the pictures they drew of the lamentable state of the poor in every part of the country. But these English censors had taken no initiative in the matter, and had only followed where Scottish writers had led the way. Dr. Alison of Edinburgh had devoted many years and great zeal, energy, and experience to the cause.  In 1839 the General Assembly of the Church of Scotland had issued a report on the general management or mismanagement of the poor in Scotland, which was presented to Parliament, and ordered to be printed.  A "pastoral address" of that body, circulated in 1840, stated that the treatment of the poor in Scotland *"was such as it could scarcely be conceived possible that a Christian country could tolerate or that human nature could endure."*  In the session of 1844 Commissioners were appointed by Parliament to inquire into the whole matter, and take evidence.  This evidence, when printed, showed, in the words of one of the clergymen who made his return, that "the state of the law which permitted such a state of things as it disclosed, or which did not authoritatively prevent it, was disgraceful to a civilised country, and at variance with the spirit and precepts of Christianity."  That this was no exaggerated opinion the following brief extracts from the testimony of some of the witnesses will show :—

The Rev. J. HUNTER, of the Tron Church, Edinburgh—" Could the poor of your parish possibly subsist on their allowances from the Charity Workhouse without other resources ?"—" Certainly not."

" Are you aware of the resources on which they rely ?" —*" Public begging;* and I fear that leads to lying, and stealing, and imposition on the public."  " Is it your opinion that the small allowance given by the Charity Workhouse degrades exceedingly the character of those receiving it?" —" Certainly."   " And destroys their moral feelings?"—

"Yes. In my parish, those who have no visible means of subsistence prevail to a very considerable extent. Except by begging, they have hardly any means of eking out the little money they have from the Charity Work-house. Some of them are *almost absolutely famished*. I visited a very poor part of my parish on Friday last, and in all the houses I found persons destitute of food, and completely destitute of fuel, without an article of furniture, without beds or bedding, the inmates lying on straw." (Vol. I. p. 54.)

Rev. T. GUTHRIE, lately of St. John's, Edinburgh—"Do you think the present allowances not enough?"—"I think them *miserably deficient*. In many cases, people have no choice but *to steal or starve*. I have trembled often when I have gone, at the call of duty, to visit these receptacles of wretchedness, because I felt that I could not relieve the misery which I must look upon in such cases; and nothing but a sense of duty could compel me to visit the poor."

"Is it common for parents to leave their children under the present system?"—"I find many instances in which parents abandon their children altogether." "May not that arise from the knowledge that the children will be provided for by the parish?"—"No; *I think it arises from the wretchedly low state into which they have fallen—so low, that I have sometimes seen parents glad when their children died*." (Vol. I. p. 559.)

Mr. JAMES MARSHALL, Treasurer of the Destitute Sick Society, Leith—"Have you reason to believe that the destitution existed for a considerable time previously to the relief being given?"—"Yes, in many cases it existed until they were compelled from necessity to make their cases known. We have found that they have been without food almost entirely for days, and without knowing where they were to find it, before making application for charity." (Vol. I. p. 226.)

Captain MILLER, Glasgow—"You refer to the report of Dr. Cowan, where it is mentioned that a number of persons died from want of nourishment. Have any cases come under your knowledge of that kind?"—"Yes, if I am able to judge. Sometimes I have seen poor creatures having no bed, nor a rag to cover them, but their miserable scanty clothes, lying in a damp dwelling, and in fever. It requires no medical man to give an opinion on this: *I have seen it frequently.*" (Vol. I. p. 328.)

Dr. FLEMING, one of the District Surgeons, Glasgow— "In the course of your visits, have you perceived a great amount of destitution?"—"Yes, in some parts. Very abject poverty in some cases." "Does it appear to you that the amount of allowance received from the Hospital fund has been sufficient to maintain them, either wholly or with regard to other sources?"—"I should say that there were many cases that came under my notice in which it was *quite insufficient.*" (Vol. I. p. 338.)

Mr. R. STEELE, Ship-builder, Greenock—"There is *much begging* in Greenock; particularly among the destitute paupers. The poor get their support more from begging than from the assessment. I hear the complaints which the people make themselves, and I hear from others who are in the habit of visiting and seeing them, that they are in a state of great want and destitution, and but for begging, they would starve." (Vol. I. pp. 530-31.)

Mr. J. DENNISTON, (lately a magistrate), Greenock— "Are the parish allowances sufficient for the maintenance of paupers who have no other means of subsistence?"— "They are never contemplated as sufficient." "How is it contemplated that the pauper is to live, when he has no other means?"—"Either *by begging,* or receiving something from some charitable institution." "Are many decent people among the destitute?"—"Oh yes, a great many." (Vol. I. p. 545.)

HUGH MILLER, Esq., Provost of Ayr—"There is a good deal of begging in Ayr, which is suppressed as much as possible; but it cannot be effectually put down, nor is it attempted. The reason is, *that people are quite aware that the allowances which these poor people get are not sufficient for them.*" (Vol. I. p. 693.)

Dr. REID, Dumfries—"What is the condition of the paupers on the roll?"—"I take them to be in a very poor state; generally with very scanty bedding, often lying on a little straw, and sometimes on the floor, with very few bed-clothes." (Vol. I. p. 571.)

Dr. W. WELSH FORBES, Inverness—"I have seen a great many of the poor receiving parish relief in a very destitute state—their supply of food generally scanty. A poor man has perhaps a suit of clothing in four, five, or six years; it becomes torn and worn out, and affords very little protection from cold in winter. In regard to female paupers, I have reason to know that several of them have only one shift—and when that is washing, they have none on their persons. Their clothing is very inadequate to protect them during the winter season. They have dunghills about their houses, and a great want

of cleanliness in and about them.   They are very ill-off
as to bedding—generally they have a little straw or ferns,
some, perhaps, chaff, and, in a few cases, they have little
of these between them and the boards.   I have seen some
of them lying on the floor, and only a little straw under
them."   (Part II. p. 465.)

Dr. R. A. MANFORD, Inverness—"Is there anything
you think it important to mention to the Commission in
regard to the poor, or any suggestions to make in regard
to improvement in their treatment?"—"I beg to suggest
that their clothing, their diet, their houses, and their
living, in general, should be better attended to.   I believe
that the greater number of complaints we are called on to
treat in the dispensary and infirmary are brought on by
impoverished and scanty diet, and bad clothing, and ill-
ventilated and damp places of abode.   They have not
been sufficiently attended to under the system of a
voluntary assessment.   It is found that their allowance is
not sufficient, in many cases, to afford them that support
which is necessary."   (Part II. p. 471.)

Bailie FORBES, Aberdeen—"What kind of houses do
the poor live in?"—"In many cases, they are exceedingly
filthy and ill-ventilated, and not water-tight.   In many
cases, the poor have only a shake-down of straw on the
floor, and three or four persons sometimes sleep upon it.
For bed-clothes, they have merely a coarse rug or coverlet;
and frequently the principal part of the bed-clothes are
their body-clothes spread over them.   These, in many
cases, are very tattered, and in a very filthy state."   (Vol.
III. p. 599, et seq.)

Captain GROVE, Perth County Police—"The poor here

are a most miserable people—*worse than in Ireland,* where I was quartered a considerable time. Their bodily appearance is most miserable; they are fully as dirty, and, from their appearance, seem to have less food than those in Ireland." (Vol. III. p. 248.)

But all the clergy of Scotland were not in favour of an amendment of the law which had produced such results. One of them—and one of the most gifted and the most eminent, the Rev. Dr. Chalmers—happened to be a political economist and philosopher as well as a divine, and contributed to the *North British Review* an article which opposed any system of poor laws whatsoever, and maintained that by church collections and the charity of the poor towards their still poorer brethren, all could be done that was necessary. In this article, the Reverend Doctor, after dwelling upon the degraded state of the population of Scotland, both morally and physically, at the end of the seventeenth century, as portrayed by Fletcher of Saltoun, quoted a happier description by Defoe, written in 1717, from which it appeared that morals in the latter period were much mended. On this the Doctor made his comments, attributing the fact to the zealous preaching of the ministers of the gospel. But, he added, that the economical improvements kept pace with the moral, and that not only the disorders, but the extreme destitution rapidly disappeared. He went on to say that—

"The only public charity then known throughout the great bulk of the nation, was that upheld by the free-will offerings from Sabbath to Sabbath at the church door—and these mainly contributed by the people themselves, or by the commonalty of each congregation, *not far removed in their own circumstances, or rather pressing hard on the very borders of pauperism.* And all this without any legal or economical expedient whatever, *without a poor-rate, without any allotment system, or cottage system, or agrarian invasion upon property, or any infringement whatever on the proprietary feelings of the upper classes;* but due altogether to a change of habit and character, which, along with the coming up of a new generation, took place upon the families—a glorious result of educational and ecclesiastical influences alone— or, as we have said already, due singly and entirely to the operation of moral causes.

" Nor should it be difficult to comprehend the process by which this result was arrived at, and which, with the revival or progress of Christianity, might be repeated with the same result at all times, and in all countries of the world."

Dr. Chalmers must have known the miserable state of the Scottish poor in 1844, which was a time when there was no lack of preaching, but a superabundance of it, consequent upon the disruption of the Scottish church into two hostile and jealous bodies, the Established and the Free, each competing for the favour of the people ; but he could scarcely have imagined that the evil could be cured, or was in process of being cured, by preaching ; —that poverty could be effectually relieved without extension of trade ;—and, failing that, by a legal assessment upon property. He could not think that the kindly dole of those who are not far removed from pauperism themselves, could do more than merely prolong the misery which it could not remove? But it seemed that he would rather allow the rich to go free, and do no violence to their "proprietary feelings," even though the poor should be miserably relieved by the poor, than forego one iota of his favourite dogma, that ecclesiastical superintendence was alone sufficient. But every page of the large blue book of the Commissioners of Inquiry proved that the ecclesiastical mode was not the mode in which the poor of Scotland ought to be dealt with. Pauperism is a sore too deep to be healed by preaching; but the establishment of a national and humane, but compulsory, system of poor laws—including the relief of the able-bodied—would render it impossible for any future Commissioners of Inquiry to record with truth such deplorable facts as those with which their volumes were crowded. It was impossible at the time that Dr. Chalmers wrote to pass along any of the principal streets of the rich and thriving city of Glasgow without being solicited for aid by miserable-looking women with squalid infants in their arms, or followed by importunate children—half clad and half starved. The streets, in this respect, were positively a disgrace to a civilised community;—the bridges swarmed with mendicants, who stationed themselves in the most public places day after day, without remonstrance;—and sturdy vagrants prowled about the thoroughfares to demand charity, in tones of insult and menace, from women, whenever they met them alone and unprotected. In the neighbourhood of Glasgow—about a mile or a mile and a half from the city—the state of matters was still worse. There the beggar would take no denial;—he exhibited his filth and wretchedness in such hideous forms, that his object seemed to be to excite disgust, as the surest means of exciting pity ; and often when it was attempted to shut the door upon him, he used force to prevent it— placed his foot inside, and launched imprecations against trembling women when he suspected that they were alone in the dwelling. Well fed and well clad citizens who were sufficiently alive to the evil, but who did not see the proper way to abate and get rid of it, urged that the police should interfere and put down this .practice of begging, by punishing the offenders as rogues and vagabonds. In the rural districts the assistance of the police was not to be obtained ;—and in the towns, where the squalid and miserable were more numerous than the sturdy and insulting, the suppression of mendicity by the police was not easy. But it was felt by the friends of an amended Poor Law, that it would not be humane, or politic, or just, to punish those who had *no* other means of obtaining a livelihood for seeking one by beggary. Many of those who resorted to this mode of maintaining life were no doubt idle and dissolute characters, able but unwilling to work ;—but how in the inforcing of such a law against mendicity, as some wished, was the police to distinguish between those depraved characters, and those who were unable to toil, or to procure any kind of employment ? The evil called aloud for redress—but could not be removed by the greater evil of inflicting punishment on the guiltless : and enlightened public opinion did not ask that laws against mendicancy and vagrancy should be enforced—except in the case of the insulting and violent—until there was adequate provision for the poor—for those who were unable to work, or who, though

able, could not procure it. Many who called for the aid of
the prison instead of the poor-house, forgot that the
authorities in many Scottish towns granted licences to
beg : that, instead of relieving the poor by assessment
upon the owners of property, they sent these wretched
people forth, armed with authority to levy contributions
from those who were not much better off than the beggars
they relieved, and that ministers of the gospel, with a
most pertinacious and pernicious, though well-meant
benevolence, actually set themselves against a legal and
compulsory relief to the poor, by maintaining, with Dr.
Chalmers, that spiritual superintendence and church-door
contributions were sufficient for their relief. Society
would not have dealt fair and even-handed justice to the
beggar, at one moment encouraged in his calling by the
warranty of civil and ecclesiastical authority, if in the
next he were punished, because, unwilling to starve, he
had sought the only relief that circumstances put in his
power, and a relief which he has been taught he was
justified in craving.

Upon the subject of legalised mendicity, legalised in
order to spare the pockets of the rich from the burden of
a poor rate, the Parliamentary Commissioners were emphatic in their denunciation of the evils it produced.
They stated in their report that in " the parish of Camp-
belton forty-nine persons were, in October, 1842, struck
off the roll by a Committee of Managers of the poor, *and
badges were given to such of the number as chose to receive
them, as a licence to beg.* Even without badges being regularly granted, we find that in most of the burghs and
smaller towns *the paupers are allowed to beg on one or*

*more days in the week,* as in Inverary, Dingwall, Thurso, Perth, Kirkcaldy, and many others. *At St. Andrews, in lieu of licensed begging, a box has for many years been carried through the town on Saturdays.* The inhabitants having complained of the annoyances to which they were daily subjected by beggars, this plan was adopted to get rid of their importunities.    *    *    We cannot close our report without remarking on the prevalence of mendicity in many parts of Scotland. The evil is most observable in towns. In many of the country districts we have reason to believe that it has been checked to a considerable extent by the establishment of a rural police ; but it is still very prevalent in many parts of the country."

These evils were not only dwelt upon in the *Glasgow Argus* and a few other journals that were bold enough to run counter to the feelings and prejudices of the great landowners, but by the press of London; and public attention was so roused to the importance of the whole subject, that shortly after the opening of the session of 1845, Sir James Graham, then a member of Sir Robert Peel's administration, announced the intention of the Government to introduce a Bill for the better relief of the poor of Scotland : a Bill that was to provide more completely for the aged and the impotent, and to abolish legalised mendicancy. The *Argus*, that by dint of hard hammering on the subject had made itself an authority, expressed its disapproval of any compromise which did not provide for the relief of the able-bodied, and insisted that the only remedy for the evils that had been so vividly exposed on every side, except on that of Dr. Chalmers and the philosophists, was a Poor-Law, as nearly as possible similar to the amended Poor-Law then in operation in England. The *Argus* urged that it should affirm the following principles :—

1st. That no man, woman, or child should be allowed to die for want of food within the realm of Scotland — unless somebody could be held responsible for the scandal and the crime.

2nd. That the aged and impotent who were unable to work, and the able-bodied who could not obtain work, must be maintained in life, not as a favour, but as a right.

3rd. That the relief given should not be so large as to make the condition of those who received it as comfortable as the condition of those who laboured for their daily bread ; but that some indulgence should be allowed, under proper advice, to the aged and impotent.

4th. That out-of-door relief might, in the discretion of local officers, be given to the aged and impotent.

5th. That the able-bodied should receive in-door relief, and that they should work for it—and that, whenever independent work out of the workhouse could be procured by or for them, their relief should cease.

6th. That the law, which should thus provide every one with food sufficient to sustain life, obviated all necessity for mendicancy, and would be justified in punishing it as a crime.

7th. That as the workhouse was merely to be considered a temporary home for the distressed able-bodied, and was not to be made so comfortable as the home of the working man : the able-bodied husband and his wife should be separated while in the workhouse, as an additional inducement to make them leave it as soon as they could obtain work, and as a reason to make them unwilling to return to it.

8th. That, for a similar reason, children, while in the workhouse should be separated from their parents, and that this separation was necessary for their proper instruction and discipline.

9th. That as the children of the poor, if allowed to grow up without instruction, were likely to be as burdensome to the poor-rate as their parents before them—it was necessary, not only for the safety of society, but for the well-being of the children themselves, that they should be instructed in the elements of knowledge and some trade or handicraft besides.

But when the Lord Advocate of Scotland introduced his bill, it was found that he had wholly omitted the able-bodied poor, and that acting in the supposed interests of the heritors, or landed proprietors, on whom, in the rural districts, the burden of the rates would fall, he had confined its operation to the better relief of the aged and the impotent only. This was not the Poor-Law that would meet the needs of Scotland, or stay the three evils that afflicted the country; first, the mendicancy of the able-bodied, having no claim except on charity; second, the conversion of counties, or half-counties into deer-forests, or into grazing farms, giving employment to a score or half a score of shepherds among the valleys, or on the mountain slopes that had formerly maintained hundreds, or even thousands of men in arable farms, and when Great Britain was in sore need of soldiers to fight her battles, had provided the very best soldiers who had ever carried her name and fame over the world ; and third, the exodus of the people into the great cities, where they could not always find work or support; or out of the country altogether to the United States, Canada, Australia, New Zealand, anywhere, so it was but away from the land of their birth. About this time the Duke of Sutherland, whose ancestors had been foremost in clearing the county of Sutherland of the tenantry and the peasantry by their famous " evictions," evictions which would not have been profitable or possible if the owners of the soil had been liable for the relief of the able-bodied poor, under an efficient Poor-Law, wrote to me on another subject, and took occasion to add :—

" I enclose you a short account relating to the state of the county of Sutherland, which has been considered as called for by late representations in the *Times* newspaper.

" Poverty and its consequent evils are undeniable, and I must confess that there, as elsewhere, the poor have *not* had all the attention given to them which ought to have been given. I shall be most desirous for all possible improvement in this respect, and hope that all may be *obliged* to do their duty, and that neither attention nor money will be grudged by those who desire to serve their country in the true sense of the term.

" Though not immediately connected with the county of Sutherland, your parentage makes you sufficiently so as to take an interest in what more particularly concerns that remote district.

" The subject would lead me to write at great length,

and the printed account which I enclose might have perhaps advantageously been made more full; but it has not been printed from any desire to boast, but in defence against an unfair sort of attack which has been published."

As the Duke had himself broached the subject, and knew my position as Editor of the *Glasgow Argus*, and also that I had advocated as strongly as I could the assimilation of the Scottish to the English Poor-Law system, I was emboldened to ask his opinion on the Bill then before Parliament. I received the following reply:—

"LONDON, JULY 25, 1845.

" SIR,

" I feel much obliged for your considerately putting in writing to me the question regarding ' compulsory assessment of all parishes for relief of the poor.' If I were obliged at once to give a vote which might decide the question, I should certainly feel it a most weighty responsibility, but my impression is that in such case I should vote for it, notwithstanding the apprehension of evil consequences, as represented by Dr. Chalmers. I fear much the effects of the feeling ' the parish is bound to provide us,' among the people, and that their present virtuous attachments, and consequent exertions in favour of each other, which in the Highlands have been remarkable, and form a beautiful feature of their character, may give place to selfish disposition.

" But as a change of system of Poor-Law is necessary,

and as the maintenance of paupers must depend on the resources of those in better circumstance, it becomes necessary to consider how the charge can be thrown as fairly as possible on all, that they may contribute their fair proportion according to their means, and it seems to me that this can be most effectively done by assessment. Those that are really benevolent and charitable will still find occasion for the exercise of their philanthropy. It would be sad to think that this may be blunted by the operation of the proposed measure, and may we hope that in Scotland this will not materially take place ?

"Dryden remarks that the character given by Homer to a Grecian, of whom he says, φιλος δῆν ανθρωποισι, παντας γὰρ φιλεεσκεν, could never have applied to a Roman. Hitherto our poorest have been generally (as we know from many particular recorded cases that the POOR were elsewhere 1800 years ago), admirably charitable, and willing to share their pennies, or whatever they have, with their neighbours, may we trust that this disposition will still continue ?

"After having stated my impression that compulsory assessment will be found generally requisite, it is right that I should say that I may not desire it to be immediately enforced, and that I think that in parishes in Sutherland, it may be better to try at first a voluntary assessment, and endeavour to see our way.

"I thank you very much for what you tell me regarding personal opinion; I should wish to deserve to be well thought of, though mere popularity can for myself be no object. I have lately had an unexpected compliment

from Mr. O'Connell in consequence of a letter having
been communicated to him by a Mr. Mackay, whose name
had been put to a Report from their Association, in
which it was stated that 'some recent clearances in
Scotland, particularly in Sutherland, showed' that the
Act for 'Letting Field Gardens' in England would
be useful in Scotland, I wrote to deny any recent clearance
in Sutherland, and to say that nearly every cottage had a
lot of land at a low rent.

"Other kind demonstrations have given me much satisfaction; but whatever one's wishes and intentions may be,
the undeniable poverty and concomitant disadvantages,
the want of remunerative employment, and the precarious
nature of that on which they have mainly to depend,
make the present and future condition of the population
a subject of anxious consideration.

"I am, Sir,

"Very truly yours,

"SUTHERLAND.

"P.S.—I sent this to London, but it has been brought
back, as you had left for Scotland.

"I hope to be able to return there too, in time to
assist in bringing the new law into operation."

In these letters the Duke, it will be observed, made no
allusion to the able-bodied poor, whose condition was the
gist of the whole controversy. And it was scarcely to have
been expected that he would. He, as well as most of the
great landed proprietors of the Highlands, were Englishmen and aliens, who did not mingle with the people or

understand their language, who had for the most part
paid enormous prices for their Highland properties, and
preferred them to English properties, for the reason,
many of them, that they could do as they liked with
them, oust, evict the able-bodied, turn them out of their
holdings upon the highway, either to die or live upon
voluntary charity, make deserts and solitudes and call
them deer-forests; and convert arable farms, employing
and feeding hundreds of people, into sheep-walks, giving
work to one or two shepherds; and reconverting the most
beautiful districts of Scotland into the primitive wilderness to afford room for grouse.   Although the want of a
Poor-Law on the English system works very oppres-
sively on such great towns and cities as Aberdeen,
Dundee, Greenock, Paisley, Glasgow, and Edinburgh,
into which the evicted tenantry and farm-labourers
flocked, if they did not take the wiser and bolder
step of crossing the Atlantic in search of the bread
denied them at home, and of the farms to cultivate,
which in the far West and the uncleared regions of
Canada might be had almost for the asking, the inhabitants of the towns dreaded the compulsory poor-
rate, for the support of the able-bodied, and remained
either apathetic, or hostile to change.   Public opinion in
Scotland was not fully awake to the importance of the
subject; the unhappy serfs, remaining to be cleared out
of the Highlands and islands had not advocates in
sufficient numbers, and with sufficient influence, to insist
upon a better Bill;—and the incomplete and illusory
measure, having the good wishes of the heritors, or
landed proprietors, as well as of the rich inhabitants of

the towns and cities who were agreeably surprised at being let off so easily, was passed into a law. The results were such as were anticipated. Still, throughout Scotland, the aged and disabled poor were relieved, by a "weekly sum, considerably less than is usually paid for the board of a dog;" and still were the casual poor allowed to prowl about the streets and highways of the country, the most abject, and yet the most impudent beggars to be found out of Spain. Still were disgusting objects allowed to exhibit their misery in the public ways—still were lunatics and half-lunatics allowed to go at large and beg—and still was Scotland suffered to lag behind all other civilised countries in her encouragement of habitual mendicancy. The framers of the Act had gone upon no right principle, and had tampered with an evil which they had neither the courage nor the skill to cure.

Such is the Poor-Law of Scotland at the present time. The prosperity of the Lowlands during the last twenty years, and the increasing immigration of the able-bodied, have greatly diminished the evils of mendicancy; but the Highlands remain in the state of wilderness. While rich English sportsmen pay enormous rentals for deer-forests and for grouse shootings, while sheep farmers dispense with all but the smallest modicum of labour, the wilderness pays the Scottish proprietors, whether they be English or Scotch, better than cultivable and cultivated lands, and gives no trouble with the people; the reason is, that *there are no people.* General Narvaez on his death bed, was exhorted by his reverend confessor to forgive his enemies. "I have no enemies," said the

dying man." "How so?" "I have killed them all."
And the Scottish landlords, if asked how they treat their
people, may reply in the same style, "We have no people,
we have banished them to the ends of the earth."

At the anniversary dinner of the French Society in
London, early in 1875, the Count de Jarnac, the French
ambassador, used a happy phrase when he spoke of " the
disinherited classes." The Highlanders of Scotland are
truly a disinherited people. The land of the Highlands
—mountain and glen—was originally the property of the
whole clan, for whom the chief was but the trustee, the
steward, and the administrator—and the meanest member of which had the same right to live upon it as he
had. On the abolition of the feudal system, the chiefs
were erroneously supposed to be the proprietors of the
fee-simple—and being in no wise loth to be recognised in
that character, they usurped possession, and in many
cases sold the land, without the slightest consideration
or thought of their clansmen. Had there been a Poor-
Law, recognising the right of the able-bodied, as in
England—even had the land been sold—it would have
been sold subject to the rights of the poor; and the
English Dukes of Sutherland, formerly Marquises of
Stafford, who inherited much property from their maternal
ancestors the Scottish Earls of Sutherland, and who
bought the Reay Forest and the Mackay Country from
Eric, seventh Lord Reay, for a very large price, would
not have been allowed to evict the clansmen of Lord
Reay from their farms and holdings without making
themselves liable to maintain them in the destitution
to which they reduced a worthy people. But the Suther-

land family were not the first to commence the system of
evictions, and in cruel fashion "to disinherit the people."
The Scottish Dukes of Athole had set the example long
before, and had reduced the beautiful and fertile Glen
Tilt into a wilderness, in order that the Nimrods of their
day—deprived of English hunting grounds by the extension of trade and manufactures and the growth of large
cities, and by the legal obligation to maintain the poor,
able-bodied, or otherwise—might have "happy hunting
grounds" within reasonable distance of London and their
country seats. There are glens that once contained many
hundreds of men capable of bearing arms, and others
that contained from two to five hundred, that have no
human occupants in our day—except a solitary game-
keeper or two or three shepherds :—

" Nimrods and hunters are lords of the mount and the forest,
    Men but encumber the soil where their forefathers trod ;
Though for their country they fought when its need was the sorest,
    Forth they must wander, their hope not in man, but in God.
" Roaming alone o'er the heather,
    Nought but the bleat of the wether,
        The bark of the colly or crack of the grouse-slayer's gun
    Breaks on the lonely ear,
    Land of the sheep and deer!
        Albyn of heroes ! the day of thy glory is done."

Should unhappily the day ever dawn when Great
Britain shall be forced into a war with any of the great
military powers of Europe, and have to struggle for her
national existence, or her place as a leading power, she
will find few or no soldiers in the Highlands, and among
the gallant people that in former days supplied her so
bountifully with the best she ever had. In that day

statesmen will perhaps regret that they had allowed it to be possible to expatriate the strongest men of the country —and made it impossible for hundreds of thousands of such men to earn their bread in the land that gave them birth. Perhaps, too, it will be found in that day that the soil of Great Britain is too narrow and limited for deer forests—and that if, to use the words of Dr. Chalmers in reference to the Poor-Laws, we should not do violence to the " proprietary feelings of the rich " by rendering deer forests illegal—statesmanship may see its way to taxing them and their produce to such an extent as to render them too grievous a burden even for a millionaire to support, and to make it cheaper for him, if he wants a deer forest, to acquire it in the shadow of the Rocky Mountains or the skirts of Manitoba. Even a Poor-Law on the English system—though it would have prevented evictions by rendering them too costly, and fixing the support of the people on the pockets of those who prevented the people from working for their bread—would not now remedy the evil; for the people are gone, never to return. But a heavy tax upon deer forests and unnecessary moorlands would tend to bring land into cultivation—and cultivation, if it would not bring back the people, would retain the next generations, and the exodus of the future would be stayed. Taxes upon luxuries are universally admitted to be the most just of all taxes, and a tax that would prevent unfeeling rich men from creating wildernesses for their selfish enjoyment, would be ultimately a boon to such rich men themselves, and an incalculable advantage to the whole community—either in peace or war—and most perhaps in war, when the nation

had need of stalwart arms, and stout hearts, to fight for a
land that had ceased to treat such arms and hearts with
cruel injustice.

[At the time (August, 1875) when this sheet is passing ·
through the press, it is announced in the *Army and Navy
Gazette*, and many other London newspapers, that " the
Duke of Sutherland has expressed his readiness to
*import some of the distressed Norwegians into his county!*"
This means that the Duke of Sutherland's ancestors,
having cleared the county of Sutherland of its brave
inhabitants, the Mackays, and forced them to emigrate
to the ends of the earth, it has become necessary or
expedient, to entice men into the desolated but beautiful
land, and that finding it impossible to re-import the
Mackays, the present Duke is glad to have the aid of
Norwegians, when Highlanders are no longer obtainable,
to turn to proper account the resources of a country,
which—wiser than those who preceded him—he has discovered to need strong arms and intelligent minds for
its proper development.]

# THE GLASGOW ELECTION OF 1847.

To be too early in important affairs is often as prejudicial as to be too late—an aphorism, if I may so call it,
the truth of which I was destined to prove in my own
person. At the commencement of the year 1847, I
conceived the idea, considering the growing wealth and
population of the great city of Glasgow, then, as now,
the second in the empire, that it would be a sound
enterprise to convert the Glasgow *Argus*, published every
Tuesday and Friday, into a daily newspaper. At that
time there was no daily paper published in any part of
Great Britain, except in London, and I thought the time
had come when such cities as Glasgow and Manchester,
and more especially Glasgow, were able to support a daily
journal, and that such a project, if aided, as I hoped it
might be, by a large advertising connection in so busy a
hive of trade and industry, might be successfully conducted. I issued a prospectus to that effect for private
circulation, basing my calculations on a minimum daily
sale of three thousand copies, with two pages of advertisements. Three of the proprietors of the *Argus*
thought well of the proposition, and were prepared to

give it their best attention. The remainder were not only hostile, but bitterly so ; and one, who claimed to be the spokesman of the malcontents, went about the city, hinting that I must be insane to have thought of a scheme so wild and so impracticable. Not meeting adequate support, I suffered the matter to remain in abeyance for some months. But meanwhile my prospectuses were handed about, and discussed in various quarters, and to such purpose, that, greatly to my surprise, and, I may add, disgust, I saw one morning in the advertising columns of the *Argus*, the announcement of a new daily paper in Glasgow, to be called the *North British Mail*. A wealthy, or supposed to be wealthy, ironmaster had been favourably struck with my idea, and seeing the field clear, resolved to be the first in it. The new journal had to struggle against many difficulties, but it succeeded in establishing itself; and on the repeal of the newspaper stamp duties, the advertisement duties, and the Excise duty upon paper, became, perhaps by slow, but certainly by sure degrees, a very valuable property. The *Glasgow Herald*, a bi-weekly journal, like the *Argus*, and edited by the late George Outram, the author of some very clever comical legal lyrics, well known in Scottish society, also became in due time what the *Argus* was not destined to be, a daily journal, and thrives exceedingly, as does an evening daily paper, an off-shoot of the *Glasgow Citizen*, formerly published only once a week. Thus I was not so very mad in desiring to establish a daily paper—as incredulous Glasgow once supposed—but only guilty of that self-damaging species of folly, which consists in being before my time, and seeing a little further ahead than my contemporaries.

The *Argus* was not destined in other respects to be a source of much satisfaction to its editor, and came ultimately to an inglorious collapse, the circumstances of which may be interesting and instructive to future literary men who may accept the editorship of journals, which are owned and governed by a numerous, and possibly an antagonistic, body of proprietors. In accepting the editorship of the leading Liberal journal of the West of Scotland, I stipulated, before leaving London, that I was to be wholly untrammelled in the expression of my literary and political opinions, subject only to the restriction that I was to support the cause and policy of the Whig and Liberal party. I did not imagine that the ardent Whigs and Liberals who were proprietors of the *Argus* would ever quarrel among themselves, and would split into two parties, each of which would strive to bring me over to its side ; and that in such a case, side which way I would, I would certainly make an enemy of the other. But such was to be my evil fortune. Mr. John Dennistoun, one of the members for the city, had made himself particularly unpopular among the magistracy—all members of the Liberal party—and especially with Mr. Lumsden, the then Lord Provost, one of the principal proprietors of the *Argus*, my kindest friend and staunchest supporter in Glasgow, whose official position in connection with schemes for the improvement of the city and the Clyde, and especially with that noble project, happily accomplished, for supplying Glasgow with the pure, clear, and abundant

waters of the beautiful Loch Katrine, led him frequently
to London with his brother bailies, during the sitting of
Parliament.  He and his associates complained much of
the hauteur, inattention, and inaccessibility of their
member, from whom they could obtain neither civility
nor service; both of which were freely and cheerfully
rendered by Mr. John Macgregor, the then Secretary of
the Board of Trade.  They also complained that Mr.
Dennistoun seemed to look upon the representation of
Glasgow as his indefeasible right, belonging to him as
long as he lived as much as his coat, his hat, or his
purse.  And not only these gentlemen, but the great
body of the Liberals of Glasgow, were dissatisfied, and
determined that, come what might, Mr. Dennistoun
should be opposed by a better Liberal at the next
election.  Mr. Dennistoun, however, had a strong friend
in the proprietary of the *Argus*—a gentleman who had
a very small share, but a considerable amount of influence, and who happened to be the legal adviser and
electioneering agent of Mr. Dennistoun.  The Lord
Provost and his friends determined to bring forward
Mr. Macgregor as their candidate—a choice that was
cordially welcomed by the great majority of the Liberal
party; and as cordially resisted by the agent of Mr.
Dennistoun, and a very small minority.  What was
the editor of the *Argus* to do under the circumstances?
He could not be neutral—he was compelled to take a
side—and he knew full well that whichever the side
might be, he would make an enemy of the other.  Acting upon his own judgment, agreeing with the majority
of the electors, and determined, moreover, on the asser-

tion of his independence, he declared for Mr. Macgregor,
and supported his candidacy during several weeks to the
best of his ability.    And this brought on an inevitable
crisis.    Taking advantage of the absence in Ireland of
Mr. Lumsden, who had more interest in the *Argus* than
any other proprietor, a meeting of the financial and
governing committee was summoned, and the editor was
formally relieved of his duties, and the doors of the
editorial office were shut against him.    The circumstances created a certain commotion in the political
and literary circles of the city, which was largely increased by the publication of a voluminous correspondence which there is now no necessity to reproduce : in
which I and my friend set forth all the facts of the case,
and in which I more especially set forth that in coming
to Glasgow I had taken " care to stipulate that there
should be no interference whatever with my opinions
on the part of any proprietor or proprietors.    I added
that this condition having been agreed to, I on my
part undertook to edit the paper on ' *Liberal* principles,
and as *an auxiliary to the Reform party,*' as expressed
in the language of the proprietors themselves, and that
I never imagined at the time that disputes could arise
as to *who* constituted the Reform party of the city of
Glasgow."

The press of Glasgow, of all shades of politics without
a single exception, ranged itself on my side, and the
following article appeared in the *Glasgow Citizen* of the
following Saturday, June 19, 1847, from the pen of Mr.
James Hedderwick, the poet, who was both editor and
proprietor of that journal, and stood in the happy

position of being able to say his own say in his own journal, with nothing to control him but his own sense of what was right and befitting :—

"A RECUSANT EDITOR.

" The dulness necessarily attending an election in which all the candidates threaten to be on the same side, has this week been enlivened by a quarrel between the proprietors of the *Argus* and their editor, Dr. Mackay. The party pleasantly known as the " Clique " fell out on the subject of the representation—Dr. Mackay refused to be the tool of a section—and hence the grand explosion which has been the seven days' tattle of the town.

" What, in the name of all that's discreet, could Dr. Mackay mean ?   Under some strange misapprehension as to the nature of the literary office, he seems to have attempted to act not as a simple manufacturer of sentences, but as a promulgator of opinions.   He, the employed, had, we are assured, the hardihood to sport sentiments of his own, in opposition to those of some of his employers.   Now, fancy the absurdity of a stone-mason cutting and building in his own way with the independence of an architect, or a block-cutter following his own designs with the fearless licence of an artist !

" In order to make the matter perfectly plain, we beg our friend, Dr. Mackay, to imagine himself for the moment a shoemaker.   What could he expect if, when his employers ordered shoes, he persisted in giving them boots ?   The misfortune is that Dr. Mackay could not put himself in the position of a shoemaker at all, but believed, on the contrary, that some of his employers were ' snobs.'

" The case is as plain as that two and two candidates make four candidates in all. A number of gentlemen, not thoroughly accomplished in the rules of syntax, are ambitious of enlightening the world with their political views. They subscribe funds—purchase types and a printing-press—and hire a person who has been at school to put their sentiments into English. The types are of the quality ordered—the press is precisely the press they wished—all the materials are in fact thoroughly obedient —ready either to tell truth with the unvarying accuracy of a mile-stone, or to lie to all time with the infamous audacity of the Gorbals clock. In one thing only are they deceived. The doer-up of their leaders professes to have a mind of his own—convictions and a conscience to be consulted—a distinct idiosyncracy to be upheld—and a right of independent action to be maintained!

" Was ever conduct so perverse ? What could be more annoying to gentlemen accustomed to carpet their rooms and paper their walls according to whatever pattern they pleased ? It was, in fact, an attempt to set mind above money, by declaring that mind should cease to be its slave. In like manner the cook in the ' New Way to Pay Old Debts ' asserts his right of free action—rebels against the orders of Justice Greedy—refuses to roast the fawn with a Norfolk dumpling in the belly of it, or to dish the wood-cocks with toast and butter ! What was to be done with such a cook ?

" The ugliest part of this business is the terrible revenge which the dismissed editor has taken on the concern he has left. The boat he has been set adrift in is the jolly-boat, and he chuckles audibly over the fact

of his having doomed the ship.   No honest man will now
trust it.   He has betrayed the rottenness of its timbers.
Puffing will be useless—all attempts at raising the wind
a jest—it may as well drop its canvas at once.   If it move
it will be moved by a secret agency, leaving its new crew
to sing with the ancient mariner :—

> ' Till noon we quietly sailed on,
>     Yet never a breeze did breathe :
> Slowly and smoothly went the ship,
>     *Moved onward from beneath.*'

Ah, cruel Doctor! thou hast left a fearful malison upon
the shrouds!   Whether any new Jason of this ill-fated
*argosy* may be successful in regaining the golden fleece
we know not; but this we know, that, whatever be his
hope of success, he must avoid the error of his predecessor
—an error which not all the enchanted herbs of Medea
could repair—and refrain from taking the flame-breathing
bull by the horns.

"At the same time, we are free to confess that our
sympathies in this case are wholly with our professional
brother.   Mean men with money in their purse may
occasionally take advantage of the necessities of men of
letters.   For ourselves, however, rather than be worried
to death by a querulous and meddling proprietary, we
would submit to carry coals.   Tools and sycophants will
never be wanting to accept the wages of unprincipled ser-
vility; but we owe all praise to Dr. Mackay for the stand
he has made for the honour and dignity of a profession,
which will only attain its legitimate status in society when
its members have learned how to respect themselves."

As I had always predicted, Mr. Oswald declined to contest the representation of Glasgow. In his anticipated default a coadjutor was found for Mr. Dennistoun in the person of Mr. Dixon, a wealthy ironmaster, the glow of whose furnaces upon the wintry sky is a familiar sight to the Glasgow citizens. The Liberals, led by Mr. Lumsden, brought forward Mr. Macgregor, and found a colleague for him in Mr. Alexander Hastie, a merchant of the city, and successor to Mr. Lumsden in the provostship; and to promote their election a temporary successor to the now hostile *Argus* was created in a little weekly publication called *The Glasgow Electors' Mentor*, which I edited and carried on until the conclusion of the contest. Messrs. Macgregor and Hastie were elected by large majorities; and at the declaration of the poll those gentlemen and myself walked to the Exchange amid the plaudits of the multitude. But the victory, agreeable as it was to me and my political and literary friends, was the death-blow to the *Argus*. After the secession from that journal of Mr. Lumsden and those who agreed with him on the subject of Mr. Dennistoun, the *Argus* languished and drooped. Its remaining proprietors lost heart, and stopped it without note of warning. Everybody expected the catastrophe. The *Citizen*, three months previously, had predicted it, and a journal that had all the elements of prosperity within it, except a united proprietary, who could understand and act upon the fact, that no newspaper could be successful that depended not upon the great public, but upon a small coterie, came to an inglorious end. And at that time and since I have often thought, and think still, that a newspaper

cannot be conducted on the principle of a republic—
where many men have their say—but can only exist
as a despotism, with one will at the head, to whom all
other wills are bound to submit.   Divided counsels are
fatal in journalism; and a true editor, worthy of the
name, ought to be the master and not the servant, and
be as imperial or imperious in his own sphere as the
Autocrat of all the Russias.

For some weeks after the collapse of the *Argus* I had
serious thoughts of remaining in Glasgow and establishing another journal in that city; but after long deliberation and consultation with my friends, I at last decided
to return to London.

END OF VOL. I.

BRADBURY, AGNEW, & CO., PRINTERS, WHITEFRIARS.